WHY I BECAME A PSYCHOTHERAPIST

WHY I BECAME A PSYCHOTHERAPIST

EDITED BY

JOSEPH REPPEN, Ph.D.

JASON ARONSON INC.
Northvale, New Jersey
London

Production Editor: Elaine Lindenblatt

This book was set in 11 pt. Times New Roman and printed and bound by Book-mart Press Inc. of North Bergen, NJ.

Library of Congress Cataloging-in-Publication Data

Why I became a psychotherapist / edited by Joseph Reppen.
    p.   cm.
    Includes bibliographical references and index.
    ISBN 0-7657-0170-7
    1. Psychotherapists. 2. Psychotherapy—Vocational guidance.
  I. Reppen, Joseph.
    [DNLM: 1. Psychotherapy personal narratives. WM 420 B398 1998]
RC480.5.B379 1998
616.89'14'023—dc21
DNLM/DLC
for Library of Congress   98-4116

Printed in the United States of America on acid-free paper. For information and catalog write to Jason Aronson Inc., 230 Livingston Street, Northvale, New Jersey 07647-1726. Or visit our website: http://www.aronson.com

Contents

Preface

This volume grew out of a wish to uncover origins: what, in the personal lives of psychotherapists, inspired their journey to becoming psychotherapists. This work is a logical extension of my two earlier books, *Analysts at Work* and *More Analysts at Work*. In those books distinguished practitioners described, either by case presentation or in a general way, their approach to treatment. Each contribution suggested many different ways of being a therapist and practicing psychotherapy. I became very curious as to what life circumstances produced such variation of thought and practice. I thought, Why not ask therapists to write about their journey to psychotherapy? And so I invited a group of psychotherapists to tell about how they came to their chosen profession.

The response to my invitations to therapists from a very wide range of theoretical orientations to write about themselves surpassed my expectations. The number of authors who agreed to participate in this project and their enthusiasm were overwhelming, suggesting that all of the contributors to this volume wanted to tell their life stories. And fascinating and enthralling stories they are.

I trust the reader will find a deeper understanding of how personal being a therapist is and how many roads there are to becoming a psychotherapist. At a time when psychotherapy and all psychodynamic treatments are under attack, these stories are a testament to the dedication, training, skill, caring, and profound humanity of those who practice psychotherapy.

Joseph Reppen, Ph.D.
October 1998

1

For Love of the Imagination

MICHAEL VANNOY ADAMS

The Imagination is not a State; it is the Human Existence itself.
William Blake

I became a psychotherapist because I so love the imagination. For me, psychotherapy is essentially an affair of images, of how people imagine—and reimagine—"self," "others" (whether they be external others or internal others), and "world." I have recently published *The Multicultural Imagination: "Race," Color, and the Unconscious* (Adams 1996b), in which I discuss what I call the "fantasy principle." I regard the fantasy principle as more fundamental than either the pleasure principle or the reality principle. Although in particular that book addresses the "raciality" of the unconscious and engages the issue of "colorism" between whites and blacks, what interests me in general is the imagination.

Why I became a psychotherapist is inseparable from what kind of psychotherapist I became. I esteem all of the different schools of psychoanalytic thought: the original three schools (the Freudian, Adlerian, and Jungian), as well as all of the subsequent schools (among them the Kleinian, Kohutian, and Lacanian). I have a particular interest in the Jungian school—and in the post-Jungian, "Hillmanian" school of imaginal (or archetypal) psychology that James Hillman has elaborated (Adams 1997a). Jungian analysis interests me because it empha-

sizes the imagination more than the other schools do. Psychoanalysis—
especially Jungian analysis—has enabled me to return to the imagination.

To "return" to something, one must have "left" something. In a
certain sense, I left the imagination. In another sense, however, it was
not I who left the imagination (nor was it the imagination that left me).
Rather, the imagination was left—left behind me for several years.
According to Richard Kearney (1988), the imagination may be leaving us all, not temporarily but permanently. In the postmodern period,
he says, we may be witnessing the death of imagination and attending, if not the funeral, at least a wake. There may be such a general
trend, but it is a quite particular experience that I wish to emphasize.
Mary Watkins, who has described the many varieties of imaginal techniques in use historically in European and American psychology (1984)
and who has recently championed the importance of what she calls
"imaginal dialogues" (1986), criticizes certain psychologists (among
them Piaget, Vygotsky, and Mead) for undervaluing or even devalu-
ing the imagination. For such psychologists, the imagination is a developmental stage that we should grow out of as we grow into adulthood. For them, the imagination is merely a "phase" of childhood.

I grew up as a child in a small town in Texas. I was an only child
until the age of 9 when my father and mother—57 and 51 years old at
the time—adopted my brother and sister, two Korean-American war
orphans, ages 4 and 5. For my parents, for my family, that was a su-
premely imaginative (or reimaginative) multicultural act. Before that,
however, as an only child, I had experienced nine years of what a
Jungian might call introversion. I do not mean that I was oblivious to
external reality in some schizoid sense or that, like Jung (1963), I had
a public "No. 1" personality and a private "No. 2" personality in any
radically dichotomous sense. Nor do I mean that I had an imaginary
companion or an imaginary world—what David Cohen and Stephen
A. MacKeith (1991) call, after Robert Silvey, who collected many
elaborate examples of such worlds, a "paracosm." I merely had an
opportunity to develop an internal, imaginal reality in relation to external reality. Others have had the same or a similar experience; I was
hardly unique. As an only child, I was sometimes a lonely child, but I

also developed the capacity to be alone without feeling lonely, as well as a respect for the necessity of privacy, even secrecy, and I appreciated what Anthony Storr (1988) calls the virtues of solitude, for it provided me with an occasion to imagine.

I had time and space by myself as a child to indulge in what Gaston Bachelard (1969) calls "reverie." My father and mother had moved a big, old house onto ten acres where one of my grandfathers earlier in the century had once had a business that he advertised, true or not, as the largest nursery in northeast Texas. On either side of that land were streets with houses in 1950s suburban style, but those ten acres were, for me, a quite separate reality, which I called "the field." Other children had yards; I had a field. In a sense, it was a field of daydreams, a field for my imagination—a field with black soil, red and yellow roses, purple irises, and white gardenias (that most fragrant flower, my father's favorite), and apple, pear, and peach trees. In that field I played for hours on end by myself, alone with my imagination.

If nature was outside, art was inside. In the house I played in a room next to my mother's studio, where she drew in charcoal and pastel and painted in oil, where she glazed clay and enameled metal and baked her creations in a kiln. There was also the farm of my other grandfather: eighty acres that a railroad and a highway divided into three parts, a house with two fireplaces (one a hearth in the kitchen, where my six-foot four-inch grandfather would warm his back while he ate his cornbread after he had dipped it in his buttermilk), a barn (where I learned to handle the udders of cows and to squirt a stream straight into the mouths of cats at a considerable distance), horses, hogs, chickens, and dogs. Jung (1927/1931) says that "the chthonic portion of the psyche"—the aspect "through which the psyche is attached to nature, or in which its link with the earth and the world appears at its most tangible" (p. 31)—grounds life in the most transparent way in archetypal images. In my experience as a child, it was not only nature—earth, plants, and animals—but also art that archetypalized my imagination. My imaginal reality was a combination of the chthonic and the aesthetic dimensions: my grandfathers' and father's world and my mother's world.

For me, the imagination was not left behind abruptly. If I were to attempt to date the experience, I would say that it occurred over the years between age 13 and 21. In a sense, the process seems to me to have been quite normal—it just happened. I do not believe, however, that it was inevitable, nor do I believe that it was developmentally desirable, as if the imagination was merely one of those childish things that I needed to put behind me. Someone else might simply regard those years as a period of necessary extraversion, or socialization. It is difficult for me to do so, however, because I sensed that I missed something, I intuited that I had lost something, perhaps irretrievably. What exactly I had lost, what precisely I missed, I would have been hard put to say, but I now know that it was the imagination.

School and university did not, at least for me, validate the imagination. Educationally, the imagination was not of much visible value. In that context, I resorted to journalism. I edited school and university newspapers, I majored in journalism, and I worked as a summer intern reporter on the *Washington Post* and the *Atlanta Constitution*. I became preoccupied with the external political reality of current events, especially civil rights and the Vietnam War. Then something happened that was to transform me irreversibly. I discovered psychoanalysis, I discovered Freud—I began to rediscover the imagination. In retrospect, I realize that an interest in external political reality can also be a very serious expression of the imagination—as Andrew Samuels (1993) notes, there is not only political imagery but also "a *politics of imagery*" (p. 14)—but at the time I did not experience it as such. The year was that year of years, 1968. As a Flower Powerist and New Leftist, I read Herbert Marcuse's *Eros and Civilization: A Philosophical Inquiry into Freud* and Norman O. Brown's *Life Against Death: The Psychoanalytical Meaning of History*. Marcuse and Brown impressed me because they both, although in different ways, called for an end to repression.

My girlfriend at the time was majoring in psychology. She had a prior interest in psychoanalysis and Freud. She was writing a senior honors essay on Freud and the scientific method, attempting to demonstrate that, methodologically, Freud had been a scientist. We engaged in intense discussions about psychoanalysis—I citing Marcuse and Brown, she citing Freud. She was extremely critical of the way that

Marcuse and Brown used the word *repression* and insisted that they were not using it in the same technical sense that Freud had used it. She challenged me to read Freud in the original, in the Strachey translation, as she had already done. I began to do so. Reading Freud was a revelation. I had never before encountered a system of ideas of such vast imaginative proportions. Freud so impressed me that a year later, when my girlfriend and I flew to England to backpack across Europe, our very first stop in London was the Hogarth Press, where, with my meager undergraduate savings, I proudly ordered a set of the *Standard Edition*, to be shipped to America to await my return at the end of our travels. Since then, I have never been without those twenty-four volumes; they have accompanied me to England for three years and to India for a year.

At the time, I was still seriously contemplating a career in journalism. While working as a summer intern reporter on newspapers, however, I had gradually begun to feel that journalism was not the life for me. The emphasis on current events began to seem superficial: too much surface and not enough depth. I now know that it was not journalism that was superficial; it was I who was superficial. I needed more depth. My recent experience with psychoanalysis had led me to believe that ideas were deeper than events. I decided to go to graduate school; I enrolled in the American Civilization program at the University of Texas at Austin.

In my very first semester in that program, I took two courses— "Psychoanalysis in America" and "Herman Melville"—that profoundly influenced me. The two courses were a fortuitous combination. I had never read any of Melville's works, but as I began to do so I discovered that there was a great deal of psychoanalytic literary criticism on his works—especially on *Moby-Dick* and on *Pierre*, the novel in which Melville, like Freud, emphasizes "the two most horrible crimes . . . possible to civilized humanity—incest and parricide" (1852, p. 351). I also discovered that one of those who had written psychoanalytic literary criticism on Melville was Henry A. Murray, the Harvard psychologist who (in collaboration with Christiana Morgan) had developed the Thematic Apperception Test (TAT). One of the inspirations for the TAT was evidently Murray's reading of the "Doubloon" chapter in *Moby-Dick,* where Melville describes the various interpretations of the gold coin by Captain Ahab and the other sailors as, in effect, a projective test. As one of the sailors says of the attempts to interpret the doubloon: "There's another rendering now; but still one text" (1851, p. 434). Another, equally important source for the TAT was Morgan's artistic renditions of her fantasies, or "visions," which Jung employed in seminars to illustrate the technique of active imagination (Douglas 1993, Jung 1997).

The immediate consequence, for me, was that I began to entertain the possibility that I might become a psychoanalytic literary critic. I also began to perceive (or, more accurately, to project) sexual symbolism everywhere in Melville's works. This interest of mine made a certain impression on Jay Leyda, the eminent literary, music, and film scholar. Leyda, who had edited *The Melville Log,* two magnificent volumes of biographical documents, visited the University of Texas while I was a graduate student there. We had lunch, during which I waxed enthusiastic about my interest in Melville and in sexual symbolism. The next year, Leyda (1973) published an essay, "Herman Melville, 1972," in which he reflected on the then current state of scholarly and critical work on Melville. He lamented that "the art of Herman Melville has been reduced from discovery to a reading assignment" (p. 163). According to Leyda, the study of Melville was now merely an academic exercise:

> What we once read for joy has been transformed into a "subject," or rather an object for criticism and interpretation. The man who wrote these works has been pushed aside (again!) by well-meaning persons who tell us what the words really mean—so that there's not much room for either man or works. Critical microscopes are brought into play, but I'm no longer sure for what purpose. [p. 163]

Whom, exactly, did Leyda have in mind? As I read the essay, I was chagrined to realize that he had me in mind. What, he wondered, is the advantage of "a close, a very close hunt for the sexual puns" (p. 163) in Melville's works? "Is it to learn more about its author than we knew before? Or to draw attention to the ingenuity of the interpreter?"

Leyda even gave me a funny name: "the hunting inspector" (pp. 163–164). My critical microscope was, of course, psychoanalysis.

In the meantime, I was awarded a Marshall scholarship (comparable to a Rhodes scholarship but granted by the British Parliament in commemoration of the Marshall Aid Plan for Europe after World War II) to pursue doctoral research at the University of Sussex in England. I proposed to write a psychoanalytic dissertation on—what else?—the sexual symbolism in Melville's works. I spent much of the next three years in the library of the British Museum, at a desk under the dome of the reading room (I felt as if I were sitting inside a beautiful blue eggshell). I tried to read every book on symbolism that Melville might have read. Many of these books were late eighteenth- and early nineteenth-century works in what we would now call comparative mythology. The more I read, the more I began to suspect that my psychoanalytic approach to Melville was woefully naive. As I discovered in those works of comparative mythology the sources of much of Melville's symbolism in *Moby-Dick*, I realized that the symbolism was not, in any psychoanalytic sense, unconscious. I began to appreciate Melville as a literary "psychologist" who had imaginatively adapted symbolism from works in comparative mythology to serve his own, quite conscious purposes. I finally decided that psychoanalysis had less to say about Melville than Melville had to say about psychoanalysis. In the process, I also inadvertently became less Freudian and more Jungian. I did not conclude that the source of Melville's symbolism was the collective unconscious, but I did believe that the source was comparative mythology of the sort that so fascinated Jung in, for example, *Symbols of Transformation*. Methodologically, Melville was a Jungian—or Jung was a Melvillian.

One morning while reading the *London Times*, I came across an article on the poet and Blake scholar Kathleen Raine. I had never heard of her, but something about the article made me feel that her own work on William Blake might have something to do with my work on Melville. I wrote a letter to the author of the article, and he forwarded my letter to Raine. Shortly I received an invitation to visit her in London. Raine served me tea and scones with double cream and fruit preserves. In her I discovered a kindred spirit who graciously befriended me. On the walls of her house were wonderful engravings by Blake. She showed me other possessions: Yeats's fountain pen, his ESP cards, and his poltergeist photographs. Then and on many occasions afterward, we talked about Blake and Melville and the fact that they had both used many of the same sources in comparative mythology. Raine's psychoanalytic sympathies were, as mine had become, Jungian, although, like me, she did not regard either Blake or Melville as unconscious in any psychoanalytic sense. In her major work, *Blake and Tradition*, she had demonstrated that Blake had imaginatively adapted traditional symbolism. My own research had become, in effect, a study of Melville and tradition.

On one of my visits to Raine, she suddenly said to me that on my return to America I must meet a Jungian analyst by the name of James Hillman. I had never heard of Hillman, and it was several years before I met him. By then, I had begun to read the books that he had written—among them, *Re-Visioning Psychology*, *The Myth of Analysis*, and *The Dream and the Underworld.* As I write this essay, Hillman's newest book, *The Soul's Code* is at the top of the *New York Times*'s nonfiction bestseller list. "Soul" sells, as Thomas Moore, a popularizer of Hillman's ideas, has amply demonstrated in recent years with *Care of the Soul* and *Soul Mates.* What so interested me about Hillman, however, was not his psychology of the soul but his psychology of the image. In those earlier books, the emphasis was on the imagination. He might be "working toward a psychology of soul," but it was, as he declared, "based on a psychology of image" (1975, p. xi). Here, finally, was a psychoanalyst for whom the imagination was primary and constitutive of internal reality, not secondary and derivative from external reality.

Through the cumulative influence of Marcuse, Brown, Freud, Melville, Jung, Raine, Blake, and Hillman, I finally returned, full circle (or perhaps full spiral), to the imagination. After graduate school, I did become a psychoanalytic literary critic for fifteen years. Then I moved to New York, where I accepted a position as associate provost of the New School for Social Research and entered psychotherapy with a Jungian analyst, the first of three with whom I have worked over the years. Eventually, I earned a clinical social work degree at New York

University. When the New School established a master's degree in Psychoanalytic Studies, I served as director of that program for three years. I now have a private practice as a psychotherapist with a special interest in Jungian and post-Jungian theories and methods.

The practice of psychotherapy is, for me, an analysis of how people have imagined—and how they might reimagine—self, others, and world. This is what I mean by the fantasy principle. I consider it a great privilege to be a psychotherapist. To be a psychotherapist is to be privy to the imagination of others. I feel honored and humbled to be in the presence of someone who shares with me, confides in me, what he or she imagines. I am fascinated by the imagination, whether it be beautiful or ugly, happy or sad, complex or simple, comic or tragic—or, from the perspective of psychopathology, healthy or sick. To me, the discovery that internal reality, psychical reality—or imaginal reality—is just as real as any external reality is the most important discovery of psychoanalysis. Psychoanalysis does not quite assert that, as Blake insists, "Mental Things are alone Real" (1810, p. 617), but it does contend that what I call the psychical construction of reality (or the imaginal construction of reality) is the basic issue in psychotherapy. "The psyche creates reality every day," Jung says. "The only expression I can use for this activity is *fantasy*" (1921, p. 52). How does someone construct reality imaginally? What images does someone employ, consciously or unconsciously? What is the internal, imaginal experience of external events? These are the questions that I, as a psychotherapist, ask and attempt to answer. When Jung first began to work as a young psychiatrist at the Burghoelzli Mental Hospital in Zurich, what astonished him was that nobody "concerned himself with the meaning of fantasies, or thought to ask why this patient had one kind of fantasy, another an altogether different one" (1963, p. 127).

The reason that I am a Jungian rather than a Freudian is that it seems to me that Freud wants to rectify the imagination—to require what I call the fantasy principle to conform to what he calls the reality principle. For me, Freud is ultimately too much of a realist and not enough of an imagist. Freud proposes a distortion theory of the imagination. According to him, the function of fantasy is to distort reality. The images in a dream, for example, are mere manifest appearances, distortive derivatives of a latent reality. They are not what they seem to be or seem to mean. From that perspective, the purpose of psychoanalysis is to expose the distortion, identify the derivation, and provide a rectification of the fantasy in strict accordance with reality.

In contrast, it seems to me that Jung wants to explore the imagination without prejudice. As Jung says:

> It is true that there are unprofitable, futile, morbid, and unsatisfying fantasies whose sterile nature is immediately recognized by every person endowed with common sense; but the faulty performance proves nothing against the normal performance. All the works of man have their origin in creative imagination. What right, then, do we have to disparage fantasy? [1931, p. 45]

For Jung, the purpose of psychoanalysis is, as Blake says, "Conversing with Eternal Realities as they Exist in the Human Imagination" (1810, p. 613)—or, in Jungian terminology, dialoguing with archetypal realities that exist in fantasy. According to Jung, the images in a dream—or in active imagination—are exactly what they seem to be or seem to mean. He proposes a precision theory of the imagination. "Precision means whatever is actually presented," Hillman says. "Simply: the actual qualities of the image" (1977, p. 69). The unconscious, Jung argues, is incredibly precise in the selection of qualitatively apt images to epitomize psychical reality. It is difficult to interpret psychical reality not because some censor distorts, or encrypts, reality in a code that we then have to decipher, but simply because the unconscious, like some poet, communicates in images with which we are only more or less familiar. We do not have to translate these images; we have to define them. We have to explicate all that a specific image implies. The imagination is, in this sense, what the philosopher of science Michael Polanyi (1966) (who also befriended me in Texas and later in England) calls a "tacit dimension," or what the physicist David Bohm (1981) calls an "implicate order." Jungian analysis employs a phenomenological (or "essentialist") method. It inquires into the essential being or meaning of images, the fundamental phenomena of psychical reality. From a Jungian perspective, the unconscious does not so much conceal as it reveals. What an image is or means is not hidden from us, as if there were some deceptive intent; it is simply unknown to us, because we have not mastered the poetic, or imagistic, language that the unconscious employs.

I marvel at the compositional autonomy of the imagination. When and how does this compositional process occur? Are our dreams gradually composed during the day while we are awake, or are they instantaneously composed during the night while we are asleep? Are our dreams born, like Athena, full-blown from our heads? In a sense, we do not dream—we are dreamed. *We* do not compose our dreams; some autonomous process, which for lack of a better word we call the imagination or the unconscious (we used to call it "god"), composes our dreams. Rather than a supernaturalistic, metaphysical account of this process, psychoanalysis offers a naturalistic, metapsychological account—as if that were an adequate, scientific explanation. Similarly, do we fantasize, or are we fantasized?

The ingenuity of the imagination—or the unconscious—never ceases to amaze me. Someone—for example, a woman—tells me a dream, and that dream tells me precisely (and often incredibly concisely) who she imagines that she is. Dreams present self-images, other-images, and world-images: what Jung calls "imagos." "Someone shoots the president," the dreamer reports. "Then there is chaos." Immediately, I know that there exists in the psychical reality of the dreamer a would-be assassin who shoots the president. Who is this president? Or, phenomenologically, what is a president, what is the essence of "president"? A president is not a dictator who dictates in an authoritarian mode; a president presides in a democratic mode. A president is the head of the executive branch of a government. What the dreamer imagines—or what the unconscious of the dreamer images to her—is an assassination attempt on the executive function of the psyche. The imaginal assassin shoots (the dream does not say that he kills) an imaginal president. The psyche experiences the attempt as chaotic—and potentially fatal to the executive function. What does this dream have to do with the dreamer? In this instance, the dream has to do with what I might call the mind–body politic of the dreamer. It has to do not only with her psychical reality but also with her physical reality. The images in this dream immediately evoked in the dreamer a spontaneous association to an injury that she had previously suffered to her spinal column in an automobile accident. A physician had prescribed a brace, but for reasons of vanity (or, if one prefers, narcissism) the dreamer had ignored or neglected—one might justifiably say "repressed"—the prescription, with the result that her condition had deteriorated. The images in the dream enabled the dreamer to appreciate that one aspect of her psyche, a vanity function, was, in effect, attempting to assassinate another aspect, the executive function, the central nervous system in the spinal column. The dream was not a distortive image of this psychophysical "political" reality; on the contrary, it was a very precise image of it.

Although it is true that the dream did not literally image the condition of the dreamer, this fact does not mean that the imagination distorted that reality, as if it intended to deceive the dreamer. The dream metaphorically imaged the mind–body state of the dreamer, and it did so accurately, with scrupulously elegant exactitude. Jung says that the "obscurity" of the dream is not a distortion but "is really only a projection of our own lack of understanding." If a dream seems "unintelligible," it seems so "simply because we cannot read it." According to Jung, we must "learn to read it," and in order to do so we must "stick as close as possible to the dream images" (1934, p. 149). It is apparently from this specific passage that the Jungian analyst Raphael Lopez-Pedraza derives inspiration for the dictum "stick to the image," which Hillman emphasizes as the basic principle of imaginal psychology. Hillman admonishes us to " 'stick to the image' in its precise presentation" (1977, p. 68). From this perspective, the language of the unconscious consists of exquisitely precise images that serve a metaphorical purpose (Adams 1996a, 1997b). Not only Jungians but also at least some contemporary Freudians appreciate that, as Arnold H. Modell says, metaphor is the very "currency" of the psyche (1990, p. 64). In short, as psychotherapists, we need to learn the language of metaphor.

I thus practice what I would call psychotherapy of the imagination. Whether the images emerge in dreams, in active imagination, or in the psychotherapeutic dialogue, I address them in one and the same way. (Even reports of experiences of real external events are what I would call "the imagination of everyday life," for what is ultimately important is not the literal, objective event but the subjective, meta-phorical experience of that event.) I believe that everyone fantasizes continuously, that fantasy suffuses reality pervasively. Psychotherapy is an occasion for me and someone else to explore the imagination to-gether. It is an opportunity for us to appreciate that fantasy is a reality just as real as any other reality, as well as an opportunity for us to appreciate the extent to which reality is also fantasy.

I do love the imagination. Interpretation is a Logos operation; imagination, an Eros operation. If I am a psychotherapist for love of the imagination, it is because, for me, images have an erotic value (which may simultaneously and perhaps paradoxically be both an at-traction and a repulsion: not all images are intrinsically lovely in any simplistic sense). If I once left the imagination, or if it once left me, psychotherapy now enables me to return to it, as, in the myth, Psyche finally returns to Eros to give birth to Pleasure. (Perhaps there is not so much difference, after all, between what Freud calls the pleasure principle and what I call the fantasy principle.)

Michael Vannoy Adams, D.Phil., C.S.W., is Senior Lecturer in Psychoana-lytic Studies at the New School for Social Research.

REFERENCES

Adams, M. V. (1996a). Flowers and fungi: archetypal semiotics and visual metaphor. *Spring: A Journal of Archetype and Culture* 59:131–155.
——— (1996b). *The Multicultural Imagination: "Race," Color, and the Unconscious.* London and New York: Routledge.
——— (1997a). The archetypal school. In *The Cambridge Companion to Jung*, ed. P. Young-Eisendrath and T. Dawson, pp. 101–118. Cambridge: Cambridge University Press.
——— (1997b). Metaphors in psychoanalytic theory and therapy. *Clinical Social Work Journal* 25(1):27–39.
Bachelard, G. (1969). *The Poetics of Reverie*, trans. D. Russell. New York: Orion.
Blake, W. (1810). A vision of the last judgment. In *Blake: Complete Writings with Variant Readings*, ed. G. Keynes, pp. 604–617. London: Oxford University Press, 1972.
Bohm, D. (1981). *Wholeness and the Implicate Order.* London: Routledge & Kegan Paul.

Cohen, D., and MacKeith, S. A. (1991). *The Development of Imagination: The Private Worlds of Childhood.* London: Routledge.

Douglas, C. (1993). *Translate This Darkness: The Life of Christiana Morgan.* New York: Simon & Schuster.

Hillman, J. (1975). *Re-Visioning Psychology.* New York: Harper & Row.

———— (1977). An inquiry into image. *Spring: An Annual of Archetypal Psychology and Jungian Thought* 37:62–88.

Jung, C. G. (1921). Psychological types. In *Collected Works*, vol. 6. Princeton, NJ: Princeton University Press.

———— (1927/1931). Mind and earth. In *Collected Works*, vol. 10, pp. 29–49. Princeton, NJ: Princeton University Press.

———— (1931). The aims of psychotherapy. In *Collected Works*, vol. 16, pp. 36–52. Princeton, NJ: Princeton University Press.

———— (1934). The practical use of dream-analysis. In *Collected Works*, vol. 16, pp. 139–161. Princeton, NJ: Princeton University Press.

———— (1963). *Memories, Dreams, Reflections.* New York: Pantheon.

———— (1997). *Visions: Notes of the Seminars Given in 1930–1934*, ed. C. Douglas. Princeton, NJ: Princeton University Press.

Kearney, R. (1988). *The Wake of Imagination: Toward a Postmodern Culture.* Minneapolis, MN: University of Minneapolis Press.

Leyda, J. (1973). Herman Melville, 1972. In *The Chief Glory of Every People: Essays on Classic American Writers*, ed. M. J. Bruccoli, pp. 161–171. Carbondale and Edwardsville, IL: Southern Illinois University Press.

Melville, H. (1851). *Moby-Dick; or the Whale.* In *The Writings of Herman Melville*, vol. 6, ed. H. Hayford, H. Parker, and G. T. Tanselle. Evanston, IL, and Chicago: Northwestern University Press and Newberry Library, 1988.

———— (1852). *Pierre; or the Ambiguities.* In *The Writings of Herman Melville*, vol. 7, ed. H. Hayford, H. Parker, and G. T. Tanselle. Evanston, IL, and Chicago: Northwestern University Press and Newberry Library, 1971.

Modell, A. H. (1990). *Other Times, Other Realities: Toward a Theory of Psychoanalytic Treatment.* Cambridge, MA: Harvard University Press.

Polanyi, M. (1966). *The Tacit Dimension.* Garden City, NY: Doubleday.

Samuels, A. (1993). *The Political Psyche.* London: Routledge.

Storr, A. (1988). *Solitude: A Return to the Self.* New York: The Free Press.

Watkins, M. (1984). *Waking Dreams.* Dallas, TX: Spring.

———— (1986). *Invisible Guests: The Development of Imaginal Dialogues.* Hillsdale, NJ: Analytic Press.

2

The Education of a Psychotherapist

LEON S. ANISFELD

The manner in which my family's losses in the Holocaust became real to me was in the way my mother looked when she told me about the death of her 11-month-old infant daughter, who starved to death as they tried to escape the S.S.

My mother bent her arms at the elbow and lifted her clenched fists to her chest, as if she were holding her baby. I had never seen my mother give up so much of her emotional control. She and I were thereby transported to that time when she ran with her baby along the Polish countryside with their papers—presumably their safe passage, since my mother's first husband (the baby's father) was Gentile, with a non-Jewish name. But he had already been killed. (A witness had reported that three Nazi soldiers killed him because he had been so frightened, because they hated how he hyperventilated when he saw them approach, marching threateningly in step [goose-stepping], as they were wont to do when out on the town.)[1]

---

1. I would like to share something with the reader. Every incident that I report in this essay is true except this vignette concerning how my mother's first husband was murdered. There is no information, as far as I know, about how he died, although my mother assumes he was murdered in a concentration camp after being seized by the Nazis. Of

"And then," my mother said, confusedly, "the train crashed and [her hands circling in front of her] there were many bodies, some of them bloody, some dead. A nice man (surprisingly, he was a German[2]) brought me to the hospital. But there was no medicine, no food for the baby. She died," my mother said, matter-of-factly resigning herself to the powerlessness with that sigh of emptiness that I had heard from survivors before. She spoke blandly (with blood boiling behind a civilized and rigid veneer) of her infant withering away, so as not to evoke in herself any feeling of tenderness or any vision of the reality that memory might reproduce. Perhaps most disheartening of all was the inevitability that accompanied her reliving, always without the tears I expected. It was the same singsong ring that characterized all of my parents' Holocaust stories (i.e., the very few I was permitted to hear). Indeed, I still cannot listen to anything regarding the Holocaust without crying.

It makes me angry, this seeming acceptance of events that simply happened to them. Becoming a psychotherapist would be the sublimation of my compulsive need to reinstate the survivor's loss of a sense of personal agency. Perhaps this is as good a reason as any for the requirement of a personal psychotherapy for the psychotherapist— that the psychotherapist feel personally and achieve personally that sense of personal agency without which the conduct of a psychotherapy would be a vicarious accomplishment rather than a personal experi-

---

course, he could have been killed for any one of a number of reasons, having nothing to do with him (which I tried to portray in my fantasy vignette of the three Nazi soldiers). He could, in fact, have been seized and murdered for being Catholic, for marrying a Jewish woman, and/or, among other things, for impregnating his wife with another Jewish life (since, in the Jewish religion, the offspring assumes the religion of the mother). In essence, whatever the actual reason for his murder, he was "guilty" for having not been a member of the Nazi party, for the paranoid reason that "what is not me is dangerous to me." My fantasy was triggered by the thought that the non-Nazi would be considered a threat to a Nazi and would be eliminated as such. In addition, the traumatic situation depicted motivated a fantasy within me that involved the major characters in a very specific sense, that is, in a manner that depicted the non-Nazi as distasteful to the Nazis, by reason of the former's normal response to the Nazis' comradely activity (which, to an onlooker, would appear hostile and threatening).

2. I must want very much to find a compassionate German, because when I checked my notes it was clear that my mother had told me that it was a nice Russian man and not, as I say in the text, a nice German man, who took her and her baby to the hospital after the train crash.

ence, the latter being a necessary component in gaining the patient's trust.

As a worker in a program for adolescents abusing (actually, addicted to) drugs in a Brooklyn slum, as in my study of psychoanalytic technique as a candidate at my psychoanalytic training institute, the feeling that my efforts were of value in a person's life made my experience meaningful for me because I thereby experienced a sense of personal agency.

It was not simply that, as a child, I had to live by others' rules, but that I could not determine the course of so much that was to happen—such as my father's death when I was 11 years old, or the fact that, years later, I would contract multiple sclerosis at the age of 23 and later be forced to give up my private practice in psychoanalysis because of the inevitable advance of the illness, the latter being another intrusion into my sense of personal agency, this time in the area of my physical being. My family history seemed to me to be a succession of losses—my parents' parents (my potential grandparents), my father's seven and my mother's seven siblings (my potential aunts and uncles), as well as my parents' first spouses and their children, whose murder, while indirectly enabling my parents to meet and give life to me and my sister, has also been the basis of a great deal of unconscious guilt in me.

The tragedy is too much to bear and makes any hope of rehabilitating the human race forever impossible. And yet, my parents' perhaps unrealistic belief in the power of education to change the world (and the immigrant's place in the world) is the light that shines in the darkness of historical tragedy. I can still believe in my own goodness; in the truth I tell myself about what I want and what I dream and what I do. I hope that what I teach to other individuals, other students, and, directly or indirectly, to other patients and to whoever takes our places will have the effect of helping them not to reproduce what has been worst in our past.

The question of personal agency seems to have been important in the lives of all of my patients, as I now look back at their histories.

I think of Martha (a pseudonym), a "black lady" (as she referred to herself) in her early fifties who dreamed she was—and saw herself, in her behavior, as actually being—30 years old. Her husband and she (although she was not acknowledged as an equal contributor or beneficiary) had established one of the first successful jazz clubs in New York City. One evening, she began her psychotherapy session in tears. Her husband had been shot to death in the course of an armed robbery of the club. Over the succeeding months of our work together, helping her to mourn, Martha used this traumatic event to realize a sense of personal agency—not in the service of becoming young again, but in achieving an important component of the identity of her real self— in living her life as the acknowledged head of her family.

I will never forget the evening that she first felt this recognition of herself—the stillness that Martha exuded in the consultation room when she told of the Easter dinner she led with her five fatherless children This was, it seemed to me, a victory of her sense of personal agency in the service of a solid belief in her right to assume leadership of the family. [Daniel Stern (1985) discusses agency as a crucial invariant in the infant's specifying a sense of a core self.]

Martha's husband's murder left a hole in the structure of a family previously filled by his often overwhelming presence. In mastering the tragedy of his death, Martha rose to a new position of power and respect. A sense of personal agency was achieved in spite of the fact that her fantasy at the beginning of treatment (of being so much younger than she was) was not realized.

Indeed, achieving a sense of personal agency is not dependent on attaining some life goal or fantasy. It does not coincide with the concept of ego competence or efficacy, as discussed by the psychologist Robert White (1959). To attain a sense of personal agency requires that the individual be aware of him- or herself as a functioning/active being in the arena of a life situation that the person is experiencing. It does not require that the individual be the prime mover or, as Julian Rotter (1966) has conceptualized it, have an "internal locus of control" concerning the things that happen or that exist in his or her life.

Rather, to have a sense of personal agency requires that one believes that he or she is involved as a significant actor in what occurs in one's own life, rather than an object who is coincidentally in the field within which something has happened. For example, one can understand why a victim of the Holocaust felt little or no sense of personal agency, a situation within which such a victim has been said to have been passive, or to have "gone like a sheep" to his or her slaughter. It may even be more accurate to speak of such a victim as having had no sense of personal agency rather than as being "guilty" of surviving. Guilt is often used, I believe, because of the psychic pain, the utter frustration that accompanies the thought that one could, in fact, do nothing to stop the murderers. Thus, to accurately assess any person's sense of personal agency requires an analysis of the major sociopolitical and moral climate within which we all function.

To take an extreme example, the acts of a Hitler affect not only his victims, but all those within his victims' sphere of influence and sphere of concern. The behavior within each individual's personal agency touches the spheres of personal agency of many others.

The psychotherapist must therefore be aware of groups and subjects far beyond the individual. It is to such an awareness that Dr. Lawrence Bloom turned in his workshop at the 1996 annual conference of the American Group Psychotherapy Association (AGPA), which he entitled, "All the World's a Group." Of course, it would require an intimate familiarity with the individual to accurately assess the range and depth of his world, his place within that world, and the resulting functioning of his sense of personal agency within a specific situation.

Having said these things, I am reminded of an experience that demonstrated to me just how successful the anti-Semitic scourge was in taking up residence in post-Holocaust, small-town, rural America, where my original nuclear family settled after the Second World War. As to why my family settled there, an answer would no doubt require that we invoke the notion of the repetition compulsion.

This is what happened. One day in the schoolyard, where I was running around mindlessly, all of a sudden, I felt a boy jump on me and bite what turned out to be a sizable chunk out of my back. He then yelled in my ear: "Dirty Jew!"

I had never heard such a thing before this. I had never been the victim of such a curse before this. As if the action had set off some innate alarm within me, I, in shock, pushed my fist into his face and knocked that kid's two front teeth through his upper lip. The next thing I heard was the sound of the principal's voice yelling at me, but not at my attacker. "I want to see your parents tomorrow morning!" I was being blamed for everything!

The next day, when I awoke, I felt two things: a burning sensation on my back where I had been bitten, and anticipatory shame (butterflies in my stomach) at the thought that my father—and his Polish accent—was to come to school with me to see the principal.

What transpired was that my father, the "grene" (greenhorn) defended me about punching that kid, in a show of courageous self-assertion of which I would previously have thought him incapable! But my reaction was not (as I feel now) gratitude, but disappointment. Yes, I was proud, but not relieved. I had wanted my father to *kill* them, to repay them all, for *everything*, then and there! But he had been persecuted as a Jew in Poland his whole life and so he didn't really expect as much as I did!

Still, it was the first time that I consciously felt his protection from a hostile external world, and it gave me what I've referred to in this chapter as a sense of personal agency, a sense that I mattered. This happened once I no longer felt powerless, helpless, and insignificant in the face of the anti-Semitic other. Quite outside my conscious awareness, I began to evolve the sense of agency that would be crucial in the forces that led me to become a psychotherapist.

My life in that rural ghetto of anti-Semites ended abruptly with my father's quiet death of a heart attack, his fifth and final one, when I was 11 years old. Almost everyone attributed his premature death to the cumulative residua of the tortures he had suffered in the war and the trials of his subsequent assimilation to a new life. I, unfortunately, felt more personally responsible, an unbearable guilt I rejected by eschewing any sense of personal agency. It was only in working through these painful conflicts that I could begin to assume a more self-fulfilling confrontation with my past and the shackles it had imposed upon me in the present.

I have discussed a number of matters in this chapter that have, as a common element, one of the major questions raised by this volume, namely, What is it that is important in the making of a psychotherapist? The specific issues that the psychotherapist helps his or her patients to deal with are often a link to problems or concerns in the therapist's own life. The opportunity that work with a patient offers to vicariously deal with these concerns (including the opportunity to experience a sense of personal agency) makes becoming a psychotherapist of such importance to those of us who have made it our life's work. By becoming psychotherapists, we give ourselves permission to be what some, including some of our own profession, would consider selfish. We give ourselves permission not only to search for errors and for understanding, but to maintain a sense of ourselves alongside our patients during the therapeutic hour.

ACKNOWLEDGMENTS

I want to thank Janet Fisher for her help in revising the original draft of this chapter and Spencer Means, Baruch College, CUNY librarian, for his help in obtaining some of the material I used in my research.

Leon S. Anisfeld, D.S.W., is a member of the Institute for Psychoanalytic Training and Research (IPTAR) and the New York Freudian Society.

REFERENCES

Rotter, J. (1966). Generalized expectancies for internal versus external control of reinforcement. *Psychological Monograph* 80:1–28.
Stern, D. (1985). *The Interpersonal World of the Infant.* New York: Basic Books.
White, R. (1959). Motivation reconsidered: the concept of competence. *Psychological Review* 66:297–333.

3

My World, the World of Psychoanalysis, and Its "Innermost Essence"

MARIA V. BERGMANN

In my first psychoanalytic consultation, my analyst asked me, "Why do you want to become a psychoanalyst?" I had heard about free association and I replied spontaneously, "I think I want to know what holds the world together in its innermost essence" (*"Ich will wissen was die Welt in Innersten zusammenhaelt"*). This is my translation of a quote from Goethe's *Faust*: Faust says he wants to know what holds the world together from within and he is willing to make a pact with the devil in order to find out. I had read Mephisto in a reading of the first part of *Faust* in my school class in Vienna, an assignment I had been very proud to execute, and therefore I knew these lines by heart. I did not know then the many implications of what I was saying. At that point in my life I was trying to hold many threads together from my own creation up to my current life, which was new and varied and so different from the world from which I had come. What springs to mind is the description by Tristram Shandy of how he visualized "the innermost essence" of how he came to be in this world:

> I wish either my father or my mother, or indeed both of them, as they were in duty both equally bound to it, had minded what they were about when they begot me; had they duly considered how

much depended upon what they were doing; that not only the
production of a rational Being was concerned in it, but that possibly the happy formation and temperature of his body, perhaps his
genius and the very cast of his mind; and, for aught they knew to
the contrary, even the fortunes of his whole house might take their
turn from the humours and dispositions which were then upper-
most; . . . Had they duly weighed and considered all this, and pro-
ceeded accordingly, . . . I am verily persuaded I should have made
a quite different figure in the world, from that in which the reader
is likely to see me.

"Pray, my Dear," quoth my mother, "have you not forgot to wind
up the clock?" . . . "Good G—!" cried my father, making an ex-
clamation, but taking care to moderate his voice at the same
time, . . . "Did ever woman, since the creation of the world, inter-
rupt a man with such a silly question?" "Pray, what was your father saying? . . . Nothing." [Sterne 1760, pp. 5–6]

This is how Tristram Shandy began to solve the problem for himself—in two volumes—of what held the world together. My questions
were different. When I was born, a terrible aura of war still hung over
my family and over the streets of Vienna, which were replete with
wounded veterans. I wondered why I was there when some of my
uncles, whom everybody knew but I, had been lost in the war. I knew
them only from pictures on the walls. Everybody loved them and my
grandmother cried about them. War and death still permeated the air
like a heavy fog.

In some ways my life was very cheerful. In kindergarten my first
boyfriend was Harry. I was invited to his birthday party and his birthday cake was an elongated chocolate cake with almonds stuck on top,
which looked like the needles of a porcupine. I still remember this cake,
which deeply impressed me. The party was an exciting event because
Harry was very important to me.

From my preschool years through part of elementary school, there
was Marika, my best girlfriend. Her parents were friends of the family. We played together for days on end. Her father would draw pictures into my diary and Marika herself could draw wonderful pictures
that looked like real things. Suddenly, Marika's family had to leave

Vienna. They went to Russia. I learned later that her father had fled from Hungary because he was a communist and now had to leave Vienna precipitously. Marika and I corresponded for years. She drew wonderful pictures about her experiences and she made a calendar for me with illustrations of the different seasons (perhaps my later love of medieval miniatures depicting the seasons go back to Marika's drawings). This was my first experience of losing a close friend and not understanding why this had happened.

My elementary school was called the Pedagogical Institute, one of two schools in Vienna that were experimentally run by modern creative methods with an emphasis on giving children space for self-expression. I revisited this school on my last trip to Vienna and saw that on the facade of the building, covering the entire front, were marvelous illustrations four or five feet high drawn by children. The illustrations were colorful and cheerful. I loved being in school. My most important encounter was my elementary school teacher, whom I had grown to love. I planted a lemon pit in a flower pot and took it to school when two or three leaves had sprouted. The tree continued to grow on a classroom window. Before I left Austria, I revisited my teacher and the tree.

We were encouraged to do crafts work, and when I was between 7 and 8 years old, I designed a pillow for Mother's and Father's Day. The design had lines, circles, and triangles in many colors. It was an overly ambitious project and my grandmother helped me finish it for Mother's Day. It was ensconced in the living room on the sofa, but when it was admired I felt I needed to tell people that my grandmother helped me finish it, and this was why the stitches were so regular. When I went through my mother's papers a few years ago, after her death, I found the design for the pillow among her papers.

My mother was an educator who received psychoanalytic training from Anna Freud. Anna Freud had two branches of psychoanalytic education in Vienna. One was for the training of child analysts and the other for the training of educators who would work with children who had problems. My mother worked with children who were in analysis, with children who had learning difficulties, and with children who had trouble with impulse control. By the time I was 11 years old,

I was able to help her. I began to realize that children could be very troubled and very unhappy. I understood intuitively that they could be reached and helped by being talked to and shown things. But I was puzzled about why they needed analysis or someone special to talk to who could somehow help them to be less unhappy. How did that happen? It remained a mystery.

My father was a mathematician and, as I later understood, one of the first topologists. He published papers and went to international congresses. (Sometimes he came home with someone else's raincoat that was not as nice as his and my mother was dismayed.) In Vienna, however, he could teach only in the gymnasium and at the university only in night school because he was a Jew.

My father opened up a different world of whys for me. When I was a young teenager, he brought home a book of Einstein's theories for teenagers and we read it together. He taught me chess, and we had exciting talks about prime numbers, which could not be divided by any number except 1, and about the strange position of the number 0. He informed me that parallel lines eventually met in infinity for which I saw absolutely no reason. To me this assumption seemed unfathomable and I could not understand why mathematicians bothered with it. Our discussions were exciting and when I was not logical, he immediately interrupted me and tried to teach me how to think when presenting an argument. He was a logical positivist with a fervor and when I was older he showed me a book he cherished. It was written in 1920 by one Hugo Bergmann and called *The Struggle for the Principle of Causality* (my translation). Many years later, I married Bergmann's son. I told my husband that I had seen this book by his father, because it was in my father's possession, and he had cherished it, but Martin had never heard of it!

The other important why had also a what and a how attached to it. It had to do with music. My parents said I could pick out tunes on the piano with one finger before I could talk. I don't know if this is true, but I do remember improvising from the time I was young. On Sundays, my parents regularly played classical music, for four hands, on the piano. When I played with my mother, she would stop when she saw me play a wrong note, and say, "Now look again. What does it say here?" My father was amused when I improvised a measure or two that I could not read properly, particularly in a fast movement, and let it pass with a smile. It was obvious in retrospect that I needed them both: one for discipline and one for spontaneity.

I had my first piano teacher when I was 6 years old. She was a sourpuss and, excited as I was to finally get lessons, I edged my way to confessing that I really didn't like Miss Paula. She always looked as if she was going to cry, and she didn't seem to enjoy music. Mercifully, I was sent to the Children's Conservatory at 6½ where a new world opened for me. I was extremely fond of my teacher, and very sad when I was skipped and sent to the Adult Conservatory after a little less than two years. This school, in which I was the youngest, was housed in one of the large concert halls in Vienna, which served me and my girlfriends well for our endless walks through the empty corridors when we were not in class and where we could discuss the facts of life, our feelings about boys, and gossip about our teachers.

I had to get used to functioning without individual instruction, and be a member of a class where I was the youngest. We had to perform for each other, and everything was discussed. All mistakes were talked about. My teacher was tall, heavyset, wore enormous hats, and everybody was afraid of her. Her assistant was thin, shy, and had a bad complexion. We teased her and terrified her perhaps in order to tolerate the terror spread by our other teacher. One of the first pieces I played was Beethoven's "Für Elise." I guess I played it like a march or like folk music. The teacher shook her head. She threw her eyes up to the ceiling, a familiar gesture usually reserved for technical errors. "One can see from the way you play this piece that you have never been in love! Don't you realize that Beethoven *loved* Elise, that he admired her, and dedicated this piece to her?" I turned crimson. I was barely 9 years old. I still loved "Für Elise" thereafter, and I still play Beethoven.

Music became increasingly important to me. When I was a young teenager, I first joined a children's chorus, and then became a member of a regular concert chorus shortly before I left Austria. The other important musical influence was an invitation to a small circle of people who were privileged to listen to concert rehearsals of composers of the Second Vienna School (the atonal descendants of Schönberg) before each performance. Each composer explained something about his composition before a concert. Most of what was being said was not clear to me at that time. But the idea that the structure of a musical composition could be described in words made a deep impression on me.

Another important influence of those years was the youth movement. We took hikes, debated politics, and there I first learned about Marx and Freud. At that time, many of us attempted to link the doctrines of Marx with the ideas of Freud, idealizing their potential of healing the ills of the world. I found that my parents had some books by Freud at home and I read *The Future of an Illusion, Civilization and Its Discontents,* and *Beyond the Pleasure Principle,* and Wilhelm Reich's *Sexual Struggle of Youth* when I was 14 years old. It appeared that there was a world beyond the immediately knowable, something beyond the obvious, visible, something unconscious, that could come to life and be known. This fascinated me. There was also the very important task of freeing the world from prejudices of various kinds. Saving the world and saving children from becoming unhappy became amalgamated ideals in my mind. I was convinced that these issues were related and that it was only a matter of knowledge to find ways to achieve both.

All this suddenly came to an end without warning. In 1934 Dollfuss was shot and a weak chancellor succeeded him. I remember that after his death the picture of Dollfuss was on posters all over Vienna with a black frame around it and one of the American children asked, "Why do they advertise a dead person?" It taught me something about culture being relative: a poster is an advertisement to an American child. The adults had been insecure about the government for four years before Hitler marched into Vienna in 1938. But this threat had been outside my emotional awareness.

I had been rehearsing Mahler's *Second Symphony* in the chorus behind the orchestra, under the direction of Hermann Scherchen. It was incredibly exciting, although my position was behind the trumpets, and I was disillusioned by all the noise they made cleaning their instruments when they did not play music. Overnight, the rehearsals were canceled and the chorus disbanded. We learned that Scherchen had fled to Switzerland. My fellow students in school were out in the streets welcoming Hitler, marching and shouting. I sensed immediately that our life as we knew it had abruptly ended. I would awaken in the morning cheerfully, the sun was shining, and all of a sudden I would remember what had happened. It seemed like a black cloud that was impenetrable. It changed our lives. There were no more public meetings, concerts, or theatres for us. My father stopped going to the café where he talked mathematics with his colleagues. The American families left Vienna, and were soon followed by the Viennese analysts, many of whom had been friends of my parents, and some of their children had been my friends.

Every day, incidents of terror against Jews were reported, and their number increased. People were yanked out of their homes, their possessions were stolen, their homes were vandalized, and their store windows were smashed. Many were wounded and left without medical care. Others were taken away to an unknown destination.

Nevertheless, my parents hesitated to leave. It meant leaving an aging grandmother and two older uncles. Since one of his older brothers had an important position in the city administration of Vienna, my father thought that our family would be safe. Other people's parents also hesitated. By contrast, all my friends wanted to leave. After a great deal of pressure on my part, and a great loss of time on the quota system for Austrians, my mother wrote to one of our American friends asking for an affidavit for us to come to the United States. Our waiting time on the quota system took more than a year. The first thing to do was to get a passport. There were interminably long lines at the passport office. In addition, one had to have a lawyer specialized in matters of emigration. Other young people and I stood in line night after night until the wee hours of the morning, because we were young and strong enough to take it.

Hitler marched into Austria in March 1938. By August, the border to Switzerland was closed. A lot of people had fled there while it was possible. I had two close friends who planned to cross the Alps to get into Switzerland. It was, of course, very dangerous, but everyone thought it was less dangerous than to stay. I was afraid to join them for fear of holding them up, for I was not as physically strong as they were. They were convinced there would be a way for me to join them once they were in Switzerland. It was agreed that once in Switzerland, if a way was found, I would get a letter with some innocuous information about the weather. It would be a folded piece of paper, and on the empty page inside instructions would be written in lemon juice informing me what I had to do. I would have to hold a lit match under the empty page and the flame would make the lemon juice turn brown, and I would be able to read my instructions—an old boy-scout trick.

In September, in a little more than one month after my two friends had left, such a letter actually arrived. I was instructed to send a photograph together with the date and time when I would board a train to Zurich. I was to occupy the last compartment of the train, and a man from the Swiss border police would come, stamp my passport, and let me go on to Zurich.

I followed my instructions. Two days before I was ready to leave, and after I had finally received a valid passport, without which one was a "non-person," the Gestapo issued an order that everyone who desired a valid passport to emigrate from Austria would have to get a red J stamped on top of the first page. However, only people with valid exit visas could get such a J. On the other hand, a passport without a J was not valid. Recently a *New York Times* article (February 8, 1997) stated that Switzerland suggested to Nazi Germany in 1938 that the letter J be stamped into German Jewish passports to facilitate recognition by the Swiss border police. Through this article I learned that the J had been a Swiss invention. As far as facilitating recognition, I remember vividly how I was struck by the difference between an Austrian passport bound in leatherette with gold letters, looking friendly to the beholder, and the ugly brown paper with black letters that adorned our passports, which looked more like something to be discarded than something to be remembered.

To have an invalid passport was like being a "non-person" again. And yet leaving without the J was risking arrest. So was leaving without a visa. I decided I had to have a valid passport with a J for the Swiss border police. This represented, as I was aware, a way of thinking which defied any logical argument, a way of thinking that I had learned from my father. I did not realize it then, but it was a way to achieve a greater likelihood of survival. I felt I had no choice. I went to a beautiful Vienna baroque palace with a double marble staircase fenced in by a wrought iron grill. At the entrance, in a large marble hall, two Gestapo officials were seated at a desk issuing the J. The incongruity of this beautiful building, seized by the Nazis for official purposes, and what these men were doing, did not strike me at the time. I placed myself in the long line of people who had exit visas, and stood there for many hours. I realized that if I would be caught by the Gestapo I would immediately and forcefully be taken to prison. I stuffed some papers into my passport, which in my fantasy made the passport look more official. When my turn came, I put the passport on the table. The man in charge put the J in mindlessly, as he had done in many passports before. This had been my great hope. Further down the line was a couple, friends of mine who had a visa for the United States. They knew my situation. When they saw me leave the line, they shook their heads, almost imperceptibly, and an equally almost imperceptible smile crossed their faces. My legs felt weak and my heart pounded. I got into the street and took the next streetcar away from that spot. I didn't even know where it was going. Then I found my way home.

On the appointed day, I took the train. I said goodbye to my parents. I had a very small suitcase with an overnight change of clothing, a sandwich, and a bunch of grapes. When we came close to the border, the train almost emptied. Two Gestapo men in uniform boarded the train. I had not counted on that. I knew that there was a prison for women on the border and I would be taken there if I tried to cross the border illegally. They demanded my passport, looked at it, and took it away. They said I would have to get off. I went back to my compartment and I suddenly knew what it felt like "to have nothing to lose but one's chains." I paced up and down, thinking over what I should do. The two men stood near the exit. One of them was holding my passport. I yanked the passport out of his hands and shouted at him that he had no right to take it away from me. I caught a glimpse of the facial expression of the man who had held my passport, and I could see an expression of astonishment, perhaps a feeling of being caught by surprise. I ran to the other end of the train to be at the back of the last compartment.

Meanwhile, the train stopped, the two men got out, and in less than a minute, we were at the Swiss border. A Swiss official entered the train. I immediately knew when he looked at me without recognition of my face or my name that he was the wrong man. He stated the obvious: "You have no visa." He turned my passport around into which he had placed an entry stamp, which he tried to cross out, but he ran out of ink. I said I was sorry, but I knew I had no visa. He tried to put "visitor" into my passport underneath the stamp, but again, he couldn't do it, as he had no ink. He told me I had to get out. I told him I knew. I followed him happily, because I was in Switzerland. He bade me to sit down in the station house. Another man came in and as soon as the first man left, he told me that he had recognized me immediately from the photo, but the other man had boarded the last compartment first, and therefore he had been unable to go there. He told me that he would get me a room in a nearby guest house that he called "cheap but clean," and that I could take a local train at 4 A.M. to Zurich. Nobody would check that train. He was on duty, and he would get me the ticket. I asked if I could make a phone call. I called my friends, who were already celebrating my arrival in Zurich. Nobody had expected that there would be a problem. During the night, the station man and I ate my grapes and talked. He belonged to a social democratic organization that tried to help refugees leave Austria illegally. But he said it was becoming more difficult. The Austrian Nazis made leaving impossible and the Swiss Nazi party made immigration impossible. When I reached Zurich as an illegal immigrant, I felt I was in paradise, in spite of the fact that I was told that I would have to be hidden, and that if found, I would be sent back to the border, where I would be shot by the Nazis.

Attempts were made to make my stay in Switzerland official, but it was too late to legalize my existence there. However, after just having escaped two life-threatening situations with the Gestapo, I could take in stride being unofficially in Switzerland. I lived comfortably, albeit very frugally, in warm Swiss hospitality. In addition, I had a circle of friends, some Swiss and some who had escaped from Austria.

After three long months, my aunt, who lived in London, was able to procure a visitor's visa for me to come to England until my affidavit from America would come through. I was a little apprehensive leaving Switzerland, wondering whether I would be questioned at the border, since I had never officially been there. I was able to leave without an incident. It was hard to say goodbye to my friends.

In England I worked as an au pair with children. I was fortunate to find two English sponsors who made it possible for my parents to come to England and for my friend to come from Switzerland. I left with my parents for the United States in a British convoy in January 1940.

Incredible as it seemed to us, once we were in the United States, my father was suddenly recognized as an important mathematician. He found work almost immediately, at the Institute of Advanced Study in Princeton. My mother became an educational director in a school. I applied for a scholarship, and got into college. I had to have perfect grades, in spite of my not-so-perfect English, in order to continue my studies. I could work with children during the summers to have pocket money, but I needed to have free tuition. I was happy that I was able to have my undergraduate and graduate education on scholarships, fellowships, and as a teaching fellow. As soon as my parents had a home, they acquired an upright piano and I could be in touch with music again. While in school, I exchanged German lessons for piano lessons. I studied psychology and philosophy, but took all my elective work in art history.

I married Martin Bergmann in 1947. Together we engaged in a life of study and exploration of psychoanalysis that still continues. Learning about art and art history became a passion that came to life particularly on some of our summer trips.

Our learning of psychoanalysis took two forms: in peer groups and learning from our teachers. In some of the peer groups I found myself once more to be the youngest, but I felt more protected than when I entered the Adult Conservatory of Music. Many of the leading peer group members are no longer with us: Joel Shor, John Herma, Edmund Weil, Moses and Giza Barinbaum. Joachim Flescher had come from Italy and worked with me in supervision for a while. My first supervisor was Esther Menaker, then Marcel Heimen, and later

Marianne Kris. Jesse Zizmor, who became a beloved friend, organized the licensing of psychologists in Albany. We had private study groups with leading psychoanalysts, who would analyze us, supervise us, and teach us in seminars, provided we would not make this public. Today, one would ask, "But how would the countertransference of your analyst or teachers have influenced your experience, keeping your training secret, and what effect did that have on you?!"

At that time, we were so grateful to be trained, albeit unofficially, by well-known analysts in the profession that we idealized our training situation. We needed to feel supported by it; we could not question it in any way. For me, having brought the atmosphere of "real" psychoanalysis from home, I felt very fortunate to have these opportunities. They were exciting and opened a new world of study and inquiry. A damper was put on our learning experience by our limited social acceptability as unofficial students. Once again, I found myself pursuing something that was extremely desirable, absolutely necessary, but could not be officially acknowledged. We sat in the last rows at the Psychoanalytic Institute (behind the rope for nonmembers) to listen to lectures.

The International Congress in Zurich in 1949 was the first congress after the war. It was emotionally very meaningful to many who met there who had not seen each other during the war years. We had difficulties being admitted, in spite of the necessary signatures by members we had obtained in advance. After we succeeded, we were the only nonmembers present. We heard the initial rendering of Rene Spitz's paper on anxiety in infants and saw his film of babies on a little screen. (This paper was published in the *International Journal of Psycho-Analysis* in 1950.) At that meeting the painful question of collaboration with the Nazis resulted in a debate whether Schultz-Henke, a German former Nazi, should be expelled from the International: it finally did happen. Emotionally important to me was the book table of the congress, which exhibited several volumes of the early psychoanalytic *Imagoes* and *International Journals* in German (!). I bought two of these volumes immediately but debated whether we could afford more. By the time I had talked this over with Martin, all the other volumes had been sold. These volumes had probably been bought by people attending the congress who, like myself, cherished the best of our intellectual heritage, which somehow miraculously had been salvaged.

Symbols of exclusion from all official organizations of psychoanalysis were shared with our peers with whom we could talk about this. It was from these first peer groups that my first patients came. Many of us went to all lectures and congresses to which we could gain admittance, and our courses and seminars on the "black market" went on for many years. Later on, becoming a member of the Holocaust Study Group of the American Psychoanalytic Association, and working within it for fourteen years, was personally very painful, but also healing. The group gradually evolved a new paradigm for the study of trauma.

Our first study group with a distinguished analyst was the study group led by Paul Federn. We read Freud's most important papers in what today would be considered great detail, pondering on the various meanings of Freud's ideas. It took the better part of the year to read *Inhibitions, Symptoms, and Anxiety*. After each study group meeting, Dr. Federn devoted a short period to explaining some of his own ideas to us. These related to what many years later contributed to a better understanding of clinical problems of borderline and schizophrenic patients. After Paul Federn's death, his son Ernst and Martin Bergmann organized the Paul Federn study group. We were able to engage Dr. Robert Waelder as our seminar leader. For many years, he worked with us for three or more hours on many Saturday afternoons. Dr. Waelder was our first systematic psychoanalytic teacher. He guided us through new and difficult ideas with the utmost clarity. He had come from Vienna as a non-M.D. analyst. By the time we came to know him, he had made important contributions to psychoanalysis.

Simultaneously, we had many visiting analysts from the New York area whose work we studied in advance and who gave us lectures or brief courses. We studied the dream with Henry Alden Bunker and schizophrenia and perversions with Robert Bak. Phyllis Greenacre, Edith Jacobson, Herman Nunberg, Rene Spitz, and many others lectured in the Paul Federn study group. I also took courses with Ernst Kris at the New School on Piaget and on ego psychology. At the same time, we were analyzed and were able to have "unofficial" supervision. (Dr. Robert Wallerstein refers to some of these events in his forthcoming book, *Lay Analysis: Life Inside the Controversy,* to be published by Yale University Press.)

Teaching the first year of courses given by the Training Institute of the New York Freudian Society, and helping to put its curriculum together, was a most important step, providing a new level of psychoanalytic exchange with a group of people who were interested and enthusiastic. Two courses I initially put together and taught on early ego pathology and fantasy formation are still being taught. Over the years and for thirty years hence, at the New York Freudian Society and in my private seminars, I taught almost every subject of interest to me and my students. Teaching became an important way of continuous learning. It became part of a new and vibrant professional life.

It was a great feeling to realize that I could impart some of what I had learned about psychoanalysis to a generation of younger professional people who wanted to join the field but who, like myself, were unable to receive such training at a medical institute. At that time, this fact was in the forefront of our joint consciousness—our zeitgeist—within our professional group, more so than it is now, when psychologists, social workers, and people from other academic disciplines have a number of choices to apply for training to a psychoanalytic institute.

I gave my first lecture at the New York Psychoanalytic Institute in 1978. My discussants were Drs. Peter Blos and Burness Moore, and shortly thereafter I published my first paper in the *International Journal of Psycho-Analysis*. It was the first time I felt seen and heard by an esteemed and official psychoanalytic forum and journal. Other papers followed. Reviewing the years of development of my thoughts, I find that much has to be revised I once thought to be the only correct and ultimate truth from which to view psychoanalytic issues. I have written about and am still most interested in the clinical situation—in the why, how, and what of cure.

In spite of the current difficulties that have beset our field, my enthusiasm for what psychoanalysis is and what it can accomplish is a prime mover of my motivation, my ideas, and my ideals. The discovery that people can improve their lives and change is by itself an incredible life experience; that one can be effective in bringing this about with the tools of psychoanalysis never ceases to be a great discovery. I have learned something about "what holds the world together in its innermost essence," and although I also had to learn what psychoanalysis cannot reveal or accomplish, I have not given up the search.

Maria V. Bergmann is a Training and Supervising Analyst at the Institute for Psychoanalytic Training and Research (IPTAR) and the New York Freudian Society.

REFERENCES

Spitz, R. A. (1950). Anxiety in infancy: manifestations in the first year of life. *International Journal of Psycho-Analysis* 31:138–143.
Sterne, L. (1760). *The Life and Opinions of Tristram Shandy, Gentleman.* London: Macmillan, 1924.

4

An Endless Becoming

HEDDA BOLGAR

Being a psychotherapist is an endless becoming. It is not doing something but rather a going on being, to use Winnicott's words. It is not something that has a clear beginning and point in time when the becoming ends and one is. It has very little to do with training programs and certifications or with what one lists on official documents in answer to the question about "occupation." Not that those things are not useful and perhaps necessary to relieve the therapist's anxiety, to confirm identity, and as a reminder that even the most unique and individual becoming and being take place in a social context.

I have been psychotherapist for over fifty years and a psychoanalyst for a little over forty years and the changes in the world around me and in the world of psychoanalysis as well as the rediscoveries and changes in myself continue to contribute to my becoming.

Writing about becoming a psychotherapist is in effect a review of my entire life. Almost everything that I remember connects in some way with what I bring daily into my consulting room, with the successful end of what Robert Stolorow calls the "search for the analog." I listen, scan the screen of my experience, and I remember the emotions surrounding an event similar enough to the patient's experience to understand, to be able to respond, and to accept the projections. The very first time I thought I knew what another person felt and would do was when I was 3 years old. I was at the dinner table with my father and mother and I refused to eat the spinach on my plate. My father, in his very quiet way, said, "If you don't feel like eating what we are eating you might as well go to your room." I do not recall being upset and once in my room I remember saying to myself, "I know we are having chocolate rice for dessert. It is my favorite dessert. Mom is not going to let me go without it. She will bring me some." And sure enough, Mom appeared with a dish of chocolate rice. I will never forget the feeling of elation about having made an accurate prediction about how another person's mind worked. Unfortunately, there was a down side to the elation that I dimly felt but did not understand—a sense of regret about my mother's defiance of my father and even a sense of contempt for her. Complex Oedipus?

My early life was a time of overstimulation, loss, and, I believe, depression. There were too many events—my parents' divorce when I was 3½, the beginning of World War I when I was 5, my mother and I moving into my grandparents' home, losing my first nanny, starting school at 6. I was my parents' only child and my grandparents' only grandchild and I had my main meal of the day with very verbal adults who passionately argued about a wide range of issues. By 7 I knew that war was bad, and that victory meant that there were more dead on the other side than on ours. I knew that women should have the vote and that the government should take care of the wives and children of the day laborers who had been drafted without notice and had to leave their families to fend for themselves. Also, by 7 I knew that there were children who did not have enough to eat. They were a special group referred to as "poorchildren" and I felt so guilty about them that I did not want any presents on my seventh birthday; I wanted the money to be used for the poorchildren and I wanted it to be an anonymous gift. My mother sent me flowers for my birthday.

There was not only a great deal of intellectual stimulation; there was also a whirlwind schedule of activities (not unlike that of the American teenager today). We were in the middle of a world war, transportation was becoming a problem, food was being rationed, and many of the basics had become unavailable, but I had to have piano lessons, dancing school, fencing lessons, and arts and crafts. There was a great deal of visiting my friends in distant parts of the city and playing with the ones who lived close by. There also were the obligatory daily walks.

It now seems to me that my family was trying to shield me from the realities of growing up with—as my mother wrote in one of her poems—the roaring of the cannons of war, and to duplicate my mother's childhood in an affluent and peaceful world. Our life during those years now feels like a manic defense against the chronic mourning everybody in the family was constantly experiencing. There were past deaths; both my grandparents had lost their mothers at age 14. My grandmother had lost three of her four children, leaving my mother as the only survivor of that tragedy to carry my grandmother's raging grief and her own guilty mourning of her sainted little brother.

On the surface life moved too fast. Events, activities, people, and ideas came and changed in such rapid succession that it seemed to me that everything happened just once or for too brief a time. Today I know that what I knew not consciously then was that very little was experienced deeply. An early memory associated with that issue goes back to a morning before I was old enough to go to school. For some reason there must have been more than the usual comings and goings that day—the arrival of the new nanny; my grandfather's daily exasperated search for his cuff links while he was dressing, to walk to his favorite café on the Corso (the promenade along the Danube) for breakfast and reading the major newspapers; my grandmother's daily conference with the cook; and everybody reminding everybody to be quiet and careful not to awaken my mother before ten o'clock.

Whatever the reasons, on that particular morning I became aware of a delicious feeling of being unattended as I dragged my toys into a deserted dining room. I sat down on the floor and carefully arranged all the toys, all the arts and crafts inventory, and my beloved stuffed black cat in a complete circle around me. When that was done I said to myself, "If I sit here with all these things around me, they will think that I am playing and they will leave me alone to think." To this day I can feel that intense craving for silence and solitude. I suspect that what I wanted to "think" about was my father and how much I missed him since my parents' divorce and how nobody seemed to acknowledge that the weekly Sunday afternoon walks with him might not be enough for me. I remember dreaming about him at night and day dreaming about his coming back. Nobody else seemed to miss him.

However, although much of my life was marked by separations and losses there were also many times when what I have described as overstimulation felt like richness; side by side with the grief there was humor and laughter and a sense of optimism. There was always a conviction that we could find a solution for every problem and that life had to be lived with dignity no matter what the circumstances were.

I was born in Zurich, Switzerland, where my father was getting his doctorate in history. He was writing a dissertation about the history of the labor movement. My mother had interrupted her career as the first and only woman journalist on the staff of a prestigious German-language newspaper in Budapest to marry my father and move with him to Zurich. They were in their mid-twenties, deeply committed to socialist ideals and rejecting bourgeois middle-class values and life styles. They took their main meal at the student cafeteria in the company of friends who happened to be students of Bleuler and C. G. Jung. According to my mother, that was where I received my prenatal psychoanalytic training, being exposed every noon to examples of enthusiastically related stories about the great professor Jung and examples of his near-miraculous skills in interpreting dreams. If so, that early training lay dormant and stayed unconscious for a long time while my life took many other turns.

At the end of my first year we returned briefly to Budapest, only to leave again, this time for the United States. My father had received an invitation from Stanley Hall at Clark University to lecture for a year on issues of labor organization. That was in 1910, one year after Freud had held a similar position there. My father had lived in the United States before in an effort to "organize" Hungarian workers in Cleveland. For my mother it was her first stay in America; she spoke fluent English and fell in love with everything American. Louisa May Alcott's *Little Women* seemed to reflect all that was good and cheerful and strong and self-reliant and spiritual in life, and Jo and Amy and Meg and Beth became my companions long after we returned to Europe. Somewhere along the middle of the year at Worcester, however, my mother became bored with being just a wife and mother when she was offered a staff job by the *Worcester Chronicle*. She accepted eagerly, and I was shipped off to Dunellen, New Jersey, to live with my father's family. I have no memory of that time, being about 18 months old. I do not know how I managed the separation from my parents but I was told that I had a wonderful time with my southern aunt who had been born as the eldest of eight children in Atlanta, ten years after Sherman marched through Georgia during the Civil War. Aunt Thressa adored and wanted children, and did eventually have eight of them herself. By the time I got there, she and my uncle already had two boys, and my cousin Rose was born while I was there. The stories I was told about that time suggest that life was safe and free and fun and games, and that Coca-Cola could cure any discomfort a child might feel. In case of a serious sunstroke, orange juice could be substituted. My younger male cousin was my hero; every morning before going to school he came to see me and brought me a "crackr," to eat. I was a little over 2 years old. I spoke English as my first and main language, although I had retained some of my earlier Hungarian and German baby words. I was right on Margaret Mahler's schedule and indeed the world was my oyster when we sailed back to Europe.

Budapest was home during my elementary school years and the place where much of my truly formative experiences took place. My parents' divorce was a highly civilized one. My mother fell in love with another man; there were only two legal reasons for divorce—adultery and desertion. My father gallantly agreed to desert my mother and left for a six-week trip to Italy. He returned with a beautiful small black sculpted vase (which I still have) as a final gift for my mother and she and I moved into her parents' home.

My grandfather was a warm, bright, affectionate, sensuous, and extremely generous man. He was my playmate, he told me stories about the animals he had loved, he took me on imaginary travels at bedtime, he walked with me in the park and spoke English with me mostly to attract attention and have people say admiringly, "Oh, she is so small and already she can speak English."

My grandmother was a most accomplished Victorian lady; she ran a comfortable home, supervised the maids, entertained everybody's guests and friends and was always immaculately elegant, wearing nothing but black or purple. I always felt very safe with and nurtured by her but also was vaguely aware of some fear of her bitterness, harshness, and contempt in dealing with most other people. She never forgave my mother for surviving the diphtheria that killed her adored little son, and my mother never forgave her for saying to her that the wrong child died when my mother, age 10, tried to console and comfort her inconsolable mother.

Ernö, my mother's lover and later husband, bright, warm and resplendent in his officer's uniform, appeared whenever he could get a furlough from his wartime service. He charmed my grandparents. He obviously adored my mother, and he wooed me with the most thoughtful and generous gifts, including seventeen books for the Christmas after my seventh birthday. He had the largest collection of jokes of anybody I have ever known and he told them well and with taste and tact. He contributed to a great deal of laughter and joie de vivre in my life. He was also the one who helped me with my math homework as needed.

There was very little overt aggression in my family. I was never punished except by my mother's disapproval, expressed in a cold tone of voice with surprise that I did not know any better than to do whatever displeased her. At age 4 I was told, "We do not make noises while eating," when I drew attention to the exquisite pleasure of loudly crunching my cucumber salad. And when at age 7 I fell from a swing and broke my wrist and screamed in pain, my mother looked at me lying on the floor and said, in that disgusted tone of voice, "We don't make such primitive sounds." I do not recall her comforting me. She did teach me one lesson very early that I have always considered invaluable in becoming a therapist. One day, when I was in first grade, I came home from school and proudly told her about my humiliating triumph over another older child by demonstrating in front of my whole class that I was smarter than she was. My mother did not share my pride but said, "And did you ever think how that other child might have felt?" My analyst seemed to think that a 6-year-old should not be expected to be as empathic as all that, and perhaps she also felt that my mother did not demonstrate much empathy for me, but all things considered it was an experience I still value.

My parents never argued; in fact I have never heard my father raise his voice. If my grandfather ever felt any anger or rage, it was controlled by an admirably adaptive degree of reaction formation. He was very kind, forgiving, and generous, taking responsibility for the misdeeds of other people, as in the case of his young assistant, whom he trusted and who embezzled large amounts of the firm's funds. My grandfather did not prosecute, saying that he was at fault for not offering enough supervision and for putting too much temptation in a young person's path. Obviously, the story had a happy ending or I never would have heard it. The young man showed his gratitude by repaying everything he owed.

My mother and grandmother argued a lot, mostly about my grandmother's treatment of the maids, but I viewed those fights as political discussions between labor and capitalism. In fact, all verbal aggression in my family was directed against the monarchy, imperialism, war, capitalism, and oppression of women and of the poor.

The war ended when I was 9. The Austro-Hungarian Empire fell apart, the monarchy was dead, the soldiers came back singing, sporting white asters pinned to their uniforms to celebrate the peace. The walls of the city were plastered with red posters screaming "No, No, Never," meaning no war ever again; the officers tore their insignia from their coats. The revolution had begun. My mother, stepfather, and father immediately became deeply involved in it. To me it was our revolution and it was glorious. It lasted a few months and then collapsed. It was replaced by the "white" terror of the counterrevolution. There was shooting in the streets and torture and executions of the leaders of the revolution. My parents managed to escape before they were arrested. They moved to Vienna and I followed a few months later. Thus started my first experience of political emigration and the deep sense of failure, shame, poverty, and loss. Before my grandparents took me to Vienna I wrote with chalk on the floor of our living room: "I will never see this place again."

I hated Vienna. The destruction of the First World War was much greater there then it had been in Budapest. The streets were in complete darkness after eight o'clock in the evening; it was cold and hun-

ger was everywhere. My mother and stepfather lived in a small furnished apartment and there was no room for me. I was sent to boarding school, and I could not see my mother except on weekends. The
horror of the weekly Sunday night separation when I had to go back
to the "Pensionat" stayed with me for many years.

I was 10 years old. I had lost everything. I had to make the change
from elementary school to a very demanding secondary school, having missed the entire first semester. I had to change from Hungarian
to German and to many different teachers instead of just one. I had to
make friends on my own and somehow manage to cope with my shame
of my tainted Communist family. I cried a lot; I bit my nails and
chewed my pencils until they broke. I lost all my creativity—I could
not write a simple story. Clearly, I was clinically depressed. I don't
know whether the grown-ups noticed any of this and whether they had
any idea what to do about it.

In retrospect, I think that it was that time and that experience that
made me a psychotherapist. I learned that even under the worst circumstances it is possible to find or to create good objects. There was
Harriet, my classmate, beautiful, rich, aristocratic, and a very unlikely
choice for a friend. But she adopted me, got me to stop biting my nails,
and begged me to say that my parents were just socialists, not Communists, because her very conservative father would not allow her to
have me for a friend. I refused and we agreed to be friends only in
school. There was my Latin teacher—the first woman to whom I became deeply attached—who made me feel special and liked. There was
Jeanette, the young French teacher who was always cheerful and care-
free and smelled of lavender perfume. There was Ludwig, a tutor at
the home who told me he was a socialist and that he loved me. Gradually I found that I was recovering, thanks to all the love I was receiving. I could console a terribly homesick roommate who cried for hours
and wet her bed every night; I gave my lunch sandwich to a very poor
and hungry old man who waited for me every day on my way to school.

I began to love and be nourished to music; one of the older students at the boarding home was a budding concert pianist and introduced me to Beethoven's *Ninth Symphony*. My art teacher discovered
my love for color and encouraged me to experiment with design. Also,

it got to be spring, the days were longer, there was more light and sunshine. Sunday nights were still unbearably painful, but I could look forward to the summer when I would stay home with my parents. They, too, seemed to find life less stressful, and a bittersweet gallows humor and a new crop of emigré jokes helped to ease their despair. Life began to return to some familiar ways. There were many scars and I learned that one can live with scars.

I also learned that there were many new things awaiting me. Suddenly sexuality seemed to be ubiquitous. One Sunday night, when I returned from my weekend at home, my two roommates confided in me—in very uncertain language—that they had experimented with sex and that they felt awful about it. I recall an initial reaction of shock and disapproval and a very quick change into what today I can only call neutrality. We talked about it for a long time and eventually agreed that it happened because they were lonely and bored and homesick. Today I would add angry, but that did not occur to me then. A few months later during a winter vacation I was molested by a close friend of my parents with whom they had left me while they attended to some business in the city. He was a famous writer and he told me that I was his muse and that his writing was much better when he could take a break and caress me. There was no forcing and no threat. I rather enjoyed the activity, although I somehow knew that there was something wrong with it. I was in no way traumatized and I did tell my mother about it. I noticed that I was never left alone with that man again.

My first experience of being a therapist occurred when I was 13. I came home from school and found my governess in a gas-filled room, half-conscious, obviously in the act of committing suicide. I must have known to open all the windows and to get her up and walk her around, but what I remember more clearly was that I made her talk and tell me why she was so unhappy. She did and I heard my first "case history" of abuse and rejection and epileptic attacks and being incarcerated in a mental institution for years. I felt rage at the perpetrators of such cruelty and a great deal of compassion. I also understood that the suicide attempt was meant to alert my mother (not me) to her need for more attention and love. My mother finally arrived and took over.

A little later I saw a movie in which Claudette Colbert played the part of a psychiatrist. She was calm and dignified and walked the corridor of a hospital in her white coat and comforted and calmed the very disturbed patients. I knew then that was what I wanted to do. It took many years and many other interests before I returned to that fantasy.

There was being a dancer and teaching in my famous dance teacher's studio. There was a continuing involvement with left-wing youth movements and politics. There was theosophy, Krishnamurti, and what today is referred to as New Age and spirituality.

There were love affairs and lifelong friendships.

And there was finally the university and psychology. The Psychological Institute of the University of Vienna was in some way a replication of the complexity of my life. In addition to the usual courses taught in psychology in the early 1930s, we had infant observation, infant testing, child psychology, social psychology, theory of language, market research, and the theory of the human life cycle. Statistics was raising its ugly head with a nod to American experimental research and behaviorism. I got out of doing statistics by doing an extensive study of suicide instead.

Academic psychology was never very friendly toward psychoanalysis but we did invite Heinz Hartmann to give several colloquia, and René Spitz was one of my classmates. He was at that time already a well-known psychoanalyst, but came to the psychology department to study academic child psychology.

Somehow during those years my interest began to shift from trying to change the social order to learning how to help one person at a time to change herself or himself. After getting my Ph.D., I started to volunteer (there were no paid jobs in Vienna at that time except in business or civil service) at a combined pediatric-neurological clinic. I learned much about pathology but very little about healing. I took the only course in psychotherapy at the university of Freud's city. It was taught in the urology department because male impotence was thought possibly to have some psychological causes. The course was taught by a very bright and dynamically informed psychiatrist and I learned quite a lot more about unconscious motivation. Through some American friends I heard about Michael Reese Hospital in Chicago, and on the spur of the moment I applied for a postdoctoral internship. To my delight and surprise, I was accepted for the year starting in July 1938.

And then in March 1938 Hitler annexed Austria and I knew I had to leave. With my political past and my recent anti-Nazi activism, I would not have survived. None of my friends nor my future husband felt any urgency, so I left alone for my second emigration to start a new life as a refugee. At Michael Reese Hospital I learned a lot about psychoanalytic theory, I met many people, and I made new friends; and once more I learned about injustice and discrimination, this time from the medical establishment. I was told that if I wanted to learn about doing therapy I had to go to medical school. However, I was allowed to treat one patient—a 10-year-old girl who was mute. She was diagnosed as severely mentally retarded. She could not be tested, but I disagreed with the diagnosis. After a few more weeks she said hello and goodbye and I knew I was right and I could be a psychotherapist. After a few more weeks she told me that she did not talk because her older brother had threatened to kill her if she ever let their parents know that she could talk. She said she was still very afraid of her brother.

My position at the University of Chicago at last made me eligible for analytic training at the Chicago Institute for Psychoanalysis. I was accepted as a "special student," confirming once more that I was special when in my analysis I was working hard to rid myself of that self-representation.

I was taught ego psychology; I was analyzed in that theoretical and technical framework. I relived much of my early depression. But when I finished my analysis, I knew that we had only scratched the surface.

There were still many years of becoming a psychotherapist or a psychoanalyst ahead of me. I feel I get closer to being there the more I learn about using myself in an object-relational or intersubjective approach. Mostly, I have learned that no size fits all and that there really is no such thing as technique in psychotherapy.

Hedda Bolgar, Ph.D., is a Training and Supervising Analyst at the Los Angeles Institute and Society for Psychoanalytic Studies (LAISPS).

5

The Republican Party, Carlton Fredericks, and Me

FRED BUSCH

Every Sunday my father played cards and argued politics with my uncles. He could have kept quiet, as my mother requested on the car rides before each of these family gatherings, and to which he assented at the time. However, my uncles, who were not under similar topical restrictions, would inevitably turn the conversation to the news of the day, leading to the inevitable recriminations on the ride home.

What would they argue about? My father was a Republican. This would not be the basis for contention in approximately 50 percent of the households in our country. However, in my extended family the two-party system consisted of liberal and moderate Democrats. Among members of our ethnic and social class you wouldn't have thought there was a Republican Party. It was like Tammany Hall was a member of the family and neighborhood. However, the Russian Revolution (Russia was my father's country of origin) plus a personal experience in business led my father to be fearful of what he perceived as the growing socialistic bent of the Democratic Party. He came to America as a teenager, with no money or language skills. Through hard work, an active mind, and a keen sense of the consumer market, he had risen to become an executive for a regional consumer company. However, after many years, the acrimonious relationships that developed with the rise of unions led him to follow his own muse. And what a muse it turned out to be! With relatively little formal education, he began a quest for personal growth and development, while following a previously dormant long-term business interest.

As an example, he became interested in the teachings of Carlton Fredericks, one of the first nutritional gurus on the radio in the 1950s. This led him to stop smoking his two packs a day of Old Golds, bring wheat germ into our meat and potatoes household, and start taking a daily regimen of vitamin pills forty years before it became fashionable. He began to study humanistic religions and Eastern philosophy in his 60s. This increasing capacity to broaden his horizons led my father to combine his entrepreneurial skills with another abiding interest of his—the mass marketing of specialty foods. Throughout his life he would roam ethnic neighborhoods in cities throughout the United States looking for interesting foods that might be developed for a larger market. This led to two creative ventures. When supermarkets were first springing up throughout the country, my father observed that in conjunction with this development there was a quantum leap forward in the technology for refrigeration. This led to his forming the first company to market shrimp in cocktail sauce to supermarkets. However, for lack of attention to details and sound business practices, "Shrimp A'hoy" is not a household name. Neither is "Hot Tangies," a spicy chip that melted in your mouth (at the time there were no alternatives to potato chips). However, he continued to explore these options even as economic necessities forced him to find a regular job. When he passed away there were 500 pounds of papaya juice in his freezer as a prelude to his next, great adventure.

This high regard for following personal directions, within the context of constantly challenging one's thinking, played a crucial role in how someone becomes an analyst who grew up thinking of therapy as something one was threatened with (e.g., "If you don't shape up you're going to have to see a psychologist") or as part of an appellation (e.g., "Boy, you really need to see a psychologist!"). Growing up I knew nobody who had been to a psychologist except, it was rumored, Danny Wolf. His parents, I was told, were Communists. Thus, I was a junior in college when I took my first psychology class to fulfill an academic requirement. I was planning to go to law school. However, I was fascinated by this introductory psychology class in ways that I was unable to understand at the time. I took another psychology class the following semester, switched majors, and stayed an extra year as an undergraduate to fulfill my requirements for a psychology major. These classes spoke to something very deep within my psychological makeup, helping me begin to understand aspects of the world around me and my own feelings. I was smitten by psychology, and have been ever since.

When I told my parents of my plan to go to graduate school in psychology my father was pleased for me, and my mother wanted to stick her head in the oven. It is an introduction to my mother that needs some elaboration. As the matriarch of an extended family, who took over as a mother to her siblings as a teenager when her own mother died, my mother needed to have a definitive sense of how things should be. Hard work, loyalty to family and the past, and following the prevailing norms, were rules I was expected to live by. If she didn't understand something, her initial reaction was to see it as a threat to her view of how things should be ordered. Over time she could be mollified. Ambitious for her children, she would willingly sacrifice for what was best for them. The clear message was that we needed to reciprocate by doing our best. My brothers followed a family tradition by staying in business, and becoming presidents of large corporations. I remained, for her, if not a black sheep then definitely a mauve one.

Family tensions can foster creative solutions, or be stifling. Certainly I have experienced both in dealing with the combination of my mother's expectation that I fit within prevailing norms, and my identification with my father's independence of mind, readiness to challenge, and risk taking. Entering a profession that was essentially unknown in our family, while hardly going off to travel with a rock-and-roll band, followed these two models I grew up with. Further, my primary area of interest has been traditional psychoanalytic theory and technique. However, within that I explored what I believe are certain inadequacies in the theory, and its implications for technique. I have attempted to chart new territory, but within the context of previously

charted areas. My particular area of interest, the role of ego psychology in clinical technique, has been considered a staple of psychoanalytic methodology. My message has been that it isn't as much a staple
as we would like to think (Busch 1995).

Freud's greatest discovery was the enormous importance of the
unconscious in all aspects of everyday life, especially the symptoms
that bring our patients to us for help. His earliest theory of the cure
process, backed by successful treatment of hysterical symptoms, led
him to posit the necessity of first discovering and then presenting to
patients the unconscious meanings of symptoms. While Freud eventually came to a more complex model of the treatment process based, in
part, upon anxiety as a signal of danger, and the presence of unconscious ego resistances, he never fully abandoned his initial penchant
for depth interpretations irrespective of the state of the resistances.
However, Freud's second model of the mind, the structural model,
brought about in large measure by the discovery of unconscious resistances, stayed alive in the work of Anna Freud, Heinz Hartmann, and
David Rapaport.

At the center of the ongoing development of the structural model
was the discovery of an ego with functions independent of the id from
birth. This was in contrast to Freud's original notion that the development of the ego is dependent on the id. That is, the ego developed to
meet the needs of the id (e.g., orientation to reality and impulse control develop so that we may more adequately meet our needs). While
the discovery of an autonomous ego had important implications for
many aspects of psychoanalytic theory, its primary effect was in the
understanding of normal developmental needs of children.

The significance of the conscious and unconscious ego in clinical technique lagged significantly. While for many years we believed
we had a fully developed psychoanalytic technique based on ego psychological principles, this was only partially true. Our understanding
of the significance of the developmental needs for healthy ego development expanded greatly. No longer were all interpretations fit within
a drive gratification/frustration model. A tendency toward unmodulated
anxiety might be understood in terms of early parent loss, rather than
the intensity of a drive. It was only with the publication of Paul Gray's

(1982) classic paper on the "developmental lag" in clinical technique that we became aware of the relative paucity of techniques with regard to the ego that we actually had. My own work has elaborated techniques for working with unconscious resistances and the more autonomous aspects of the patient's ego functions. My views are heavily based on the following observation:

> Listening to discussions of the clinical process, one is impressed with how many interpretations seem based less on what the patient is capable of hearing, and more on what the analyst is capable of understanding. We too often confuse our ability to read the unconscious and the patient's ability to understand it. We are frequently not clear enough on the distinction between an unconscious communication and our ability to communicate with the patient's unconscious. What the patient can hear, understand, and effectively utilize—let alone the benefits of considering such an approach—are rarely in the foreground of our clinical discussions. Getting to the real unconscious fantasy still seems to be our primary therapeutic goal. [Busch 1993, p. 153]

It took me approximately twenty years of clinical work to come to this understanding. It is only in retrospect, though, that I can see echoes of this same theme through much of my earlier writing and thinking. My first solo paper (Busch 1968) was a critique of attempts to predict transference paradigms from psychological testing. In this paper I suggested it was an overambitious reading of the unconscious, and this same date could "be fruitfully looked at in terms of insights into the structural functions" (p. 311). This same theme reverberates through my current work as I emphasize the structural components of the clinical interaction (i.e., the readiness of the ego to hear interpretations, the state of the resistances against the thematic material), while criticizing those who I characterize as "deep divers" (i.e., ready to bypass the ego for interpretations of the deepest unconscious material).

In my early training as a psychologist we did a lot of psychological testing. Rapaport's (1967) work in this area had brought an entirely new dimension to test interpretation, and I was fortunate to be trained by those who understood the implications of Rapaport's application of the new ego psychology toward testing. This approach emphasized the significance of the mind's structural components in psychological testing. I came to understand how the questions psychological testing could answer best were those of differential diagnosis based on the degree to which the ego was interfered with by conflict. While most referral questions were posed in terms of the unconscious significance of this or that, the referral source was most frequently interested in the state of the ego as a basis for differential diagnosis. Thus, evaluating the state of the ego became an invaluable part of my early training.

Two elements of my training as a child psychologist had a significant impact upon my interest in the role of the ego in psychoanalytic treatment. Most of my training as a child therapist plus much of my observational research was done in conjunction with people trained under Anna Freud. Her pioneering efforts in understanding the importance of the ego in child development and psychoanalytic treatment had a profound effect on my views. Thus, my earliest research, done under the tutelage of a Hampstead-trained analyst, Christoph Heinicke, involved understanding those ego factors that led to differential adaptations of children to nursery school (e.g., Heinicke et al. 1973). My later studies, in conjunction with observation in nursery school and toddler groups, also focused on the development of certain ego functions in self soothing and peer relations (e.g., Busch 1974, Horner et al. 1976). Further, in my therapy work with children, I often experienced the discrepancy between the nature of the interpretation and what I believed was the child's level of comprehension. Only after many years of clinical immersion could I put this dilemma into a historical perspective, and understand how one might use understanding the ego as an anchor of good therapeutic technique.

One of the hallmarks of an ego psychological perspective is that a goal of the analytic process is an increasing freedom of thought. This is in contrast to those methods that conceive of the analytic process as revolving around the uncovering of those factors that led to symptoms. It isn't that this isn't important; rather, it is incomplete. It leaves the analysand thinking that what he or she learns in analysis will be helpful, in contrast to those methods designed to encourage freedom of thought. As described by Nina Searl (1936) sixty years ago, that which is important is not the extent to which we may be able to impart to the patient our knowledge of his life and psyche, but it is the extent to which we can clear the patient's own way to it and give him freedom of access to his own mind. [p. 487]

From this perspective, analysis allows one to become freer to explore thoughts. In thinking about the particular type of analyst I became, I found my thinking going in two directions. First, I was surprised by the degree of continuity in what I have been thinking about over the last thirty years. In the different realms of psychology I've become involved in (psychological testing, child development, psychoanalytic treatment), my perspective has always included one aspect or another of the ego. Clearly this has been multidetermined. Second, I find myself returning to the work of Paul Gray. Those of us who have been involved in the evolving area of ego psychology owe an enormous debt to him. Two papers, published about a decade apart (Gray 1973, 1982), served as a beacon for those of us interested in this area. His felicitous use of the term *developmental lag* (Gray 1982) captured a problem in psychoanalytic technique, but obscured the radical nature of his thinking. In one sense he was doing nothing more than articulating a shibboleth of classical technique, that is, the necessity of resistance work prior to depth interpretations. However, at another level he was challenging the way psychoanalysis was actually being practiced at the time. This readiness to question a widely held perspective, while staying closely tied to traditional psychoanalysis, fits closely with my own style of thinking. Thus, his influence on me was profound not only because of what he thought, but in the way he thought about things. It is how the son of a Republican businessman who studies Eastern philosophy might end up thinking about psychoanalytic issues.

Fred Busch, Ph.D., is a Training and Supervising Analyst at the Michigan Psychoanalytic Institute.

REFERENCES

Busch, F. (1968). Transference in psychological testing. *Journal of Projective Techniques and Personality Assessment* 32:309–312.

———— (1974). Dimensions of the first transitional object. *Psychoanalytic Study of the Child* 29:212–229. New Haven, CT: Yale University Press.

———— (1993). In the neighborhood: aspects of a good interpretation and a "developmental lag" in ego psychology. *Journal of the American Psychoanalytic Association* 41:151–177.

———— (1995). *The Ego at the Center of Clinical Technique.* Northvale, NJ: Jason Aronson.

Gray, P. (1973). Psychoanalytic technique and the ego's capacity for viewing intrapsychic conflict. *Journal of the American Psychoanalytic Association* 21:474–494.

———— (1982). "Developmental lag" in the evolution of technique for psychoanalysis of neurotic conflict. *Journal of the American Psychoanalytic Association* 30:521–555.

Heinicke, C. M., Busch, F., Click, P., and Kramer, E. (1973). Parent–child relationships, adaptation to nursery school, and the child's task orientation. In *Individual Differences in Children,* ed. J. C. Westman, pp. 159-198. New York: Wiley.

Horner, T., Whiteside, M., and Busch, F. (1976). The mutual influence of the positive cohesive self, mental representational structure, and interactive behavior in the child's involvement with peers. *International Journal of Psycho-Analysis* 57:461–475.

Rapaport, D. (1967). *The Collected Papers of David Rapaport,* ed. M. M. Gill. New York: Basic Books.

Searl, M. N. (1936). Some queries on principles of technique. *International Journal of Psycho-Analysis* 17:471–493.

6

How I Came to Be Who I Was Supposedly Not

GERARD CHRZANOWSKI

It was Emerson who commented on peripheral communication when he said, "I hate quotations, tell me what you know." In this spirit I present some comments about what I presume to know.

The trouble with knowing is that we are invariably confronted with at least three possibilities: the fictive side of life; the factual side of life; and, more often than not, the black holes of our ignorance. But once we are cognizant of the pitfalls of knowledge, we can emancipate ourselves from the German philosopher Fichte's dictum that "life is but an act, rather than a fact." There are plenty of facts important to life beyond taxation and cremation. The human tendency to be compulsively cause-and-effect oriented, although often representing an overkill, still leaves room for constructing historical sketches. It is also not useful to dwell on a search for specific childhood traumas, since they were perceived by childhood eyes, as Schachtel (1959) pointed out. Neither is there a need to apologize for exploring a figure of the truth, rather than nothing short of the unvarnished, three-dimensional truth; nevertheless, this does not minimize the merit of being truthful.

It has long been appreciated that largely predictable behavior occurs in the domain of mental disorders. A person with a pronounced mental disorder such as a paranoia, depression, obsession, hysteria, or even the mental disorder of total normalcy does his or her particular thing with a measure of predictability in a variety of interpersonal settings. However, a moderately well-integrated individual may have a larger experimental and experiential range for trying on an appropriate, novel attitude. Close adherence to one's acquired style resembles a security blanket in its own right, but freedom to try on new things for size, to venture into unfamiliar territory, to be flexible, is not in conflict with basic reliability. Cultural styles are not in the category of acting, but are a distinctly nonvolitional phenomenon. For instance, my personal style has a so-called Continental flavor, due to my initial inoculation with European culture. My time as a New World denizen is close to twice as long as my previous existence as a native Old World product. Culture has a remarkable staying power and does not yield to time alone. It contains a prewired, built-in developmental barrier that accounts for the fact that only in rare instances do people get infused with a new culture once they are past adolescence. The audible result of a partial cultural adaptation is an obvious accent, since language constitutes culture in action. It means that my deviant, cultural phonemes are a strictly involuntary manifestation, not part of a personal style.

It is of interest that particularly among my numerous European colleagues I am considered to be a representative of American culture. They are keenly interested in what I have to say about American politics, psychotherapy, and so on.

I have a long-standing interest in cross-cultural as well as transcultural phenomena, an interest that enters into my psychotherapeutic stance. In this connection, I have come to realize the illusion of blending diverse cultural ideologies. The myth of an ethnic and cultural melting-pot theory has long been discarded. A shift has taken place toward the construct of bridging as a means of interchanging variant perceptions without invading or penetrating cultural integrity. Relevant data transmitted across a mental bridge require particular means of translation by the receiver of the message.

I developed a curiosity about the nature of depressive manifestations when I was an adolescent of about 19. At that time I was friendly with a young dancer who had to be hospitalized when she suffered a major depression, leading to her withdrawal from social contacts. Around the same time I became cognizant of a depressive manifestation in a member of my family. My vague recollection, which may be entirely fictive, suggests that my motivation to enter the field of medicine had something to do with my desire to obtain information about the phenomenon of depression.

The choice to become a physician clashed sharply with my father's conviction that women were temperamentally best qualified to be at the beck and call of sick people. In his opinion men were better suited to become engineers or lawyers. He himself had had a hard life; his own father died shortly before he was born, and he had to quit school and support his family from the age of 14. He wound up as one of the very few Europeans with a true Horatio Alger story.

At the age of 9 or 10 I was sent to Switzerland by our physician. He thought my lungs were not in good shape. I grew up at a Swiss school. I had a good time in that setting, where I learned all kinds of exercises, skiing, playing tennis, and at a later time, unknown to my parents, I had a motorcycle as well as a bicycle.

I had a genuine interest in many aspects of medicine, but in my last year of medical study I was determined to become a psychiatrist and a neurologist, which were then considered to be interrelated fields. My early professional experiences were within psychiatric hospital settings that brought me in contact with predominantly schizophrenic patients. Following my graduation I spent two years as a live-in resident and associate psychiatrist at the Psychiatric University Clinic Burghoelzli, the prestigious University Hospital in Zurich, Switzerland. It was world renowned and respected; Freud, Jung, and Herbert Binschwanger had worked there. I had many moving experiences there, such as with the dancer Nijinsky, who was in a very disturbed state. Eugen Bleuler, a living legend, was still around, for one year as professor emeritus. He preceded Sullivan in his dedication to people with schizophrenic disorders. Bleuler made history in humanizing Kraepelin's construct of dementia praecox. Bleuler was also one of the early supporters of Freud's psychoanalytic theories. Bleuler's basic credo was the Protestant work ethic. After I came to the United States I added five additional years of psychiatric inpatient work.

During my training in Switzerland at Burghoelzli, my chief of service was Herbert Binswanger, who was in tune with his brother Ludwig's concept of existentialism. Fate played a complicated game with me: my first supervisor was Lotte Sachs, who had been in analysis with Frieda Fromm-Reichmann. In the university hospital setting I also had exposure to organic psychiatry, which ranged from insulin to cardiazol application to fever induction and sleep treatment, and included electric shock intervention. In the realm of theoretical and clinical conceptions I became acquainted with Ludwig Binswanger's writings as well as the work of Jaspers and other philosophical thinkers. My pluralistic exposure in my professional fledgling years are, as far as I can tell, without an overt connection between these experiences and my present-day professional thinking.

In 1940 I came to the United States on the last boat to leave Genoa before World War II. I worked in state hospitals, as did many of the psychiatrists who fled Europe at that time. I also received further training at Columbia-Presbyterian and the New York Psychiatric Institute, and I was affiliated there for many years. I made many lasting friends at those places, among them the late Silvano Arieti, with whom I wrote a number of books.

In my new environment I had a number of novel experiences. It is strange to recall today that I introduced prolonged-sleep treatment in the United States. Previously hydrotherapy in straitjackets was done, where patients were "boiled." (I witnessed patients dying of scalding.) I devised a chemical formula with a chemist from Hoffmann–La Roche in New Jersey. Next came the details of inducing sleep, maintaining it while carefully monitoring the patients, and educating the nursing staff. It was a big job and I was fortunate in having Dr. Milton Zaphiropoulos as my coworker. The patients would get two weeks of ongoing sleep and their main confusion on awakening occurred when Milt and I introduced ourselves by our full names: Chrzanowski and Zaphiropoulos. The venture came to an end when our own insomnia went out of control. It was induced by around-the-clock attention to the patients' physiological status.

I also became a "movie person" with *The Snake Pit*, a movie based on a book written by a patient I treated. It was an account of her hospitalization and treatment by me. The film starred Olivia de Havilland, and Leo Genn played my role, Dr. Kick (a nickname I was given at the hospital because my name was considered unpronounceable). Darryl F. Zanuck's (1948) breakthrough film, the first about mental illness and psychotherapy, received six Academy Award nominations.

My recollection of this and related parts of my professional life at that point is hazy in my mind, almost like a screen memory. My "biophysiological period" was already intermingled with a keen interest in psychoanalytic ways of thinking.

I also founded the Bleuler Clinic in Queens, with the help of New York State. It is a large clinic for children and young people, which I directed until 1982. I opened it in 1967, and it is still in existence under the same name. It has been a very active place over the years. I was the medical director as well as the founder, and it served the factions within the community—the police, the meat packers, religious organizations and their leaders, as well as students with problems. This included pregnant students who were afraid to tell anyone, who we could treat at the high school and follow them consistently. At its height the clinic had 1,500 patients, in individual, family, and group therapy as well as pharmacotherapy.

At that time psychologists were not accepted to the William Alanson White Institute without two years of accredited training. I provided it, devising a program that gave psychologists the chance to have the required training. This was the first program of its kind.

When World War II came to an end in 1945, I became deeply involved with the investigation of psychotherapy in the Third Reich under Hitler's regime. I went to Europe immediately after the war and interviewed physicians and analysts who had lived through this experience. This investigation was done over a long period of time, eventually with two collaborators, Dr. Arthur Feiner and the late Dr. Rose Spiegel. It led to another important project.

In 1962 the International Federation of Psychoanalytic Societies (IFPS) was founded by Dr. Erich Fromm of the Mexican Psychoanalytic Society, Dr. Werner Schwidder of the German Analytic Group, Dr. Igor A. Caruso from the Austrian organization, and myself as representative of the William Alanson White Institute. It created a bridge between the United States and the remnants of postwar Europe. It took a long time to unify the different factions that made up the IFPS. The initial founders did not get along with one another. I assisted in the initial organization of the IFPS. To this day there is still antagonism between the two German societies involved. I am the sole surviving founder of the organization, which is doing well.

As I look back today, I fail to see any euclidean straight line to my present-day theoretical and clinical conceptions. The clearest statement that I can make about the impact of my early professional activities and experiences is that they fostered a certain sensitivity, in that I have a minimal need for "walking on eggs" when confronted by profoundly disturbed patients.

HOW THE PSYCHOTHERAPIST AND HIS PERSONALITY MATCH

My personality and my theory have had their ups and downs, their controversies and disagreements. With the passage of time they have made adaptations to each other and have been bridged in terms of an alliance. At present my theoretical construct is not a custom-fitted suit, but rather a loose, comfortable garment. The theoretical layers permit me to move with relative ease without feeling restraints in any particular way.

Today I am genuinely turned on by my professional work. I experience distinctly difficult patients as a challenge as well as a stimulation. There is much variety involved in my approach, since each patient evokes a distinctly personalized game plan and strategy. I feel more creative and inspired in my work today than I have felt at any previous time in my career. I consider the complex relation between fictive and factual aspects to be central in the ongoing therapeutic process, and it leads to novel constructs and novel experiences.

HOW HAS LIFE SHAPED MY IDEAS?

I am thankful for the unconscious impact of a number of existential components. But it is difficult to track the origin of ideas and to come across the particular sources for specific experiences that put an idea in our head.

HOW THE PERSONAL AND PROFESSIONAL EXPERIENCES HAVE INFLUENCED MY CHOICE OF THEORY AND PRACTICE

In looking at my psychotherapeutic passport, I find among the pages a variety of entries akin to the stamps of the different countries I have visited. This stimulating exposure to other points of view has not disguised my particular citizenship as a psychotherapist. On the contrary, other points of view have broadened my clinical horizons without remotely turning me into an eclectic.

My cultural perspective is one of the unconscious experiential dimension of my theoretical and clinical work, and my ongoing interest in the contemporary and past literature. I read a fair amount of professional and general material. My four decades of teaching my version of Sullivan have been significant in acquainting me with interpersonal approaches to psychoanalysis. At the same time that interpersonalism has encouraged me to broaden my theoretical and clinical horizon, it has opened for me a flexible approach, which includes psychotherapy, without forcing me to abandon my basic theoretical platform.

A final comment about the impact of professional experiences that have influenced my choice of theory and practice: In my training at the White Institute, I started with a middle-of-the-road classical analyst for about two years. Then I switched to a familiar figure for my analyst. In my initial dream I depicted her as a chubby Buddha figure sitting cross-legged with pleasant incense rising from an urn. I doubt that this image influenced my theoretical or clinical stance. Clara Thompson was never confrontational with me and I seemingly could never do wrong with her. She made me feel like one of her favorite children, which had its obvious pitfalls. In spite of my genuine attachment to her, I never had any desire to imitate her way of doing analytic work. This was not a rejection of her, but rather a difference in temperament and personality.

Today I am entrenched in an interpersonal tradition within the framework of present-day knowledge. In my role as a psychotherapist, I am who I am. My personality comes to the fore in my ongoing resonance to the patient's mode of verbal and nonverbal communication. Comments and interpretations on my part are neither true nor false, but focus on the impact they evoke in the patient.

Finally, an overemphasis on the past in thoughts and dreams tends to turn into a "Perils of Pauline," where an ambiance of cliff hanging was required to assure a return to the hero's or heroine's dilemma.

Gerard Chrzanowski, M.D., is a Training and Supervising Analyst at the William Alanson White Institute.

REFERENCES

Schachtel, E. (1959). *Metamorphosis*. New York: Basic Books.
Zanuck, D. (producer). (1948). *The Snake Pit* [Film]. Screenplay by F. Partost and M. Brand, from a novel by M. J. Ward.

7

Becoming a Psychologist-Clinician

MORRIS N. EAGLE

For me, becoming a psychologist is the primary story and becoming a psychotherapist is one aspect of being a psychologist. I cannot imagine doing only psychotherapy, that is, doing psychotherapy full time. I would not be happy doing that. Indeed, I must confess that I don't understand how one can do, say, forty or fifty patient hours of psychotherapy per week in an attentive and effective way. I assume others can do it. I do not think I can. In short, my professional identity is primarily that of psychologist and only secondarily that of psychotherapist, although I have been doing psychotherapy for more than forty years. I have always firmly believed that being a psychotherapist cannot be divorced from being a psychologist. In this regard, I differ from some of my psychologist colleagues who view themselves solely as psychoanalysts and do not feel any special connection or identification with the discipline of psychology. During the time that I was president of Division 39 (Division of Psychoanalysis) of the American Psychological Association, I always felt that there was some degree of tension around this issue between some Division 39 board members and myself with regard to the place of psychoanalysis in psychology, and the place of Division 39 in the American Psychological Association. There are those who view themselves as psychoanalysts period, and those, like myself, who view themselves either as psycho-analytic psychologists or psychologist-psychoanalysts.

More and more, I have come to believe that the single most important factor in determining the effectiveness of at least psychodynamic psychotherapy is the personal qualities of the therapist (or perhaps the interaction or match between the personal qualities of the therapist and patient). I think that the therapist's personal qualities are more important than theoretical persuasion or, perhaps, the years of experience. Thus, simply becoming an advocate, say, of relational theory does not necessarily make one authentically related as a therapist, just as becoming a self psychologist does not necessarily render one more truly and organically empathic as a therapist. Qualities such as personal presence, empathy, understanding, and authenticity are not, I strongly suspect, a matter of theoretical orientation or the years of experience. They are a matter of who one is as a person. But who one is as a person is a product of one's history and one's personal experiences, including the experiences that led one to becoming a psychotherapist.

One, of course, does not know the full range of experiences that shape one's life decisions. But, in thinking about the question of becoming a psychotherapist, it is clear to me that certain family experiences were extremely important. One of the first things that comes to mind is the degree to which I was, in many respects, a parentified child. I learned early on to become exquisitely sensitive to my mother's nervous moods and knew precisely what to do to reassure her and calm her. For example, I learned that if I were overly sympathetic and expressed much concern, she would become even more anxious—it meant to her that something was seriously wrong if even I was worried. I had to convey a sense of not being overly concerned, almost a subtle kind of gruffness and casualness. I became quite expert at calming her down and at modulating the usual spiraling nature of anxiety. I just knew what to do. And to this day I have naturally made use of that intuitive skill. Over the years, I reenacted a version of the above interaction with my mother countless times with friends and in other intimate relationships. I am less conscious of specifically reenacting this interaction with patients. I suspect that this is so because the "conditions of safety"

(Weiss and Sampson 1986), represented by the therapeutic situation and frame, inherently—at least to some degree—constitute such an interaction. However, I do believe that I convey to at least some of my patients something of what I conveyed to my mother during her nervous spells.

In writing this chapter, I was struck by the thought—not for the first time—that I may well be at my best as a therapist with my very close friends, not because I am trying to be a therapist with them, but because I am vitally concerned about their distress and I want to be as helpful as I can be. This makes me wonder about what Irwin Hoffman (1994) refers to as the dialectic between ritual and spontaneity. By the former, he means the therapeutic frame and its corresponding rules and rituals, and by the latter he means the personal presence and sponta-neous response of the therapist that cannot be totally defined by or limited to the frame. Although, as Hoffman notes, the mystique of the ritual very likely contributes to the healing potential of the therapeutic situation, it is also very likely, as he also suggests, that the spontane-ous personal response, presence, and style of the therapist—qualities that cannot be fully specified or dictated by the frame or one's profes-sional role—contribute at least equally to the healing properties of the therapeutic situation. Hoffman proposes what seems to me the intu-itively correct idea that one aspect of being a bad object is rigid ad-herence to ritual.

I am not referring here to the question of intentional and explicit self-disclosures; my own view is that such disclosure frequently serves the therapist's needs and can be experienced by the patient as burden-some. Rather, I am referring to the natural and inadvertent self-disclo-sure that is simply conveyed by one's personal presence and style (Stechler 1996). I believe, although I have no way of proving this, that such ongoing and background self-disclosure is far more important than periodic and punctuated bouts of explicitly identified self-disclosure.

As Friedman (1994) has observed, the therapeutic situation is a peculiar one, one that involves some inevitable degree of illusion and perhaps deception. As therapists, we implicitly encourage patients to develop intense expectations of what we will offer, expectations that will not and cannot be fulfilled. We offer intimacy, but for a price and with clearly demarcated and safe boundaries and limits. I wonder if this is one of the unconscious motives that is involved in becoming a thera-pist—intimacy and emotionally intense interactions but with safe and clear boundaries, to use Hoffman's terms; spontaneity made safe through its being embedded in ritual. A very nice compromise formation.

My good friend Sophie Freud tells me that a large number of social workers were parentified children. I wonder if this is also true of psychotherapists in general. As I indicated earlier, I certainly was a parentified child. It occurs to me that becoming a psychotherapist might represent the continuation not only of one's parentified role—that is the more obvious part—but also of that role in a safe and limited way. That is, one becomes a therapist not only out of parenting impulses and tendencies, but also out of, so to speak, opposite impulses and tendencies—that is, out of the need to *limit* one's parenting impulses and express them in a safe and bounded context. Although I believe that the personal formative experiences that shape one's character play a dominant role in determining how one does psychotherapy, I have always been impressed with the fact that for many people the profes-sional role of psychotherapist brings out the most constructive and healthiest aspect of their personality. This suggests that the frame, what Hoffman (1994) refers to as the ritualistic aspects of psychotherapy, play a constructive leveling role that, to a certain extent, modulates or dilutes the influence of one's idiosyncratic formative experiences.

I believe that although this is true, it has its limits—contrary to what appeared to be assumption some years ago that the single most important factor, perhaps the exclusive factor, that determined the com-petence and effectiveness of an analyst was how well trained or how well analyzed he or she was. I recall that when I was shopping around for an analyst many years ago, the dominant view among classical ana-lysts was that virtually all well-trained, well-analyzed analysts were essentially interchangeable (the way, perhaps, that all well-trained surgeons or cardiologists or gastroenterologists were presumably in-terchangeable). The implicit and explicit assumption seemed to be that the personal, idiosyncratic individual characteristics of the analysts—those shaped by their personal formative experiences—were unimpor-tant. They were presumably washed away by one's training and one's training analysis. Of course, such a view was easy to maintain when the analyst was seen primarily as a blank screen. After all, blank screens are, indeed, interchangeable—one well-trained blank screen is as good as another so long as it remains blank.

It seems to me that the most important and challenging tasks in becoming an effective and authentic psychotherapist are how to integrate the personal and idiosyncratic formative experiences that shaped one's character and determined who one is with one's training and with the ritual and frame aspects of the therapeutic situation, how to adhere to and use the legitimate aspects of the ritual as a framework for the constructive and therapeutic expression of the authentically personal, in Hoffman's (1994) language, and how to integrate ritual and spontaneity.

Some formal experiences influenced my becoming a psychotherapist. As I have noted, my becoming a psychotherapist was secondary to, and an outgrowth of, my becoming a psychologist. And my becoming a psychologist was inextricably linked with the psychology department at the City College of New York (CCNY). I do not know what direction my life would have taken without CCNY. For me, as for many others, going to college meant being accepted to City College. There was no alternative. One of the honors that I am most proud of receiving is an award for outstanding contribution to the advancement of psychology from the CCNY psychology department on the occasion of its 75th anniversary.

I came to City College during the glory days of the psychology department. Its faculty included Gardner Murphy, Joseph Barmack, Max Hertzman, Lawrence Plotkin, Daniel Lehrman, Alexander Mintz, and Martin Scheerer. I became a psychology major after taking a course with Scheerer. I was completely fascinated, not only with the brilliance of his lectures, but also with the theatrical and charismatic style with which he delivered them. I still have quite a clear visual image of Scheerer deeply inhaling on his cigarette, followed by the cigarette smoke continuing to pour from his mouth and nose—seemingly endlessly—as he lectured and paced in the classroom. I also still remember how impressed I was with Scheerer's demonstration of the role of distance cues in the experience of size constancy. In a totally darkened room, we observed two phosphorescent triangles and perceived them as equal and as equidistant from us. The lights were then turned on and we observed that one triangle was twice as large as the other, but twice as far away. This was a compelling and dramatic demonstration.

After I graduated from CCNY, I was accepted into its very special and extraordinary M.A. program in clinical psychology organized by Joseph Barmack, following his experience as a research candidate at the New York Psychoanalytic Institute. Among the faculty offering lectures and courses were Ernst Kris, David Beres, Ruth Munroe, Bela Mittleman, Roy Schafer, Kurt Goldstein, Katherine Wolf, Ulrich Sonneman, Karen Machover, and Lois Murphy. The program was heavily psychoanalytic and was, quite simply, the most stimulating and exciting educational experience I have ever had. Although the classes were quite large, only five or six of us were matriculated in the special, rather elite, M.A. program. We were invited to sit in the first rows in each class and each semester spent at least one evening at the home of each faculty member. All of us were Fellows (i.e., teaching assistants) in the psychology department. We spent a great deal of time together, became close friends, and we lived and breathed psychology—by now psychoanalytic psychology—all day, every day. These were truly heady and fantastic days. It was clear to all of us that we wanted to become clinical psychologists, in particular psychoanalytically oriented clinical psychologists. Given the extraordinary experiences we had, it would have been perverse to make any other choice.

After completing the M.A. program at CCNY, I was accepted to the Ph.D. program in clinical psychology at New York University. I entered the Veterans Administration training program, and worked for a few years as an intern at a number of VA psychiatric hospitals. Clinical experience with seriously disturbed, hospitalized patients was extremely useful and sobering. However, given the deadening influence of a heavily bureaucratic system, I would have to say that I decided to become a psychotherapist despite rather than because of my experiences in the VA program.

I have been extremely fortunate in my educational experiences. After my VA internships I began working at the Research Center for Mental Health, which was codirected by George Klein and Robert Holt, both of whom had recently been brought to NYU from the Menninger Clinic. My fellow graduate students and colleagues at the Research Center included Leo Goldberger, Irving Paul, Fred Pine, Don Spence, and David Wolitzky. I spent more than eight years, both as a graduate student and, after receiving my doctoral degree, as a staff and faculty member at the Research Center and they were, like the City College experience, remarkable years. In a steady and intense way, we thought about, did research on, and wrote about psychoanalysis and psychoanalytic theory. The visiting faculty and presenters included, among others, Merton Gill, Hartvig Dahl, and David Rapaport. Although our work may not have transformed psychoanalysis, our experience at the Research Center certainly shaped and transformed all of us.

Klein and Holt personified and instilled a broad perspective toward psychoanalysis. They were psychoanalytic psychologists, but psychologists first. This perspective has continued to influence me throughout my career. Klein and Holt were interested in and knowledgeable about a good deal of what was going on in psychology. Holt and I have maintained and deepened our friendship over the years and I continue to be amazed at the range of his interests, curiosity, and knowledge. And Klein was notorious for his mercurial and intense interest in a wide variety of psychological phenomena.

To this day, I continue to believe—as, I believe, Klein did and Holt does—that if psychoanalytic practice and theory are to remain vital and grow, they must be open to developments, thinking, and findings in other fields. As far as practice is concerned, and particularly in regard to such clinical syndromes as depression, agoraphobia, and eating disorders—and I refer to these syndromes as illustrative—one has the responsibility as a psychotherapist to be conversant, as much as one possibly can, with relevant findings from a wide range of perspectives, nonpsychoanalytic and psychoanalytic.

There were other experiences, such as my analyses and training that influenced the kind of therapist I became, but they did not play a central role in my decision to become a therapist. That decision had already been made when these factors were operating.

Finally, I want to comment on the question of whether I am identified as a psychotherapist. Although, as I noted earlier, I have been engaged in doing psychotherapy for more than forty years, throughout my career I have been told by a number of colleagues—particularly in New York, less so when I lived in Toronto—that they think of me as a theorist (and researcher) rather than as a therapist. I must confess that I have been bothered by this perception, particularly the "rather than" part, and I have wondered about the basis for this perception. I think it is based on a number of factors, including the fact that I have always done only part-time psychotherapy and that I am not strongly affiliated with any of the psychoanalytic institutes in New York nor with any particular psychoanalytic school. However, I think an additional factor is the implicit assumption made by some in the psychoanalytic community that concern with and interest in the epistemological, conceptual, and philosophical issues raised by psychoanalytic theory is somehow incompatible with doing clinical work or at least with *really* doing clinical work. I know that this implicit assumption is something that Benjamin Rubinstein and Emanuel Peterfreund—both of whom were in full-time clinical practice, but who were vitally interested in epistemological and conceptual issues—had to deal with all their professional lives. There is an unfortunate typecasting tendency to assume that those interested in theoretical and conceptual issues are less likely to be astute clinicians.

There is also a related unfortunate tendency to think that clinical work can rest solely on vague and poorly articulated intuitions and feelings and does not require any precision and clarity of thought, and indeed that it is handicapped by clearly articulated thinking. I have seen the operation of this sort of assumption in some of my graduate students and I believe it seriously interferes with their ability to learn and to discipline their clinical work and their understanding of clinical issues. I have tried various ways of dealing with this problem (including the assignment of Meehl's [1973] wonderful article entitled "Why I Do Not Attend Case Conferences"), but muddle-headed and undisciplined thinking can become quite entrenched and, unfortunately, finds support in some of the role models available among clinical faculty.

The shoddy thinking that often passes as clinical intuition does a serious disservice to the reality of clinical work, which requires a great deal of thought and a wedding of intuitions and feelings with clearly articulated thinking. As I have noted, this whole matter has irked me a great deal and I am aware that I am exploiting the opportunity provided by the writing of this chapter to air a long-standing gripe.

Although, as I have noted earlier, the theoretical position one takes does not necessarily determine the kind of therapist one is, there is, I believe, a relationship of a particular kind between psychoanalytic theory and practice.

It has seemed to me that at least one important function of shifts in psychoanalytic theorizing is that the new theory that suddenly captures may analysts' imaginations provides a legitimization of their personal intuitions and sense of things (Eagle 1986). For example, I think that one of the more important contributions of Kohut's self psychology lies not in its etiological account of the origins of self or of narcissistic personality disorders, but in the legitimization it provided for what many therapists and analysts knew all along, but were afraid to articulate—namely, that an empathic stance is far more likely to be therapeutic than an aloof and rather cold blank-screen role. I wonder to what extent our different psychoanalytic theories represent shifting expressions and attempts to legitimate and find a larger frame for personal visions that were shaped a long time ago.

Finally, in my subjective experience I became a psychotherapist not when I first began doing psychotherapy, but gradually and over a period of many years, when my personal qualities and my sense of who I am began to fit more and more naturally with my professional role as a psychotherapist. This meant that within the context of the therapeutic frame I could be experienced by my patients in a way that was somewhat, but not entirely, different from the way that I am experienced by my friends, students, and perhaps even my mother a long time ago.

Morris N. Eagle, Ph.D., is Professor of Psychology, Derner Institute of Advanced Psychological Studies, Adelphi University.

REFERENCES

Eagle, M. (1986). Theoretical and clinical shifts in psychoanalysis. *American Journal of Orthopsychiatry* 57:175–185.

Friedman, L. (1994). *Work and illusion in psychotherapy.* Paper presented at the annual meeting of the Rapaport-Klein Study Group, Stockbridge, Massachusetts, June.

Hoffman, I. (1994). Dialectical thinking and therapeutic action in the psychoanalytic process. *Psychoanalytic Quarterly* 63:187–218.

Meehl, P. E. (1973). Why I do not attend case conferences. In *Psychodiagnosis: Selected Papers,* ed. P. E. Meehl, pp. 225–302. Minneapolis: University of Minnesota Press.

Stechler, G. (1996). *Self-disclosure and affect.* Paper presented at the Spring Meeting of Division 39, New York City, April.

Weiss, J., and Sampson, H. (1986). *The Psychoanalytic Process.* New York: Guilford.

8

Shivers

MICHAEL EIGEN

My work as a patient is what made me an analyst. But many factors went into making me a patient. I slept in a crib in my parents' room until age 5. From the earliest age, I listened for sounds in the night. I've never stopped listening. Some of my earliest dreams were primal scene dreams.

I hated the crib. It meant being a baby, held back, compressed, imprisoned, suffocated. The crib played a role in my becoming a sort of lifelong rebel. As a young adult, I couldn't be free enough. I'm lucky to be alive, given the crazy things I did to feel free. The rock musician who wrecks his guitar makes me wonder if I've spent my life, in part, breaking cribs. The sense of being compressed, looking for spaces to pour myself into, never left.

When I was 6 my parents bought a house and I had my own room. I still tried to hear what they were doing at night, but having own space was a blessing. My new neighborhood had kids and I played all the time. I've never needed much to be happy. Walking down a street, looking around, swinging my arms is enough to make me smile. I used to whistle while I walked and now my older son hums and whistles a lot.

I didn't understand school until college. Classes in grade school were leaden. Listening to teachers felt like being in a soundproof chamber. No soul echoes. No flashes of mind. A lot of memorization of things that didn't mean much to me. In college things opened. I finally understood what was going on. I loved learning. I fell in love with James Joyce, Socrates, Kandinsky, Klee, Ormandy's Bach (my first real girlfriend took me to see the Philadelphia Orchestra a lot). I bought a motorcycle, got girls on the back, saw Miles Davis, Bird, Bud Powell. I could fly.

In high school I'd play hooky sometimes and go to hear big bands at the Palace. Playing in bands helped get me through. Music was real nourishment. It was something I could feel inside out, soak up through my pores, feel soul's porousness. Psychotherapy is musical. It lives by improvisations of spirit.

The movement from my parents' room and crib to a room of my own, from a lonely neighborhood to an active one, from public school to college, are examples of living in a cocoon for long periods of time, followed by periods of rapid expansion. Similarly, my move from Passaic, New Jersey, to New York City. As a boy I could see Manhattan's skyscrapers from my block and thought, "I'm going to live there."

Making the move to Manhattan wasn't easy. It took several false starts. I rented a room and couldn't move into it. I couldn't tear myself from my parents' home and Passaic, even as I desperately wanted to. College was over. Now was the moment of truth. I was too weak to make the move. Therapy demonstrated its practical power by enabling me to leave home to find my way.

During my first year of analysis (three times a week) I read Jack Kerouac's *On the Road* and D. H. Lawrence's *The Plumed Serpent*, and wanted therapy to help me go to Mexico and just live. It was like having a genie in my corner. Make a wish—boom, a new life materializes. My analyst was somewhat skeptical and hoped I'd continue with him. But empowered by the therapy genie, I got on a bus and went off to Mexico, played in a band, wrote, followed the moment.

I became a believer in the primacy of ecstasy. I remember one morning on a hill looking down on San Francisco in an empty lot. I decided to stare at a tree in the middle of the lot and try as hard as I could not to become ecstatic. But the tree won and, after a struggle, my heart burst with ecstasy. Such moments convinced me that primary emotional reality is orgasmic ecstasy.

Yet my raw naked self was also a ball of agony. My ugly agony did not fit San Francisco's beauty. I met many friendly people and never was at a loss for things to do. I had more friends in San Francisco than in New York, yet my loneliness was more intense than ever. My loneliness did not fit the West Coast life I led. One day I got the idea that my loneliness fit New York.

Perhaps I was latently too hostile or wretched for San Francisco. It was easier for me to be wretched in New York. I felt New York could absorb my blackness better. New York was a better mirror of my ugly self. There was a better fit between inner and outer isolation, loneliness, rage, paranoia, depression, excitement. I began to feel emotionally confined in San Francisco. In New York I felt free to go as deeply as I dared into my personal prison. New York was a better place for a tormented, ecstatic soul.

I reentered analysis (five times a week) within a year of returning to New York and eventually sought refuge in the world of therapy. I began working with disturbed children in schools and camps and in Blueberry, a treatment center for schizophrenic children, was actually called a therapist. I loved looking at and listening to Mira Rothenberg, the clinical heart of Blueberry. I felt her feelings, intuitions, gropings. I loved the immediacy of her work. We fought a lot but when I was with her I felt the warmth and breath of a living soul. I was, at first, put off by Helmuth Gumprecht's ego (he was Blueberry's intellectual guru), but thrilled to his talks and his belief in our patients (mostly schizophrenic children). It is an attitude I felt at one with and it has grown ever since.

For some time analysis continued to be a wish-fulfilling vehicle. I wanted more beautiful girls—analysis helped me get them. I wanted to travel—analysis paved the way. I wanted to write—analysis encouraged me. I wanted to be me living the moment—and analysis said, "Let there be the living moment." The moment stretched into years. What I did not quite notice was that I was falling in love with analysis and, as Roustang (1983) writes, analysis never lets go. I was hooked.

My analyst began to worry as I entered my late twenties. He feared our work could go on forever without my piecing a life together. The living moment was not enough. He felt I should go for my Ph.D., get married, dig into something besides my flowing psyche. I guess my love of or addiction to analysis began to bother him. I spoke in his tone of voice, used his locutions, smoked a pipe like he did, read the same books. Analysis was my life and he was pushing me away. He reduced my sessions to four, three, and then two times a week.

Something was wrong. I was contracting rather than expanding. He had gotten me focused on him; now he feared it went too far. His own life fell apart. His marriage ended badly. He left the city for a university position. I was left hanging with a painfully ruptured bond. I hated him. I hated him like I hated my father, whom I loved so deeply, too. I hated him for making promises he couldn't keep, also one of the reasons I hated my father. My analysis was repeating wounds of my life, broken promises, broken hearts, broken connections. As deep as I could go, the wound was there. It seemed it was there before time. And now time intensified it.

I started graduate school a year after my analyst left the city. Apparently I needed to lose him before starting to build a life. In school a fellow student, Susan Mulliken, recommended me to her ex-husband, Richard Mulliken, who ran a training program at New Hope Guild, a psychiatric clinic in Brooklyn. I took to it like a fish to water. More important than courses and supervision was the chance to be with patients in sessions.

Sessions are holy. They convey a sense of the sacred. Sessions mediate the growth of souls. Being with patients in individual therapy changed my life. Session life was something I felt at home with, something I could feel from inside, connect with. It was like finding an atmosphere or medium I could live in. Being in sessions as an adult in my early 30s felt as natural and creative as being in bands when I was younger, something I could sink my soul into.

Socializing has always been difficult for me. I've had friends and close relationships. I've been OK when there's a feeling between another and myself or a deeply shared interest. But a lot of social life occurs outside personal links and I've suffered from fear of people in impersonal settings from an early age. Therapy provides a safe haven for being with another person. I could hide behind my therapy mask but more often therapy is a vehicle for emotional exploration and very deep contact. Therapy exists to explore the nature of links and ruptures between people, and it can do so in vivo in raw yet graceful ways.

I feel lucky to have grown into therapy at a time when there was no rush to finish quickly, when therapy itself and what went on in it dictated its length. New Hope Guild supported the relationship between therapist and patient, and there was no pressure to abort or warp it for extraclinical reasons. My patients gave me a chance to learn what I could do, what we could do, what could be done. We stayed with each other long enough for me to begin appreciating and studying some of the psychosocial ingredients that constitute therapy, a bit like an artist learning about materials by using them, discovering what he and they can do, the ever-undulating limits of the possible. I summarized basic aspects of my New Hope Guild work in a chapter entitled, "Working with 'Unwanted' Patients" in *The Electrified Tightrope* (1993).

I stayed with my patients longer than my analyst stayed with me. I was trying to complete my analysis and heal myself through them. My analytic work was motivated by my need to repair my own broken analysis. It was, too, trying to mend the unmendable. My younger brother was killed by a truck when he was almost 11 and I was 21. My mother never fully recovered and to say I felt guilty does not even come close. I suspect I became an analyst partly to bring my brother back to life. This is one reason why I have been attracted to the impossible and worked so long with many patients who had been given up on by others—the psychotic (Eigen 1986); the unwanted, undeveloped, malignant, recalcitrant, or otherwise maimed self (Eigen 1993); and the dead (Eigen 1996).

Some patients have stayed with me more than two and three decades, and I have indeed witnessed the dead come alive, the blind see, the lame walk. These therapies take me places I might otherwise not go, mute wounds accessible only by tears of awe and outrage. Life is miraculous. To our horror, miracles of destruction often prevail, but we grow more delicately alive trying to better the balance.

Books have been integral to my development. They open seas of experience beyond the confines of one's life, which enables one to dig more deeply into the bit of life one lives. In high school I was blessed with three moments of real reading. The first happened when I had to stay after school for some infraction that I don't remember. I was alone in a classroom reading Gaisworthy's *Strife*, which suddenly came alive. I don't remember this play except for a fire that still burns in me. Perhaps the destructive fire united with unconscious images of eternal flame, hell, fury—the pulse, heat, and violence of life. Whatever it was, it was more real for a time than the drab teachers and walls surrounding me.

The second occurred when I was a senior, confined to bed with bronchitis. I read Thackeray's *Vanity Fair*. Again, I remember little of this book except some descriptions of Becky Sharpe. What stays with me is the feel of another world, an imaginative reality more real than most people, a world I could lose myself in, better even than staring at the sky.

The veil dropped more compellingly the third time, later in my senior year. I went with a friend to Philadelphia. He was thinking of going to Temple University and I to the University of Pennsylvania. He fixed me up with a date who was pleasant enough but nothing happened. At the end of the evening, he made out with his girl in her room, while I waited alone in the living room. My hand fell on a book by e. e. cummings and that was the end of me. My soul's jaw dropped. Words melted. Language was alive. Meaning danced everywhere. A bar between me and my insides dropped away. Wow! This was great! This was home! Unlike other books in high school, I still can quote lines from e. e. cummings.

Over the year such moments link with each other and build momentum. In college James Joyce, Plato, and sex taught me experience is infinite. I fell in love with the stream of consciousness, the good, the infinities of soul worlds. Soul orgasms, body orgasms, mind orgasms, being orgasms. I've spent much of my life dumbfounded as the kaleidoscope of experience keeps turning. Now and then I try to do a bit of work with multiple realities that do and don't get along. Most often I'm overcome with awe or laziness.

I hung on to readings in depth psychologies and mystical traditions as rafts in strange waters. I read Jung and Fromm before Freud,
although I read parts of Freud more intensely than ever now. I read
existential psychology and philosophy in my late twenties, although I
was hit by novels by Gide and Camus in my late teens. In my early
thirties a paper by Searles (1961) meant a lot to me. I loved two papers by my major analyst (Elkin 1958, 1972), true affirmations of the
human spirit. I began reading Winnicott (1958, 1971, 1992) in my
thirties and I get even more from him today. I've been reading Bion
(1965, 1970) for more than twenty years and Lacan almost as long,
and have been giving seminars on Bion, Winnicott, and Lacan for many
years. Kohut (1971) helped me immensely after my analysis broke up.
I always get something from Melanie Klein (1946). Marion Milner
(1957) helped link my basic intuition with psychoanalysis, particularly
passages on symbolic life expressing facets of creative experiencing,
including orgasmic joy of creativeness. I summarize aspects of my
meetings with Milner, Winnicott, and Bion in the Afterword of *The
Electrified Tightrope* (1993) and Chapter 7 of *Psychic Deadness* (1996).

For years I went over childhood traumas that mis-shaped me. My
mother went to work when I was about 8 months old and the maid we
had was devastating. She would put cream on her pimples, wrap herself in a sheet, then pretend to be a ghost and tell me I'd never see my
parents again. When the doorbell rang, she sometimes hid in the closet
and took me with her. My parents did not act on my complaints and I
felt a growing helpless fear and rage.

The trauma list created by my father was endless. I was terrified
of his rageful outbursts. He drank a lot during my childhood. At the
same time, he was fearfully overprotective. I fought for years to get a
bike, never got to go to sleepaway camp, scarcely ever was allowed to
go to public swimming pools. It was a nightmare. My mother was a
soft, kindly woman, and her basic good-heartedness fooled me into
thinking she understood me. Both parents installed in me a sense of
basic goodness, at enormous expense.

In my ongoing self-analysis, particularly with Winnicott's and
Bion's writings, I've tasted how frightened my mother was of me as a
baby. She has since verified she was terrified (more than normally) of

injuring me as a baby. My experience with her when I was a little older suggests she didn't know what to do with my aggression either, that she also feared being injured. A melding of panic-joy-goodness-destructiveness characterized the emotional air I breathed. I've had to work long and hard to become a little less afraid of myself and others and to find constructive uses of fear and anger.

After years of reciting permutations of my traumatic upbringing, I began losing interest in how hurt I was. The wound that never heals meets the fire that never goes out in never-ending ways. I became less interested in my past than in getting on with my life. Suffering, ecstasy, inspiration were facts. My history made me part of the human race. As time went on, I became more interested in what went on in therapy for its own sake, as a process of soul making. Therapy is not only a soul searchlight. Interactions between patient and therapist actually create being and new nuances of being.

Therapy is far more than rehashing the past, understanding patterns, and freeing oneself from destructive tendencies, although all these may be important. Therapy is part of being and, as such, is ever created by being and creates being. The model of a high-velocity particle collider creating new particles is too narrow. A physicist, perhaps Eddington, said, "Something unknown is doing we don't know what." This applies to therapy, too. Bion (1965, 1970, Eigen 1996) is especially helpful in keeping the unknown-unknowable open. What hasn't happened may be more interesting and helpful than what has happened. And what is happening may never have happened quite this way before. Whatever we know about therapy, there is more we don't know, more we have not begun to live.

We work on becoming better partners with our capacities. There is no end to opening. Patient and therapist are ever on the brink of opening with each other in fresh ways. Two people coming together to create being is not unique, but to set aside time specifically for this purpose is not usual. I originally entered therapy in pain, to strengthen myself, fulfill wishes. Now it is more thrilling to let therapy teach me what therapy can be.

I could not continue to progress in therapeutic work without my interest in religion. Mystical experiences provide models for aspects

of therapeutic processes, and therapeutic processes tie mystical experiences to real living. I have seen individuals lost in mystical experiencing without a clue to what they were doing to themselves and others. On the other hand, there are individuals so mired in the confines
of a narrow therapy, that they are blinded to the impact of the infinite.
In *Coming Through the Whirlwind* (1992) I depicted an individual
dedicated to psychological truth at the expense of spirit, and an individual dedicated to spirit at the expense of psychological issues. In
Reshaping the Self (1995) I use the Job story as a frame for therapy.
The intersection of the psychological and spiritual is important for us
today. Each amplifies and strengthens the other. They evolve together.

I'm not a scholar, systematic reader, or follower of any school.
I've loved aspects of most religions I've dipped into. In my twenties I
nearly became a Catholic, but got ill during instruction, and abandoned
this idea as part of my recovery. St. Augustine and Meister Eckhart
are among those who have had an enduring impact on me. I've been
sustained by parts of Taoist writings for more than four decades. I enjoy
Rumi and imagine myself a Sufi. My contacts with Buddhist and Hindu
masters have been intriguing and worthwhile. The Bible and *siddur*
have exercised my imagination since childhood.

One of my proudest moments was on a *Simchat Torah* (the holi-
day of Torah joy), when the rabbi called me up for a blessing, then
whispered in my ear, "You're a Hasid!" We made a *L'chaim* together
and danced like crazy. The Hasidic movement originated in a joyous
heart connection to God, although it can reinforce narrowly parochial
elements in Judaism as well. Jewish prayer, song, and stories touch
my heart and energy centers.

I use Buddhism partly as a psychic cleansing system. Emptiness
and selflessness act as antidotes to this or that version of self. People
narrow, even destroy themselves, defending this or that identity. The
"I'm right–you're wrong" structure produces nightmares. A good dose
of Buddhism protects one against destructive self-definitions—nationally, racially, and personally.

To say I'm a Hasid in my heart and a Buddhist in my head would
be too simple. But the neutrality of open awareness keeps one mind-
ful that there is more to go, that more is going on than one may be

imagining, that something is happening beyond the identities we have constituted for ourselves. If pain is real, so is the joyous light through and beyond pain. Can one stop working with walls of personality short of anything less? Going through the light whets an even deeper, fuller appetite.

I married for the first time in my mid-forties and having a family has had an enormous impact on my work. The opening of my heart upon having children made me view my patients in a new light. I think my work was more strident and brittle before children. Caring for children made me care for my patients more. My capacity for love grew. I became, too, better able to appreciate the complexity of family life from a variety of perspectives—that of different parents (husband, wife) and of different children. I made peace with my own parents as well.

To really endure and make a go of family life involves dimensions of personal sacrifice not required by the single life. Either I would find ways of growing in order to help make things work or we were in trouble. The pressure put on personality by family life is mind-boggling. One is besieged by problems that can't be solved, impossible demands by loved ones, differences in time worlds (the time worlds of infancy and childhood challenge normal adult living, and vice versa), new levels of pain through deeper bonds with those you most want to benefit but struggle with, and so on. I've grown more in my marriage than in any period since my early twenties.

Catholic and Buddhist writings have viewed married life as second best. Marriage saps strength and resolve necessary for spiritual development. Daily chores eat energy that might have been poured into prayer and meditation. Marriage is sacramental for the masses who can't pursue God full time. My experience has been the opposite. Marriage has acted as an accelerant for my spiritual as well as psychological growth. The Holy Spirit thrives on and nourishes the soul ground to bits and pieces by daily torments. Nowhere does the soul grow more through its own demise than in everyday clashes with those one loves.

To grow enough to encompass multiple antagonistic pressures with those one loves makes the idea of going beyond polarities more than an abstraction. The work in the trenches required on a persistent basis by family living has broadened my sense of what therapy does. It has made me far more respectful of what people actually achieve in the way of real living in spite of themselves. Work with patients and family living feed each other.

Today my patients inspire me. I'm inspired by what they have gone through and what they must yet go through to work with themselves. Therapy helps sensitize people to their lives in ways they missed or couldn't reach on their own. It helps people become more respectful of what is possible and fosters the capacity to be inspired by the lives they and others live. It helps the capacity for inspired living grow in less destructive ways.

We work with suffering, yet serve *jouissance* (Lacan 1977). We mediate *jouissance* for each other at the same time that life's pressures mutate us. We learn and keep on learning to work with our wondrous mutant selves. The work forces us to dig into experience and keep opening. We go ever deeper into the faith–despair helix and shiver as a mysterious joy ripples through the agonies we encompass and that encompass us.

Michael Eigen, Ph.D., is a Training and Supervising Analyst at the National Psychological Association for Psychoanalysis (NPAP) and Associate Clinical Professor, New York University Postdoctoral Program in Psychoanalysis.

REFERENCES

Bion, W. R. (1965). *Transformations.* London: Heinemann.
——— (1970). *Attention and Interpretation.* London: Tavistock.
Eigen, M. (1986). *The Psychotic Core.* Northvale, NJ: Jason Aronson.
——— (1992). *Coming Through the Whirlwind.* Wilmette, IL: Chiron.
——— (1993). *The Electrified Tightrope.* Northvale, NJ: Jason Aronson.
——— (1995). *Reshaping the Self.* Madison, CT: Psychosocial Press.
——— (1996). *Psychic Deadness.* Northvale, NJ: Jason Aronson.
Elkin, H. (1958). On the origin of the self. *Psychoanalytic Review* 45:57–76.
——— (1972). On selfhood and the development of ego structures in infancy. *Psychoanalytic Review* 59:389–416.
Klein, M., (1946). Notes on some schizoid mechanisms. In *Developments in Psycho-Analysis,* ed. M. Klein, P. Heimann, S. Isaacs, and J. Riviere, pp. 282–320. London: Hogarth, 1952.

Kohut, H. (1971). *The Analysis of the Self.* New York: International Universities Press.

Lacan, J. (1977) *Ecrits*, trans. A. Sheridan. New York: Norton.

Milner, M. (1957). *On Not Being Able to Paint.* New York: International Universities Press.

Roustang, F. (1983). *Psychoanalysis Never Lets Go.* Baltimore, MD: John Hopkins University Press.

Searles, H. (1961). Phases of patient–therapist interaction in the psychotherapy of chronic schizophrenia. In *Collected Papers on Schizophrenia and Related Subjects,* pp. 521–559. New York: International Universities Press, 1965.

Winnicott, D. W. (1958). *Collected Papers—Through Paediatrics to Psycho-Analysis.* New York: Basic Books.

——— (1971). *Playing and Reality.* New York: Basic Books.

——— (1992). *Psychoanalytic Explorations,* ed. C. Winnicott, R. Shepherd, and M. Davis. Cambridge, MA: Harvard University Press.

9

A Psychotherapist in Mexico

LUIS FEDER

I became a psychoanalyst for various personal and historical reasons related to war, heroism, danger, salvation deeds and fantasies, pioneering, naïveté, idealization, disappointments, unconscious factors and motivations, and other psychic factors.

The only family survivor of Nazism on my maternal side was my mother, the oldest of thirteen living children, and the only survivors on my paternal side were my father and his older brother. His brother had left earlier for the United States. But it was my father's leadership that saved the rest of us. Already heroic at 14, he ran away from a seclusive Jewish orthodoxy to study in the Russian system and finished at the gymnasium. During the First World War, he was named a lieutenant in the Quartermaster Corps, Cavalry Division. During the Battle of Erzurum against the Turks, my father always aimed at nothing. "I have never killed anyone, as far as I know." This message goes deeply into my paternal superego, which was reflected in my difficulty in facing the bloody side of medicine. I had already operated on cats and other animals, but could not do so on humans. The image of my family being exterminated by the Nazis certainly haunted me.

Responding to a friend's warning, "Being an ex-Czarist officer has placed you on the list of those to be shot tomorrow," my parents, with a 6-year-old child, gave up, within hours, a lovely furnished home in postwar revolutionary Russia. The requirement to save lives was renunciation of material goods; this is what saved us, as it did many other people in Germany and Russia, and many other people in similar circumstances. They had a split second to flee! Unfortunately, later on my European maternal and paternal sides had no choice under the Nazis. We lost about eighty family members in Russia. My father, leaving material comforts, chose to migrate to Mexico in 1926, almost twelve years before the Nazi invasion on Poland.

At the University of Texas, shaken and pained by the extermination of most of my European family, I volunteered for the Air Corps, Latin American Division, but I was rejected because I was not yet 21. I organized a very successful radio program sponsored in Washington, giving news to the Southwest Mexican and Spanish-speaking population. As a postgraduate in Berkeley, shaken by the knowledge of atomic warfare, I proposed an international strike of scientists working with agencies and states dealing in lethal weapons. Since I was then an unknown speaker, with a naive message and a deaf and indifferent audience, I wasted my fantasy. All this took place before my psychoanalysis began. Years later, as a more mature psychotherapist, I received better responses, such as one in London, in front of close to 3,000 members, to my protest against the Soviet psychiatric hospitals for their jailing of dissidents under the guise of doing psychotherapy.

In Mexico, I ran into Santiago Ramirez, freshly returned from Buenos Aires and authorized to carry on training analyses. I was most fortunate. I knew whom to pick and why. But how do others know? This is a question that remains open.

After selecting my psychoanalyst and later my supervisor, I was not fully aware that both my analyst, Ramirez, and my first supervisor, Parres, would become the pioneers of bona fide psychoanalysis in Mexico. I would become one of the second group of founders of our Mexican psychoanalytic movement. After selection came payment. Financing the treatment is where the curtain really opened and the drama began. Finding work was easy: I was appointed Head Translator, Division of the Liga Mexicana de Salud Mental. But there were many financial struggles and some exploitations of my naïveté.

I was the first fully trained graduate of the Asociación Psicoanalítica Mexicana. My becoming a psychoanalyst guided me to apply other forms of dynamically oriented psychotherapy, such as analytic group psychotherapy. It enabled me to be gainfully employed, to bring relief to others, and to experience freedom from fear and pain. It gave me the opportunity to be a pioneer within psychoanalysis in creating group analytic programs covering most socioeconomic levels and most psychiatric disorders, including one experimental group with chronic patients, plus the daily harvest of discovery through the individual or collective therapeutic modalities.

Music has been my accompanist. From an early age up to the present it has accompanied me daily in the stages of my life. Lately, musical composition and psychoanalysis have become integrated. To honor our first International Psychoanalytical Association (IPA) Latin American president, Horacio Etchegoyen, I composed a string quintet "Mestizajes" performed by psychoanalysts at the Amsterdam IPA Congress. Two years later I was commissioned to compose the music at Delphi, for the IV International Symposium on Adult Sexuality and, for the artistic program, a symphonic ballet with the same name. It was performed by the Delfos Ballet Group of Mexico.

My therapeutic psychoanalysis unleashed pent-up aggression, differentiated from hostility, and redirected it into creative energy in me and in my patients. I have had an unusual number of professionals as patients who became creative in the arts and sciences.

My first psychoanalytic paper was "Psychoanalytic Technique and Salvation Fantasies" and many years later, in 1990, my first symphonic chorale, "Themes for Survivors," with the Spanish preface of my text read by Arrigo Coen and the English by Merton Gill, was performed at the Elementos de la Orquesta Sinfónica Nacional (National Symphony of Mexico). Musical composition has been my second profession and my first hobby.

Another thought about becoming a psychotherapist: Some of us, given equal training requirements and opportunities, prefer clinical work, while others are more interested in the theory of technique, and still others in the psychogenic aspect of psychoanalysis. Becoming a

therapist requires a thorough acquaintance with one's own oedipal, psychic, and social reality.

Luis Feder, Ph.D., is a Training and Supervising Analyst at the Mexican
Psychoanalytic Association.

BIBLIOGRAPHY

Feder, L. (1973). *Incesto y fraticidio institucional y la adoctrinación.*
    Presentado XII Congreso Nacional de la Asociacón Mexicana.
———— (1974). The adoption trauma: oedipal myth/clinical reality. *Interna-
    tional Journal of Psycho-Analysis* 55:491–493.
———— (1979). *Los asesinos de la fantasía.* Unpublished.
———— (1980a). *La vocación psicoanalista.* Preámbolo de una investigación
    en la APM e Instituto Copal. Rio de Janeiro, Brasil.
———— (1980b). Preconceptive ambivalence and external reality. *International
    Journal of Psycho-Analysis* 61:161–178.
———— (1985). At work. In *Cuadernos de Psicoanálisis,* ed. Asociación
    Psiconalítica Mexicana, pp. 1–25. Mexico, DF: Asociación Psiconalítica
    Mexicana.

10

Remembering a Quiet Place

GERALD J. GARGIULO

As I sat in the large, book-filled office, frightened yet somehow strangely comforted by the white-haired doctor sitting behind his desk, I had a sense that I had found a safe place. I was 10½ years old, too young to last much longer in my battle to try to figure out what was going on in my life, in my mind, in my family.

Fifty years ago, child therapists were not particularly common and school counselors were not as available as they are now. Consequently, I spent considerable time in my family physician's office and the principal's office, since I was refusing to learn anything, despite the fact that the tests I was given indicated that I should be performing on a much higher level. I will never know whether it was these school officials or our personal physician who prevailed upon my parents for me to see a child psychiatrist, but one day I found myself walking up the stairs of a brownstone, on the Upper East Side of Manhattan, with my father. My father, a self-made man who had achieved a comfortable middle-class life with a home in the rural northeast Bronx, was quietly angry at his failure to control this second son of his who was causing him such embarrassment.

I cannot remember my psychiatrist's face, but I know it was kind and interested in me. I recall his buying me a magic set and that we talked and talked and played some games together—on equal ground between us. And slowly, as each Sunday morning session came and went, I began to sense that I did not have to learn other people's answers to school questions before I had figured out what was going on in me. I was finding out that it was okay for me to be me; I was finding out that I could talk to someone about my father's constant puzzling demands, my older brother's special place, and my mother's distracted attentions, and I would be listened to and not reprimanded. Something positive occurred since ever so slowly the capacity to learn, which had eluded me so far and caused me such embarrassment with my peers, was showing itself. But as it became obvious that my therapy was progressing my father announced that he could no longer afford the twenty-dollar weekly fee and, since I seemed better, I would have to stop. I can still feel my bewilderment and grief at this fiat decision. I retreated. Angrily. I believe I had seen my white-haired doctor for about eight or nine months. I cannot remember our last session. It must have been locked away in a timeless place.

Twenty-five years later I would establish my own psychoanalytic office on the Upper East Side of New York. Was I, perhaps, looking for my old friend as I walked those streets, studied the brownstones, and caught sight of the libraries behind the bay windows? Those twenty-five years were turbulent, painful, enlightening, and fulfilling—ending with my being married, having two life-giving children, and graduating from a psychoanalytic institute. Why I became a psychoanalyst is hidden in the recesses of those years and the childhood that preceded them. But, aware of the inevitable distortions that accompany such a task, I will try to rescue some of those reasons and bring them to light.

If we cannot love the world, we cannot learn from it and we have no place to stand. I was unable to learn because as a child I had too much anger and confusion in me, as well as a yearning to find a place from which to take my first steps into a personal history. What I have come to understand, paradoxically, is that to learn the most is to stand nowhere, so to speak, neither in the past nor the future. As for the present, it is always slipping by us anyway. So if I can stand nowhere for a while, I hope I can tell about my still ongoing journey, tell of events that have given me one view rather than another. I will try to do this without the intimidation of a conscious history, of a linear chronology that might make more conscious sense but that ultimately belies the truth of a life. T. S. Eliot is correct, I believe, when he muses that both past and future are rooted in the now, that time is simultaneous. If we know the past, we know the future, most dramatically in the sense that to know of our birth is to know of our death, and more modestly that to know of our past struggles is to know of our future goals. Analysis taught me that. As my deciphering goes on, I continue to find myself around this becoming a psychoanalyst.

The past, as we know, does not exist, except as it lives again in our different readings of it. So we are seemingly lost, but not quite. Despite what I have just said about a conscious chronology, let me recount a few events while recognizing that their meaning is constantly changing. By the time I was 13, building on the help given to me by my psychiatrist and a special reading teacher, I decided to make friends with the world. So I finally learned to read and tell time. I read everything I could, starting with Homer and the classics, with Freud's (1905) "Three Essays on the Theory of Sexuality" thrown in by age 17. During my adolescence, the turbulence in my household continued with my mother, whose depression finally found intermittent and prolonged expression. This period of her life lasted for four years; my sense of having a safe and quiet ground out of which to grow was again undermined. As her depression progressed, love, grief, rescue fantasies, and anger danced ominously in my soul. Fortunately, a series of supportive organizations and some electroshock treatments brought this period to a definitive close. It was not until after my first year of college, however, that, unrelieved of my emotional conflicts at home and within myself, I decided to flee to a Carmelite monastery, intent, somewhere inside me, on finding a new family.

For ten years I lived a semi-monastic life filled with study, friendship, and ideals into which I was to funnel my desires and ambitions. There was also the absence of sexuality in any form. During my last year of study in the seminary, I elected to see another psychiatrist, this time a pleasant, highly perceptive middle-aged man, whom I visited once a week. During this treatment period, which lasted for about eight months, my growing discontent with monastic life came clearly to the fore. I eventually decided, not without a great deal of anguish, to leave this safe place and my close friends—just three weeks prior to my ordination to the Roman Catholic priesthood. I returned home, became a lay professor of religious studies at a local Catholic college, and within a year and a half met and married my wife.

Within three years of leaving the seminary, I was completing my studies for a doctorate in theology and psychology at Fordham University and had started my psychoanalytic training at an institute founded by Theodor Reik, the National Psychological Association for Psychoanalysis. I committed myself to this training with an energy that now bemuses me. While teaching a full schedule of college courses, increasingly with a focus on the psychoanalytic understanding of religious symbolism, I had a five-time-a-week analysis, took eight academic courses a year, and completed the requisite hours of supervision and control analysis. This took five years to complete. By 1970 I had completed eight years as a college teacher, all the required analytic training, and most of the courses for my doctorate. I left full-time teaching, with some reluctance, and found a new monastic cell, so to speak, a quiet office on the Upper East Side that I shared with a colleague, who soon became a friend.

These are just some of the facts, yet it is their trail of memories, fantasies, and needs that I have to unfold if I am to get closer to their meaning.

My search for a new "mother" church and a new "father" God found expression in my Carmelite decade. I had not been brought up overly religious and so my choice was fueled from many sources. Had I been ordained, it would have been my father who would have had to address me as "father"—not only an oedipal victory but a reversal of the humiliation and submission he had demanded of me as a child. Happily I had resolved enough, albeit waiting to the last minute to do so, not to stamp my life irrevocably with that fantasy. I had to choose an alternate route—I chose further understanding and hidden knowledge. Having achieved firm ground intellectually, I needed to do so emotionally.

Psychoanalysis, I hoped, would offer me not only a reversal of my childhood humiliations, but a broader intellectual terrain than my seminary training afforded. By becoming the one who knows, not only of the obvious but of the hidden, I would find the respect and the power that had eluded me in my childhood. But feeling respected is just another way of feeling real. I needed to feel real as much as I needed to keep faith with that little boy in that big, book-filled, psychiatric office. I needed to find him again, inside me, and continue his treatment— a treatment that my learning to read had attempted to continue, and did, to some extent, but necessarily left too many empty spaces that only another ear could fill. My early readings had brought me to Plato, Socrates, and the Greek classics, to the discovery, to my bewildered delight, that I was not alone in a foreign world. I had found friends, mind to mind, albeit two thousand years away, yet still present. It was this most obvious of discoveries, of what reading could bring, that spurred me on. That made me realize that I loved understanding other people as well as myself, that I loved the inner world as much as the outer, and that I had, quite fortunately, found a terrain I could travel on safely.

Although I have no clear understanding as to how this knowledge came so early in my life, I always knew that emotional pain could be a bridge to others, not just a personal prison with mirrors. I remember George, a classmate in my grammar school, who was, in all likelihood, autistic. He would stand alone in the school playground just watching the other children, almost always silent. I remember standing by him, telling him that it was OK, that other people were afraid also. He would look at me and let me know, with his eyes, that he heard me. Did I sense, then, that I would have to help another to help myself? Was that a private fantasy, or a preconscious awareness of our human interconnectedness? And if I follow D. W. Winnicott's thoughts today, in my practice, have I simply found a corollary intellectual model to Freud, or have I remembered both being injured and seeing injuring before my eyes?

With this history behind me, I was both ready and surprised to hear about psychoanalytic training that was available for those who had not taken the medical route, when a close friend of my wife came to visit, a graduate of New York Psychoanalytic Institute. I knew, despite all the work I had done with my second psychiatrist, that I was still curious about my ten-year seminary stay, about my capacity to have sublimated my sexuality, and about my growing alienation from organized religion. Such sublimation, I was convinced, had its roots in more than oedipal soil—I had had to put my self together. I knew that although I was happily married, the task of self consolidation was still in its beginning stages. The promise of an analysis was a powerful lure; I had had enough therapy to know that I needed a sounding place. Having re-created myself from the superego down in my seminary years, I needed to put my hand to the same task and try it from the id up, so to speak. I needed to find my ambition(s) and my anger, my yearnings and my competence, if I was ever to complete this task of self-ness.

It was also true that these, as well as other, motives were brewing beneath my conscious desire to be of help to others, to find myself through that activity. As a college professor, a profession I truly loved, my income was modest and very frustrating; as a psychoanalyst in private practice these constraints could be removed and I could show my competence in the only way my family could recognize. My mind also echoed with my father's constant advice: that one should work for oneself—just as he did.

And so I became a midwife of memories, fantasies, and desires, my own and those with whom I worked. In the gathering of days that has marked my twenty-five years of practice, I have done some foolish things as well as some helpful things. My own analysis was enormously helpful in my finding my voice and my name, but it left some unaddressed issues as well, issues that have echoed back to me in my work with patients and that I have had to address, address in a quiet way, similar to how I try to work with patients—self-forgetful when possible, speaking whatever insights the moment brings. And I have wondered, at times, Are we analysts voyeurs of ourselves? Have we had a growing appreciation of narcissism as we have been slowly able to hear ourselves with our patients?

I still wonder about my being a psychoanalyst, whether or not it was a necessary path I deluded myself into thinking I had chosen freely.

And about the cure we provide, which, of course, is no cure at all. "If we are merely sane we are poor indeed" (p. 150), D. W. Winnicott (1958) would write, as he hoped to enable people to achieve personal aliveness rather than the given-ness of existence. Is that what I do, help aliveness? My own as well as others? Who are these others, anyway, if not ourselves?

These are my thoughts when I think about my becoming a psychoanalyst. I have other thoughts as well, and as my life goes on I will, I hope, come to know them.

Gerald J. Gargiulo, M.A., is a Fellow of the Institute for Psychoanalytic Training and Research (IPTAR) and a Training and Supervising Analyst at the National Psychological Association for Psychoanalysis (NPAP).

REFERENCES

Freud, S. (1905). Three essays on the theory of sexuality. *Standard Edition* 7:125–243.

Winnicott, D. W. (1958). *Collected Papers*. London: Tavistock.

11

Influences: Parents, Teachers, Colleagues

HELEN K. GEDIMAN

I dreamed and daydreamed of being a psychotherapist when I was in high school. At that time, the only kind of psychotherapist I had ever heard of was a psychoanalyst, so naturally my fantasies were of being a psychoanalyst, but at the age of 14 I do not think I believed that joining that august body would ever materialize into a real possibility. A beloved uncle was then studying to be an analyst. During summer vacations that our families spent together on Cape Cod, he "practiced" giving Rorschachs to me. He seemed very impressed that I saw ice-cream cones and sundaes on quite a few cards where nobody to his knowledge had ever seen them before. I was absolutely delighted when he interpreted my orality to my parents, cousins, aunts, and uncles as indicating that I had a creative and original turn of mind as well as a lust for life. Although nobody to whom he bragged about me could know for sure whether he was right or wrong, deep down I must have had an unflagging trust in his judgments about me. My favorite uncle also had Freud's *Collected Papers* on our communal shelves, and I dug into them in the wee hours as though I were surreptitiously sneaking into me all the ice cream I could possibly get, and that was the beginning of my addiction to and my burgeoning love affair with psychoanalysis. His Havelock Ellis books did nothing to retard the process.

As I write this mini-memoir, I am struck by how my adolescent enthusiasm, excitement, and idealization of my psychoanalytic heroes is reactivated, now in the present. It would be a while before the initial love affair and infatuation was gradually transformed, in the process of "becoming," into the more mature forms of passionate love, devotion, and respect, along with that quieter, more reserved love that I bring to my being a psychoanalyst, today.

A few years later, as a freshman at Harvard (we called it Radcliffe, then, and I still call it Radcliffe today as a testament to my strong feelings of support for top-quality education of women, and to my firm identity as a woman psychoanalyst) it still had not dawned on me that I, the little girl from Brooklyn, could actually become a psychoanalyst. There was also a similar feeling of disbelief that it was actually I who walked the streets of Cambridge, and had become a regular habitué to Harvard Yard. Despite those initial feelings of disbelief, of unreality, I can now look back and say I was at the right place at the right time, and blessed with very good fortune. I began my serious voyage by following my anxious parents' advice to seek out a major that would qualify me for a teaching license in the New York City public school system, which is where my parents and most of my aunts and uncles worked. Knowing how hard my parents worked to send me to what I believed to be the best college in the world in order to prepare me for teaching in the only world they knew well, I decided to major in English. However, that decision was very short-lived, because my final grade in English 1 was a B, and I hated the course, and my final grade in Social Relations 1a (Harvard's program for human psychology), taught by Gordon Allport, was an A, and I loved the course. Social relations became my major. In the years to follow, I became fairly well acquainted with the works and the persons of Robert White, Daniel Levinson, and most of all Henry Murray, who was a faculty affiliate of my dorm. Once a month he would have dinner at the table of all the social relations majors living in Cabot Hall, and once a month we would have dinner at his gracious home in the lovely Back Bay area of Boston. In those days, psychoanalysis was the only game in town for a psychology major at the undergraduate level, and Freudian thinking permeated every course I took. Even my forays into literature and art brought me into direct contact with the basics of psychoanalytic interpretation and ideas. I was so smitten then that when I analyzed Yeats' poem "Leda and the Swan" wildly, as though it were some unknown person's random dream, completely ignoring the poet's intent, my English instructor rewarded me with a D- grade. Perhaps that lapse in judgment signaled the beginnings of the lifelong process of reining in some tendency to unbridled excitement about psychoanalysis and psychoanalysts that had begun when I was a teenager.

My career path was direct and unambivalent from the beginning. Those were very peculiar times. Dean Mildred Sherman, Radcliffe's dean of women, was convinced that a liberal arts education for women should have the sole and simple goal of preparing them to be good wives to successful men, culminating in their being good conversationalists at formal dinner parties, and while pouring the demitasse that followed in their wake. I fought her all the way, however, and managed to graduate magna cum laude, having written an honors thesis on cognitive processes under the tutelage of Eugenia Hanffman. By that time, although I probably did not know it yet, I clearly was beginning to find my own voice (I think I thought I was simply a lucky overachiever), and I did not have to rely so much on the proximity to idealized successful people to bolster my self-esteem. I now enjoy the pleasures of connections to accomplished colleagues for myriad other reasons. Strange as it may seem, I was among the puny 5 percent of Radcliffe graduates in my class who went on to graduate school immediately upon graduating (it is now closer to 95 percent), and on that account was considered a rebel by the dean, who gave me no support whatsoever and did her best to discourage me from going on to graduate school in my chosen profession. Thank goodness my own parents, anxious as they might have been about the unknown-to-them career path I chose, gave me the loving support and encouragement that I sorely needed. Although I was not headed in a direction that would land me a license to teach in the New York City school system, it was unheard of to my parents that any child, boy or girl, be sent to away to an expensive Ivy League college (the cost for tuition, room, and board was then $1,000 per annum!), supported by both of their hard-earned incomes, and not go on to some profession or career. My choice was closer to my parents' aspirations than to Dean Sherman's. However, possibly as a concession to the latter, I did marry on the afternoon of my graduation. It took subsequent divorce, remarriage, and two analyses to understand the full meaning of that action.

One cannot write an account of how one became a psychoanalyst without reference to motivations that spring from personal history. So, in the brief digression that follows, I choose not to go into the details of either of my two analyses, but will supply the readers with some selected relevant background information, preferring that they use their own imagination in interpreting my particular motivational route to becoming a psychoanalyst to their being burdened with my explicit analyses.

To begin, I did not need the support of the feminist movement, which was to gain momentum a decade after my college graduation and would flourish two decades later, in order to maintain my resolve in pursuing life goals involving marriage, motherhood, and my profession. I had the support of my father, who had emigrated to the United States from the Ukraine at the turn of the century, and of my mother, whose parents arrived here from Vilna, Lithuania, during the blizzard of 1888, before she was born. My mother was the eldest of eight, and she remained single, working as an English teacher, and supporting all of her brothers and sisters until they had graduated from college, graduate school, or law school. Only then did she marry my father, continuing on in her profession. My mother, a feminist without knowing she was one, was my role model, cheering me on, completely uncomprehending of and baffled by the stifling antifeminist bias, like that held by Dean Sherman, of the 1950s. Her life was not an altogether easy one, and she suffered the tragedy, at the age of 39, of losing her first child, Marjorie, a 2-year-old girl who died from a strep throat complication of scarlet fever.

I was born two years later, to a mother who was still depressed. I was not expected to survive the first year of my life, being afflicted with a condition that was at that time diagnosed simply as diarrhea, so my mother, more depressed than ever, then became pregnant with my twenty-one month younger sister, Cecil. Thanks to my stalwart father's daily trips, after his workday as a school principal ended, to Manhattan from our home in Brooklyn to buy some kind of special milk to treat my condition, I survived. My parents, whose lives were not directly touched by the Holocaust because their families came to this country earlier to escape the programs, were thus blessed with two "replacement" children. I grew up with a mother who never stopped grieving for a lost daughter who, judging from the picture of Marjorie that never left her bureau top, looked exactly like me. And she was a mother who never stopped protecting and overprotecting me and my younger sister, Cecil, in her determination that we survive well in every endeavor of our lives.

This brief historical capsule provides some background for understanding how I got in touch with my own vulnerabilities and those of others around me, and how I must have been driven to distinguish myself in unusual ways simply to survive and to be loved. That sense of vulnerability has been a major source of my love of learning doing and teaching psychoanalysis, and has always rung out as a critical counterpoint to what some others might easily (mis)understand simply as a very ambitious wish to achieve and to be admired.

After graduating from college and defying the dean of women, I went on without missing a beat to graduate schools, earning my doctorate in clinical psychology from New York University, which at that time was heavily focused on psychoanalytic thinking. I was invited by George Klein to join the staff of NYU's Research Center for Mental Health, which he codirected with Robert Holt, both of whom were schooled in the traditions set by David Rapaport at the Menninger Foundation, and who were determined to carry on his mission. My five years as a National Institute of Mental Health (NIMH) predoctoral research fellow in that heady environment kept me on track. Among those with whom I lunched, usually at the Cedar Street Tavern of Beat Generation fame, and with whom I schmoozed almost daily were Morris Eagle, Leo Goldberger, Paul Lippman, Irving Paul, Fred Pine, and Donald Spence. This list of names and others that appear throughout this chapter, while subject to misconstrual as name-dropping, are intended solely to convey my extreme good fortune in having had the opportunity to connect all along with myriad colleagues who have become major contributors to psychoanalysis in all its facets.

Looking back, it is easy to see that once again I was fortunate to be in the right place at the right time, thriving on the benefits of shared passionate concerns with people of like minds. We were all doing some kind of psychoanalytically based empirical research. I was working on my dissertation, sponsored by George Klein, on the topic of ambivalence and stimulus ambiguity. We were all doing something on cognitive style and psychoanalysis, and most of us were very involved in tachistoscopic studies of subliminal stimuli, and with studying the effects of LSD on manifest dream content. To accomplish the latter, all of us staff members were soberly encouraged to take the drug, and then either look at subliminal stimuli or spend the night sleeping at the dream lab at Downstate Medical School, reporting our dreams each time we were awakened during a period of REM sleep. We were also expected to describe at staff meetings our personal experiences with our own altered states of consciousness. We didn't know then that we were "tripping"—I do not believe the term had yet been coined. Robert Langs was the medical consultant on that dicey project. In the end, we were all left with an unflappable conviction about the existence of the unconscious. And we all served as subjects for each other's studies, which were discussed in weekly conferences, along with some talmudic style seminars in such areas of interest to Rapaport and his disciples as Chapter 7 of Freud's "Dream Book."

During one of my graduate years, I was a school psychologist in training at the Bureau of Child Guidance of the New York City Board of Education. That work did indeed qualify me for a license that my parents had heard of, but I opted out and headed in other directions. Courses in the clinical psychology program, headed by Bernard Kalinkowitz, were all psychoanalytically oriented. I took the psychotherapy practicum and was supervised by Esther Menaker, one of the few nonmedical analysts in New York at that time who had been trained at the Vienna Institute. Since she had been analyzed by Anna Freud, I thought of Sigmund Freud as my great-grandfather, thus acquiring another relative as a psychoanalytic ego ideal in addition to my Rorschaching uncle. Although I am certain that by this time, my adolescent excitements and infatuations with highly idealized individuals of great accomplishment were on their way to being tamed, I am equally certain that in writing this chapter those older and much more raw feelings have surfaced once more, and I am reliving them, knowing they will have to be worked over again and again, with less and less time and effort, I hope, than in the past.

I knew by then that the next step would be formal psychoanalytic training, an idea that had moved out of the fantasy land of my adolescence into the more thoughtful world of viable and more sober reality, but I did not yet know where or how. Sad to leave the Research Center and my friends, I moved on to do a two-year NIMH postdoctoral fellowship in psychotherapy—and still the only kind of psychotherapy I was taught was psychoanalytic—in the Department of Psychiatry at Albert Einstein College of Medicine, headed then by Milton Rosenbaum. My mentors in the Psychology Division there, at Jacoby Hospital, were Walter Kass and Sybille Escalona, who had sprung from the same Menninger tradition as Holt and Klein, so there was considerable continuity and consistency in my training. I was fortunate enough to be at Einstein during the halcyon days when just about everyone on staff was an analyst, and nearly every resident in psychiatry and intern in psychology eventually became one. Once again, the right place at the right time with people of like minds. Among the psychiatry residents there at the time of my training were Sander Abend, Anna Burton, Robert Kabcenell, Theodore Jacobs, Arnold Richards, Elyse Snyder, and Martin Willick. Among the psychology interns and fellows were Sheldon Bach, Doris Silverman, and Joyce Steingart. My first personal analysis was in full swing, and I was privileged to be in psychotherapy supervision with Robert Grayson, William Grossman, and Lester Schwartz. In addition, I took seminars with Jose Barchilon, Eleanor Galenson, Norman Margolis, and Andrew Peto. The exciting smorgasbord continued into weekly grand rounds when presentations by Robert Bak, Edith Jacobson, Margaret Mahler, Sandor Rado, John Rosen, and Harold Searles, to name but a few, contributed significantly to a broad range of exposure to psychoanalytic thinking, even before my formal training had begun. Space limitations force me to give just the menu, but the food was delicious and nourishing even though it took years to digest in the continuous process of finding my own preferences to be expressed in my very own voice. And it took years for my vociferous and gregarious hunger to be transformed into a passion for the richness of psychoanalytic work.

Following the Einstein years, I became chief psychologist at the Tappan Zee Mental Health Clinic at Phelps Memorial Hospital in Tarrytown, where Lawrence Friedman was also on staff. My work consisted exclusively of psychoanalytically oriented psychotherapy in a suburban community setting. My case load there was large and was added to in 1961 by cases in my private practice, which I had just started in Riverdale. It was definitely time to start psychoanalytic training.

My psychiatric colleagues at Einstein who were affiliated with the New York Psychoanalytic Institute encouraged me to apply there as a waiver candidate. My research background made it likely that I would have been accepted, but I was mostly interested, then, as now, in clinical psychoanalytic practice. I did not want to get where I wanted to go through the backdoor, and had I gone that route I could not have gotten what I wanted to get: full recognition of my identity as a clinical psychologist-psychoanalyst. So I decided to study at the NYU postdoctoral program, a decision I have never regretted, because it helped to consolidate my identity as a psychologist-psychoanalyst, and laid the foundation for understanding the balance between diversity and common ground that are so much at the forefront of psychoanalysis today, worldwide.

I matriculated in 1962, one year after the program had been founded, the very first psychoanalytic and psychotherapy training program for psychologists affiliated with an academic institution. Although I identified myself as Freudian, the program, which taught both Freudian and interpersonal psychoanalysis, did not then have separate tracks, as it has now. I took courses with such diverse faculty members as Avram Ben Avi, Leopold Bellak, Ruth Jean Eisenbud, Erich Fromm, Rosalind Gould, Robert Holt, William Menaker, Esther Menaker, and Edward Tauber. My supervisors were William Menaker, Ruth Jean Eisenbud, and Leopold Bellak. Among the candidates in my classes were Abby Adams Silvan, Sheldon Bach, Shirley Feltman, Mark Grunes, Marvin Hurvich, Edwin Levy, Martin Nass, Irving Steingart, and Mark Silvan. Yes, another list, but the privilege of being connected with people such as these, as well as their predecessors and successors, was yet one more instance of being at the right place at the right time, and my good fortune constituted a critical part of the process of becoming a psychoanalyst. Before my graduation in 1968, I was invited to join a research project funded by the NIMH and directed by Bellak on "Ego Functions in Schizophrenics, Neurotics, and Normals," eventually culminating in the book with the same title, coauthored by Leopold Bellak, Marvin Hurvich, and Helen K. Gediman. The project was based at the NYU postdoctoral program but located near Roosevelt Hospital where most of the research was conducted. Others participating in the project were Morris Eagle, Nancy Goldberger, Milton Kapit, and Mark Silvan. The work was exciting, and took us to Washington on trips to the NIMH, which was hanging fire during its last years of funding research in psychoanalysis. I also learned the ins and outs of writing a grant proposal. Although this was the last formal empirical research project in psychoanalysis that I had been involved in, the increasing focus on my practice of psychoanalysis and psychoanalytic psychotherapy have enabled me to continue my interests in research in the more general sense of arguing psychoanalytic issues with illustrative case material.

Since then, I have practiced primarily psychoanalysis, averaging during any given year four analytic cases, and psychoanalytic psychotherapy. However, there was a considerable period of time when I worked no more than half time. That began in 1964, when my son was born, and when I left the Tappan Zee Clinic. My office was in my home, and I had no daytime commutes to take me away from my child and my work, and was able to combine my analytic control work with active involvement in my son's school and social activities, an arrangement I will never regret. I eventually opened a second part-time office in Manhattan, and by the time I moved there in 1977, my practice was back to full time, and in Manhattan only. Presently, all of my psychotherapy, even my work in one-time-a-week individual and couples therapy, is guided by psychoanalytic principles and a psychoanalytic attitude. So, in the broad sense I would say that all of my time currently is devoted to psychoanalysis, although not strictly speaking, if we are going to take into account specifics such as frequency and so forth.

An important part of my development as a psychoanalyst came with the founding of Division 39 of the American Psychological Association. I was in on that from the very beginning, and was a founding member of Section I. I remember the now long gone pleasures of intimate groups holding meetings at small tropical resorts. The first was at Ixtapa, Mexico, in 1981, and several others followed at other lovely beaches before Division 39 grew to its present size of thousands. My identity as a psychologist-psychoanalyst has been fortified by becoming a Diplomate in Psychoanalysis through ABPsaP, the American Board of Psychoanalysis in Psychology. I am also a member of the New York Freudian Society and its training institute, and the International Psychoanalytic Association (IPA). The American Psychoanalytic Association accepted me this year, with no strings or waiver. While I had mixed feelings about joining an organization that had excluded nonmedical analysts for far too long, I could exact some personal satisfaction from entering through the front door with their belated acceptance of me, while at the same time maintaining my primary identity as a psychologist-psychoanalyst.

Becoming a psychoanalytic therapist is a process that never ends. Most of my continuing education is a by-product of my psychoanalytic practice, teaching, and supervision. I teach classes in clinical theory and technique, as well as continuous case seminars. Presently, I am clinical professor of psychology at the New York University Postdoctoral Program in Psychotherapy and Psychoanalysis. I am also on the faculty, and a training and supervising analyst at the New York Freudian Society. I find that the best way to keep current is to read all the recent psychoanalytic journals, as well as to attend and present at regular meetings of local, national, and international psychoanalytic organizations. I have attended most Division 39 meetings, all but one IPA meeting since 1979, and this past winter participated as a presenter in a study group of the American Psychoanalytic Association, and one at the Federation of Latin American Psychoanalysts (FEPAI), with a group of clinicians from North and Latin America. I tend to publish my work and new ideas as soon as I am able to formulate them. I also participate in several peer groups in which senior and junior colleagues present their clinical work, and in which literature at the cutting edge of theory and technique is priority reading. In addition to teaching and peer groups, I am actively involved in psychoanalytic administrative activity, chairing committees, evaluating candidates' progression, and am on the board of directors of the New York Freudian Society. I publish and deliver papers regularly, and am presently preparing several articles for edited books. I have published two psychoanalytic books in the past year. The first, *Fantasies of Love and Death in Life and Art* (1995) is a work on applied psychoanalysis and the culmination of many years of prior work. The second, coauthored with Janice Lieberman, *The Many Faces of Deceit* (1996) deals particularly with deception and gullibility in the analytic dyad. I am currently working on a new book on the subject of successful women.

I designate my professional framework as a contemporary Freudian psychoanalyst with a multiperspectival bent. Following Pine's schema, and others with multiperspectival underpinnings, I look at clinical material from the points of view of drive, object, ego, and self. I have never regarded object relations, ego psychology, and the psychology of the self as outside of a contemporary Freudian framework, which includes more than a technique involving the interpretation of conflict and compromise formation. Additionally, my work is influenced by Melanie Klein and the contemporary Kleinians of London. This multiperspectival view is not to be confused with an eclectic view. I am respectful of the basic Freudian technique as it has evolved over the years, particularly with respect to developments in the principles of neutrality (which does not mean indifference to the patient, but does mean respectfulness toward all sides in a conflict); anonymity (which does not mean being a blank screen, withholding of personal responsiveness and information, but does involve disclosure of all personal responses that are relevant to the patient's knowledge of how the process works toward development of his or her own self understanding); and abstinence (which does not mean nongratifying of the patient, as any good interpretation or empathic understanding is a gratification essential to the process). I believe that the therapeutic action of psychoanalysis involves more than the imparting of insight by interpretation, depending also on the establishment of a real and therapeutic object relationship, which is integrally related to the transference and countertransference. I believe that enactments, and relational and intersubjective components enter into the analytic process in a contemporary Freudian analysis, but, as opposed to certain other orientations, the patient is always at the center. In what I have just summarized, I have been influenced by the work of Freud, Glover, Strachey, Klein, Hartmann, Jacobson, Winnicott, Loewald, Kohut, Stone, Rangell, and, more contemporaneously, Boesky, Renik, Chused, Arlow and Brenner, Kernberg, Mahler, Stern, Busch, Jacobs, and Pine.

I have always managed to practice, teach, and write, and I am now reminded of another anecdote relating to my family. One day, having returned from my August vacation, my father called to ask if any of my patients had returned to me after my absence. I said, "Don't worry, Dad. If they don't come back, I can always write." To which the anxious, and obviously ambivalent man replied, "Does anybody read that stuff?"

Becoming a psychotherapist, especially a psychoanalytic psychotherapist, is a full-time process and a lifetime proposition, and certainly not a one-time goal to be achieved and maintained in any static manner. One does not simply arrive, but continues to learn and to develop, and if one is lucky, remains young at heart in the process. In what other field can an individual reaching an age that in other fields signifies retirement time still function at peak levels?

These can be regarded, in Dickensian terms, as the best of times and the worst of times. With the constant challenge of keeping up with evolving theories and techniques, and of balancing the virtues of diversity and common ground, my life as a psychoanalyst has never been more exciting and productive than it is right now. It has also never been as exasperating and frustrating, what with the encroachments of managed care on such indispensable conditions as autonomy and confidentiality for psychoanalytic therapists and patients alike. But the ills of the managed care system are so horrendous that I cannot believe it can do anything other than self-destruct, helped along, of course, by our own concerted outreach into the broader community to revive and revitalize psychoanalysis as we once knew it, and as it has the potential to evolve into being more of. I hope for everybody's sake, particularly that of the younger generations that I have been privileged to teach, that those misanthropes who share my father's ill-founded apprehensions will be outnumbered by those trusting souls who share his obvious pride in the work that his daughter chose for herself.

―――――――――

Helen K. Gediman, Ph.D., is a Training and Supervising Analyst at the New York Freudian Society and Associate Clinical Professor, New York University Postdoctoral Program in Psychoanalysis.

REFERENCES

Gediman, H. K. (1995). *Fantasies of Love and Death in Life and Art: A Psychoanalytic Study of the Normal and the Pathological.* New York: New York University Press.

Gediman, H. K., and Lieberman, J. S. (1996). *The Many Faces of Deceit: Omissions, Lies, and Disguise in Psychotherapy.* Northvale, NJ: Jason Aronson.

12

The Multiple Origins of a Professional Identity

ANDRÉ GREEN

If I try to remember when I decided to become a psychotherapist, my memory fails to find a single event or a precise date. It is as if I am so convinced of having wanted to be one that I had never really thought of becoming anything else except during my daydreams. In fact, I am not sure whether I wanted to be a therapist, a healer, but I am sure I have always been interested to be something having to do with psychology. This interest preceded my interest in therapy (like Freud!). Even at the time I was in school, I was always considered, among my peers, as the one who was interested in finding psychological reasons to explain the behavior of others or to try to enlighten what was happening to me. Of course, most of the time these were rationalizations, but the trend was already there.

I remember that I used to be a good reciter, and so I was frequently asked to read aloud the pieces of literature that we were studying in the classroom. My peers were quite amazed to see how seriously I used to perform this task. Reading aloud scenes of Racine with such an amount of passion surprised everybody. I seemed to have identified very early on with Phaedra, Britannicus, Orestes, and other heroes and heroines of classical French tragedy. The other schoolboys could not understand why I put myself in such an emotional state, as all this was only fiction. To me it was more truthful than reality. I understand today that this was a precocious sign of my interest in the enigmas and complexities of the human soul through the characters of literature.

A memory comes back to me while I evoke this period. One of my father's friends asked me what I would like to be when I grew up. I don't remember exactly what I replied, but I am sure that what I said related to the fact that I wanted to study the human mind. It is interesting to note that my father did not ask me this question, but it appears to me obvious that my reply was addressed indirectly to him. What were the reasons for such an interest? My father at the end of his life was a very silent man, at least with me. He used to talk a lot with others and was also interested in psychology, the understanding of human behavior, and so on. And he was also a reader of literature. When I used to ask him a question, he first tried to explain to me, and if the answer was too complicated and led to another question, he used to say, "You will understand later," a sentence that I never forgot and that has probably influenced me more than I can say. But if I try to go back earlier in the past, as I have learned from my own personal analysis, the first experience that led me to want to understand psychic activity had been my mother's depression when I was 2 years old, which led to a temporary separation from her. When I look at her photographs of this period, there is no doubt that she had been depressed. She was sent away to rest and recover in a warmer city. I am sure that this type of experience, apart from the strong process of identification, is accompanied by a sense of loss of meaning and enhances intense psychic curiosity. I suppose that this far-remote experience has played a significant and decisive role in my future professional orientation. Before wanting to cure my patients, the main question for me was to understand why. What has happened to them? What were the causes of their condition? What happened to their mind to lead them to think as they did? All these questions probably have their origins in that remote past.

If this early experience had been the cause of my later orientation, another event had been of great importance to me. At the age of 16, suffering from a severe scoliosis, I had to stay in bed for nearly

nine months, encased in a plaster cast. This is not exactly the ideal condition for an adolescent. Fortunately, however, it was a very rich and
fruitful experience for me. Although I was deprived of all the pleasures and activities that my friends enjoyed, I did have the opportunity to read, to prepare for my examinations, and to think. My sister
and brother-in-law gave me a copy of Shakespeare's complete works,
which I started to read immediately, despite the fact that, being of
Egyptian birth, my English at that time was poor. I remember having
started with a tragedy that was appropriate for my age—*Romeo and
Juliet*. Again, the experience of tragedy was an incitement to deepen
my ideas on the human mind through the fascination of the beauty of
poetry. This experience of being alone, though not a day passed without being visited by friends, has been an excellent initiation to the
exercise of solitude as one may experience it when one becomes a psychoanalyst.

   After this period, if I had had absolute freedom of choice regarding a career, I would probably have chosen philosophy. My second
choice was the study of biological sciences but I was dissuaded from
this path. I was going to do research, but I realized that I would have
to accept a more modest career. Because of financial limitations, I could
not go to medical school. But I wanted to become a psychiatrist, and
medicine was the only way to do it. I thought that psychiatry was a
meeting point of my interests in philosophy, literature, and biology,
leading to the study of the brain. In the end, financial help came from
distant family members, as my father was not alive anymore, and I
received scholarships.

   I was terribly bored during my medical studies, which were so
far away from my personal interests. During the first two-thirds of my
medical studies I neglected my medical work and read a lot of philosophy, psychology, and literature. Reading Dostoyevsky has been
more useful to me than studying anatomy, histology, or parasitology.
I have learned more from all the opportunities Paris offered me, where
I resided since the beginning of my medical training—attending per-
formances at the theatre, and going to art exhibitions, lectures, and
concerts. I remember how my companions at the time used to think
that I was not a very serious student, wanting only to enjoy himself

instead of working hard, and how I felt that going to the theatre, visiting exhibitions, or attending lectures or concerts was part of my training—not so much of my medical training, which I found so narrow-minded, but as a preparation for the study of the human mind. Those who knew me as a student have been very surprised to hear that I am considered to be a very hard-working psychiatrist and psychoanalyst. I did suffer from not being able to explain to them why it was so important for me to do what I did. I now remember how much I agreed with Bion when he wrote that for him Bach or Beethoven were great psychoanalysts, more than many celebrated names of our discipline. Of course, this could extend to all the fields of culture.

It was also during my medical studies that I joined a university theatre group, Le Groupe de Théâtre Antique de la Sorbonne, which used to perform Greek tragedy, in a very different spirit from commercial theatre. My encounter with Aeschylus, Sophocles, and Euripides was an opening to a new world. Their plays and their characters were, to me, beyond psychology. I think their approach is an excellent initiation to the unconscious. I played some important parts; I am sure that what I played had an essential importance in knowing the human mind, but if were asked why or how at the time, I am sure I could only give foolish answers. Years later I devoted an essay to the *Oresteia*, in which I could finally explain to myself what I was performing.

The reader will be struck, I am sure, by my many references to theatre. I feel that the characters in a play, more than in any other literary genre, look like real persons, expressing themselves through a poetic language that gives indirect access to their inner world.

Surprisingly, when I started my psychiatric training, I was very reluctant to accept any kind of psychological explanation of behavior. I believed firmly in the role of brain mechanisms. I took a great interest in the study of the higher functions of the brain, neurophysiology, and brain pathology. I had been very lucky in meeting J. de Ajuriaguerra, whose field of expertise extended from neuroanatomy to child psychology. At the time I had hoped to find a continuity; he opened my eyes and ended my illusions. I have been a pupil of Henri Ey, the greatest French psychiatrist who was an organicist and a phenomenologist. But the most crucial experiences came from my interviews with psychiatric patients.

As our training gave us ample time to do our work as we wished, psychiatry being a dormant discipline by then, for the first time in my life I had the opportunity to examine madness, with its mysteries and enigmas. I spent many hours with each patient. At that time psychiatric services were not very active, as I am speaking of a period before the discovery of psychiatric chemotherapy. The wards were only busy in the morning; the afternoon was free. There were no doctors on the premises, and I remember being alone on the ward, trying to cope with patients, talking with them and wanting to understand what was going on with them. Most of them were schizophrenics with paranoid delusions. It was there that for the first time I understood the limitations of good will and naive understanding. It had no effect on patients' conditions, and made me more and more perplexed and despairing. I did not understand anything.

During the summer, in order to earn some money, I substituted for a colleague on vacation at a luxurious institution where wealthy people were hospitalized. I remember how surprised I had been. Psychiatric disorders had always been associated in my mind with poverty and misery. To experience it in this new context of luxury was puzzling. It helped me to understand that madness had little to do with social conditions. I was now more and more convinced that I had to come closer to the inner world, which I tried, up to now, to escape from.

One experience was decisive. When I was a resident in Saint-Anne Hospital, I took care of a woman who was hospitalized for a transient paranoid state, which is usually labeled in French as *bouffée délirante aiguë* and which has no equivalent in the Anglo-Saxon nosography but is usually included with the acute schizophrenic states. This woman, called Odile in my first psychiatric writing, presented a structure that is called in French nosography *délire d'imagination,* an imaginary delusional state, to distinguish these cases from the delusional states of interpretation or from the hallucinatory states. The *délire d'imagination* can in fact be considered very close to hysteria. I started interviewing this patient and I was interested enough by her condition to use the case material she offered me as an illustration for a work on the more general question of the imaginary delusions. What finally happened was inevitable. The patient developed a very intense transference to me, which I couldn't control. I was overwhelmed by her feelings, could not make any progress in my understanding, and felt more and more unable to help her. About the patients I mentioned before, there was no question of help, it was just a problem of understanding. But now, as I progressed in my medical training, I needed more than understanding; I needed to treat the patient. When these uncontrollable transference feelings appeared, I felt that I had failed with the patient. It was then that I decided to undertake a personal analysis.

This patient had been my practical introduction to psychoanalysis, but it wasn't my first contact with Freud. In a philosophy class in college, we had to present a reading. I chose the *Introduction to Psychoanalysis* by Freud, and at the orals my examiner asked me to discuss Freud's main hypotheses. After this experience, in which I was successful, my interest in psychoanalysis was replaced by an absorption in psychic activity and psychiatry. Odile reawakened my interest in Freud through her transference feelings. I had already started rereading Freud, and his interpretations appeared to me arbitrary and unconvincing. But after my personal analysis and as my experience as a therapist developed, I began to see what I thought were his contradictions in a different way. My interest in psychoanalysis increased, absorbing my mind and becoming exclusive as the years went by.

After Odile was discharged, he kept in contact with me, writing often or from time to time. I saw her three or four times in twenty years for some occasional sessions when she felt she needed them. She never was rehospitalized or treated with psychiatric drugs. Her delusion, I realized, was a defense against an empty life, and it helped her to stay alive. I also met with her children, and helped them to understand what was going on. They confirmed for me how important I remained for Odile. She died at the age of 65. Her children told me that she mentioned my name in the last moments of her life. Such was the power of transference.

Later on, after having been so much involved with psychiatric patients or parents of schizophrenic patients, I became interested in borderline states. I am sure that these early experiences had decisively captured my attention and fostered my interest in madness rather than in neurosis. My years of apprenticeship had paved the way.

André Green, M.D., is a Training and Supervising Analyst at the Paris Psychoanalytical Society.

13

The Midwestern Roots of a Los Angeles Psychotherapist

JAMES S. GROTSTEIN

When I look back across the years and try to probe the origins of my choice of careers, I come to realize that the potential answers available to me are multidetermined. It would seem that I chose, and paradoxically that I was chosen by fate, to be a therapist.

I was born and raised in a very small Midwestern town that was on the outskirts of a larger city. I am perhaps one of the last persons I know of who lived in a Norman Rockwell[1]-type of community where everyone was my babysitter when my parents were at work. I am grateful for having had the experience of that intimate village warmth. Most of them were Scots immigrants who had come to work in the nearby rubber factories in Akron. My family was one of three Jewish families in that town, but we seemed to have culturally assimilated with the townspeople. For this and other reasons that I shall mention in a moment, I felt that I had three nonconflictual identities—American, Jewish, and Scots. Though Jewish, I was thrilled every time our neighbor, Angus Ballantyne, would "blaw a pibroch or twa" on his bagpipe.

---

1. It was a shock when I learned that he, to say nothing of my favorite poet, T. S. Eliot, was anti-Semitic.

My father also took me regularly to the meetings of the Robert Burns Society in Kenmore. As a matter of fact, I wrote a long-hand history of Scotland when I was 11 years old.

Though they belonged to the lower middle-class economically, my mother and father were enormously cultivated, had attended college, and were well read on a vast number of subjects. My father generously founded the Kenmore Public Library in the back of his little general store—free of charge. I remember his bringing home three newspapers every evening, including *The New York Times* and also his bringing home at least three or four books a week from the Akron Public Library. He could talk on a vast number of subjects, and wrote letters to the editor of the *Akron Beacon Journal* with such frequency that he became a minor celebrity for many years. For a brief time he also served as its music critic. My mother's father was famous rabbi at the time and a noted intellectual, whose mother had actually been the doctor for the Pittsburgh ball club (later the Pirates).[2]

Our home, though quite modest, seemed to be a place where interesting people would congregate. It was before television and even before the spread of telephones, so people would just come around at whim. I recall that when I was very young I sat on the lap of a man wearing a turban. I was told later that he was Rabindranath Tagore, winner of the Nobel Prize in literature and translator of the *Upanishads*.

My mother confided in me that when she pregnant with me she became very anxious. She and my father had read a good deal of Freud that was available to laymen and were very impressed by it. There was no such thing as psychotherapy, to say nothing of psychoanalysis, in our town—or in the whole Midwest, other than perhaps Cleveland and certainly Chicago, where formal psychoanalysts worked. My mother decided to consult a Christian Science practitioner and remained in therapy with her for a short while after I was born. Few people today realize that these Christian Science practitioners actually founded the psychotherapy movement in our country. I was to learn later that a great many intellectual, free-thinking Jewish women went to practitioners

---

2. I swear that this is not apocryphal. I recall stories as a child about her most famous patient, Honus Wagner.

in those days to get help. The "Christian" aspects of it were of little importance. What stood out was that somebody empathically listened and reminded their clients that "God is love."

After the Anschluss of Austria in 1938 many Viennese emigrated to the United States, and some came to Akron. I recall one of them who had been a student of psychology in Vienna and had attended some lectures at Freud's home. He was a frequent guest in our home and I would eagerly listen in to the fascinating conversations he and my parents (and older sister) would have. I recall once they were discussing phallic symbols. I somehow thought that that was not a suitable subject for the little likes of me to be listening in on. I felt like a privileged voyeur. My understanding of the idea of phallic symbols, however, was possibly to be fateful. I thought they meant "breast." Without my having realized it then, I may have destined myself to become a Kleinian.

I was nurtured in the bosom of ideas and creativity and also with a deep respect for and tolerance of other peoples. I find even today that, though Jewish by birth and religious preference, I am closer to Christians than many of my psychoanalytic colleagues. Recently, I wrote a monograph, "Why Oedipus and not Christ?" It did not fare so well with many Jewish colleagues or even editors. The reasons may have had to do with the inherent lack of value of the manuscript, but I somehow think that that is not the whole story. I believe that psychoanalysis has both benefited and suffered from its being practiced predominantly by Jews.

When I entered the University of Akron, I was primarily interested in English literature and saw myself as being an academic. However, I also took some premedical courses because my mind was not decided. When I returned home from the war, I continued my literature major and the premed courses—until a momentous realization came to me. While doing an in-depth study of the history of the critiques on *Hamlet* over the centuries, I came to realize that the critiques centered on the issue of Hamlet's putative motivation in postponing avenging his father's murder. I then chanced upon Ernest Jones's *Hamlet or Oedipus*, and went through a sudden internal paradigm shift. I realized that literary criticism (this was before critical studies had entered the humanistic disciplines) was often concentrated on the subject of character motivation—and that was the preserve of psychoanalysis. I swiftly shifted my academic major and decided upon a career in psychiatry and psychoanalysis.

Once I entered medical school, however, I became enamored of medicine generally. I felt as if I were being inducted into a privileged order—like knighthood or something. I loved being introduced to the ancient mysteries of therapeusis and of being shown how to attend to a vast number of body ailments with techniques that were excitingly new as well as with others that date back to the beginning of time. Medicine was like a second, elite family or brotherhood. Wherever I would go in the course of my travels around the world, I would be known as a doctor to other doctors. I have found in my experiences that this idea of a medical brotherhood generally applied wherever I went in the world, but, strangely and sadly, did not apply so closely to psychoanalysis.

Though I enjoyed medicine, internal medicine in particular and even surgery, my zeal for psychiatry and psychoanalysis never slackened. I was particularly fortunate my medical school demonstrated a highly favorable attitude toward psychiatry and psychoanalysis. I was fortunate also that the Department of Psychiatry at the school was headed by a noted psychoanalyst and that there were several leading analysts in the department. Their graciousness and their personally extending themselves to me meant a lot.

During my junior and senior years I found myself regularly going to the medical library on campus. While there, I would with regularity glance over a wide assortment of medical journals, some well known, others obscure, such as the *Royal Naval Medical Journal*, in which I learned a great deal about tropical medicine. Gradually, I began scanning the psychoanalytic journals. I enjoyed most of what I read, but I remember reading Melanie Klein's articles in the *International Journal of Psycho-Analysis*. I was struck by the fact that I had a hard time following her—almost as if she were paradoxically and magically using ordinary English to speak a foreign language—but was even more struck that I felt something profound happening in me while reading her while not really understanding it. I stored her away for the future.

When I left medical school, I began a year's internship at Michael

Reese Hospital in Chicago, which had a distinguished psychiatric wing and was directed by a famous psychiatrist/analyst who had been analyzed by Freud. I prized my rotation on the psychiatric wing. Listening to the residents' case conferences and attending grand rounds, I knew that my destiny had been sealed. Chicago in those days was like a psychoanalytic Camelot. Franz Alexander was the president of the psychoanalytic society and had an aura about him. Psychoanalytic training was very highly prized, and the atmosphere was alive with psychoanalytic interest. It was jokingly said that at Michael Reese Hospital even the mice were classically oriented. All the residents had couches and spoke about their patients' transferences, and I couldn't wait to begin my own residency.

As it turned out, without having planned it ahead of time, I served in a residency that was divided among three principal places. In my first year I went to the Pennsylvania Hospital in Philadelphia. It was an ancient hospital (eighteenth century) that was unique for residency training. First, it featured long-term care. Second, it favored the use of psychoanalytic psychotherapy as the preferred treatment for psychotic disorders, including especially schizophrenia. That was a halcyon time for psychoanalysis. An aura of idealism hung over psychiatry in those days. The older, organically oriented psychiatrists resented it, but the new fields of psychopharmacology and neurobiology had yet to make their impact. Whereas attending psychiatrists could hospitalize their patients there, the psychiatric residents were in charge of the cases and conducted intensive, long-term treatment when indicated. I cannot think of a better way of being trained. I was at first baffled by the ease with which the residents ahead of me approached their patients. I had become familiar with some of the language in Chicago, but this was my first hands-on experience. Eventually, I got to throw the lingo with the best of them. I had already been influenced by the use and success of psychoanalytically informed psychotherapy for borderline and psychotic disorders in Chicago and now even more so at the Pennsylvania Hospital. That impression was to be a profound one for me because it determined my future direction in analytic and especially postanalytic training.

While in Philadelphia I arranged to begin a personal analysis with

Robert Waelder, a very famous analyst who had been analyzed by Freud. At the time I consulted him he had just broken away from the Philadelphia Society for Psychoanalysis and helped found the Philadelphia Association for Psychoanalysis. This was my first brush with psychoanalytic institute divorces. I knew already that there were divergences of views in the Chicago Institute, mainly between Franz Alexander and Thomas French on one hand and the more classical ones on the other, but Alexander's leadership was such that he was able to hold the institute together. Interestingly, the divisive issue in Philadelphia at the time was one between orthodox and classical analysis, a distinction that would puzzle people today. "Orthodox" meant id analysis, whereas "classical" (at least in this country) meant ego psychology. I laugh to myself when people consider Waelder to be an ego psychologist—despite his now-famous paper, "Principle of Multiple Function" (1936). I know him to have been a serious orthodox analyst. Many of the European-trained analysts had been trained and analyzed in the orthodox tradition and did not take easily to ego psychology—Fenichel, for instance. I was disturbed by this rent in the symmetry of my analytic idealism.

For personal reasons I decided to move to Los Angeles the next year. I regretted leaving the residency and also having to abort my plans to enter analysis with Dr. Waelder. My family had in the meanwhile moved from Akron to Southern California, so I decided to join them there. I transferred to the Brentwood VA Hospital in Los Angeles for my second year of residency and was despondent for a long time over its glaring inferiority in comparison to the one I had just left. Veterans were not the ideal patient population for the long-term treatment of primitive disorders for a variety of reasons. Further, the psychiatric climate in Los Angeles was such that it was no Camelot. The psychoanalytic treatment of psychotics and borderlines was not condoned. The residents did their best and often received good supervision on their cases from analysts practicing in the community, but the atmosphere was missing something. When I was a resident at the Pennsylvania Hospital, there existed an inspired ring of psychoanalytically informed psychiatric hospitals that extended from the Institute of Living in New Haven and down the East Coast through the Pennsylvania Hospital in Philadelphia to Sheppard and Enoch Pratt in Baltimore, the Chestnut

Lodge in Rockville, Maryland, and even to Appalachia Hall in Asheville, North Carolina, and westward to Menninger's in Topeka and to three hospitals in Chicago—Micheal Reese, University of Chicago, and the Illinois Neuropsychiatric Hospital (INI). That was the magic ring. Austen Riggs in Stockbridge, Massachusetts, also became a member in this ring and sprang to prominence when analysts from Chestnut Lodge and Menninger's converged there, particularly Eric Erikson.

Not only did I carry away with me an incredible enthusiasm about the psychoanalytically informed treatment of psychotic and borderline disorders; I carried away some of the techniques as well—particularly the so-called therapist-manager method in which the therapist who sees the patient is virtually quarantined and constrained to see only the patient, whereas another psychiatrist sees the family, writes the hospital orders, talks with the nurses and ancillary therapists, and so on. I actually introduced this technique to therapists in Southern California— to my great sorrow. Psychotherapists who lacked the training and the background in this form of treatment began employing it dishonestly in private practice (e.g., the "manager" would see a patient for a few minutes and bill the insurance company for a whole hour; the insurance companies soon caught onto the scam and ended the practice). I had initiated it naively—not realizing how it could and would be misused.

During my residency at Brentwood VA Hospital, I learned that a new residency program was to be developed the following year at UCLA Hospital and Medical School. I applied for a position, was accepted, and became the first chief resident at UCLA. The experience was a good one. Most of the staff were either analysts or in analytic training. It was downright homey; a ward chief of mine borrowed my car one day so he could attend his own analytic session. Early on in this third residency I applied for formal psychoanalytic training to the Los Angeles Psychoanalytic Institute and was accepted. I then arranged to begin my training analyst with a man who, by strange coincidence, had analyzed Robert Waelder before the latter went to Freud. This analyst had also been analyzed by Freud, so I felt that I was in privileged company—and a grandson of the master, to boot. The analyst was orthodox, and though friendly toward ego psychology (classical),

analyzed in the older model. In the meanwhile I had been disturbed by
yet another split. The one in Philadelphia was unnerving to me. Now I
came into this prestigious institute in Los Angeles on the heels of a major
division that resulted in the formation of yet another institute. I was still
too new to the profession to figure these things out, so I continued, but
thereafter with a little skepticism. My analysis was helpful, and I got
married and sired what was to become a happy and wonderful family.

Soon enough I graduated and was by this time in private practice.
In the meanwhile, three other colleagues, one from my own institute class
and the other two from an earlier class, got together to form a postgraduate study group. We enjoyed our weekly evening meetings. We
started by reading Erikson, Jacobson, and many other classical writers.
The other three members of the group had either been analyzed or supervised by a local analyst who was originally from Oklahoma, had
encyclopedic knowledge of the psychoanalytic literature, and had a profound interest and involvement with the works of W. R. D. Fairbairn,
whom we had not studied in the institute seminars. We began reading
Fairbairn and became transformed. I was in the ending phase of my
analysis about this time, and happened to mention my enthusiasm for
Fairbairn. My analyst was less than receptive to the announcement, but
when I mentioned the name Melanie Klein, with whom Fairbairn's works
were often linked, he became irate. It would take me years to learn the
significance of his aversion to Klein and British object relations theory.
By the time I did, however, I had become an active participant in the
second generation of one of the most tragic internecine battles in the
history of psychoanalysis, the war between Anna Freud and Melanie
Klein.

As we progressed in our study group, I had terminated my analysis with my training analyst and entered another one with the
Fairbairnian analyst, which was to prove very helpful. In the meanwhile, however, our study group took on a new member, one who was
to become pivotal in my own future and the future of psychoanalysis
in Los Angeles—and beyond. He had been in supervision with my
Fairbairnian analyst for twelve years and had become thoroughly
steeped in Fairbairn. Somewhere along the line while vacationing in
England, he met Herbert Rosenfeld. I will condense the events of the

next several years by saying that from Fairbairnians we all became Kleinians. Wilfred Bion, Albert Mason, and later Susanna Isaacs Elmhirst moved to Los Angeles from London and many of us entered analysis and supervision with them. The reaction of the institute, the community, and the American Psychoanalytic Association was devastating.

The battles have ebbed, and there is now a measure of peace in our community. In the meanwhile, the fifth provocative member who had introduced us to Klein was soon enough to become the founding father of self psychology in our community and to found a new institute for its promulgation.

Psychoanalysis is profound as a technique but is unsafe as a subject for institutes to propound. What seems to happen is that the ones in charge feel it is their responsibility to protect psychoanalysis and those undergoing it as patients, so that a veritable inquisition with a star-chamber cast of characters ineluctably emerges in order to protect the innocence of the sacred. Psychoanalytic training organizations are not immune to the development of group psychosis, as Bion so cogently pointed out. A newer way has to be found if we are to survive.

I have not become disillusioned with psychoanalysis. On the contrary, since my experiences with my various analysts and supervisors in the Klenian and Bionian perspectives, it has been a joy to practice— despite all the expected and unexpected disappointments. Institute training, however, has always been a bane, and its well-meaning leaders still fail to grasp the extent of the institutional morass and collusions in which they are embedded. This is one of the reasons why Bion, my third analyst, left the British Institute and came to Los Angeles—and did not apply for institute affiliation, and, in return, was not asked by any institute here to affiliate. I take it that even his ideas were felt to be unacceptable to London Kleinians after he began irreverently, I have good reason to believe, to explore "Transformations in O," which were felt to be too mystical, if not "psychotic."

Today, Los Angeles is a psychotherapy city like many others. There is a great diversity in product, ranging from puristic classical psychoanalysis through object relations (now a hybrid term), through self psychology and intersubjectivity to others now developing and others yet to come. The irony is that while psychoanalysis seems to be on the wane for the moment, the interest in psychotherapy that it spawned is growing by leaps and bounds in the United States and in other countries.

Psychoanalysis will survive the naive, well-meaning injunctions of its self-appointed sentinels because it represents a fundamental truth that is comparable to the laws of gravity, evolution, and relativity. It is the high priest in each of us who self-appointedly monitors and protects it that ironically endangers it—yet what would happen if we didn't?

Finally, I have been practicing psychoanalysis long enough and have been trained or seriously exposed to enough of its languages, techniques, and paradigms to have an opinion about how a beginning therapist should proceed in his/her training. It helps—and hurts—to be idealistic. It is fatal if one is not. One ideally should be well versed in all the classics, humanities, and mythology; one should be trained in philosophy, linguistics, medicine (optimally), and in many other disciplines—or, if not, acknowledge the handicap and seek to make up for it to the best of one's ability. Above all, it is the experience of one's own analysis of one's gifted supervisions that makes the difference— and the sane encouragement to transcend. I often wonder about the huge discrepancy between the joyful enthusiasm we had in our postgraduate study group and its fateful culmination in the ultimate creation of two new psychoanalytic institutes in our city—with all the attendant disappointments and disillusionments in each of them respectively. Earlier, I spoke of knighthood as a metaphor. I think that the analyst, by virtue of the isolation and consequent solitude of his/her practice, is analogous to the knight errant of "once upon a time." Similarly, even the knight errant had to return from his glorious adventures and report in to Camelot, where he encountered no end of intrigue, corruption, gossip, politics, and pettiness—but also recertification as to his purpose through the mutual sharing of adventures with his fellow knight errants who had also come in from the cold. We may all be Don Quixotes at heart, but, if we are, we need to be in touch with our Sancho Panzas to maintain our equilibrium.

James S. Grotstein, M.D., is a Training and Supervising Analyst at the Psychoanalytic Center of California (PCC) and the Los Angeles Psychoanalytic Institute.

REFERENCE

Waelder, R. (1936), Principle of multiple function: observations on over-determination. *Psychoanalytic Quarterly* 5:45–62.

14

Meetings with Humankind[1]

ANDRÉ HAYNAL

When piecing together a history, we tend to get a sense not only of the inevitable but of luck: a feeling that things could have turned out altogether differently, and that it only took a tiny, seemingly random detail to change everything—a little fluke that pointed the way to the final destination.

The modern and postmodern sciences have tended to proclaim, and we have more or less accepted, that causality can no longer be thought of in Newtonian terms, acting like one billiard ball knocking into another and eventually producing an "effect" after a chain of such events.

Where, then, should one start in a review of a life whose final choice of profession was psychotherapist-psychoanalyst? With a retrospective fantasy of discovering a state of harmony that may have prevailed in the womb or else in the very earliest relationships, not only with a very available and generous breast, but also in the arms of a loving woman? Or in parental dissension—a discordant couple. Did their only son find himself cast from the start in the role of peacemaker?

---

1. Translated from the French by Daphne Briggs, Oxford, UK.

Did he try to understand what their conflicts were about and strive to reduce or even "cure" them? This, with a father who was himself a doctor, pursuing healing with a passion that matched his impressive intelligence, and who became an important figure in his country—a country that was caught up in pre-Fascism and Fascism. This father believed that being a doctor also meant helping people who were suffering—a fortiori ones who were suffering persecution and injustice. He had the courage to intervene in struggles to help all these people. One of that same nation's poets, Illyés, actually described him as "doctor to a whole nation," and a journalist friend, J. Katona, felt he had become "the nation's conscience."

Was this man's son embarking upon his own career of "reparation" and healing when, in adolescence, during the Nazi occupation, he hid people despite his mother shaking physically with fear? Or, again in adolescence, when besides activities that were self-evidently praiseworthy, he also had to reconcile parents who had already split up at such a difficult time? The trauma of being deserted by his father—Oh! but Yes!, he was certainly still involved with him, despite being physically absent for years on end—further emphasized the importance of his role in reconciling his parents. All of this not only played a strong part in motivating the adult man to become a psychotherapist, but also impelled him toward situations in which he would go on trying to reconcile the protagonists of his profession, the leaders of different schools and different local orthodoxies. Is this perhaps why he has always been rather eclectic?

To offset all these fears, insecurities, and anxieties, a college with a fine tradition provided him with outward security and gave him the early benefit of the psychotherapeutic effect that some of his masters and teachers had upon him, although neither he nor they were aware of it at the time. Certain adolescent experiences showed him the power of words and imagination, and the force of human interaction and relationships, making a lasting mark upon him. At the same college he met a professor who had come back from the Sahara, where he had been studying various different expressions of Islamic religion, including the Dervishes and other fascinating people, whom he tried to imitate by organizing language classes and holding collective hypnosis sessions. This professor's influence inspired him, as a young adolescent, to immerse himself in the literature on hypnosis and similar mysteries, counter to which reading Freud had a beneficial, distancing effect. He was prompted to do this by others in his circle, especially at the end of his time at college and early in his university studies in psychology. This afforded him an experience of sitting back to think and of distancing himself from any attempt actively to dominate the situation. It led to the study of philosophy, psychology, and, later, of medicine—a long, roundabout journey on which he almost lost sight of the obvious aim of making a final choice of profession. The first direction he set out in—philosophy—changed when he considered making verbal communication his profession—journalism, at that point—and then changed again, later on, when he wanted to go back to healing activity, and therefore to medicine. The latter choice must be viewed in the context of life at that time in an Eastern Bloc country, Hungary, under Soviet Communist domination. At that time, in order to survive, it was necessary to choose a pursuit that had little connection with ideology, which finally ruled out philosophy and psychology, so he turned to an activity that was beyond reproach and at the same time did some good—medicine, nowadays so much criticized, as the authoritarian shape it took at that period certainly led to abuses, in contrast with which psychoanalysis, in particular, took pains to present itself as a good remedy for alternative medicine and nonauthoritarian. This, however, proved to be just another illusion, given the astoundingly authoritarian structures of the psychoanalytic institutes and the arbitrary element in the way opinions and "truths" were formulated by the leaders of a movement, which, besides being curative, also became powerfully ideological.

So far, this account has been written in the third person. Some questions are clearly easier to formulate if one puts oneself, experimentally, outside the picture for a moment. Looking in from outside. Speaking in the third person.

Budapest, 1948; and maturity arrived, still under the "ancien régime," at a great Catholic college. The next year, during my studies in psychology and philosophy, everything changed. At the beginning of the year there were, at the University of Budapest, Georg Lukacs; a

Jesuit Father, Janossy; and an aged Jewish writer of enormous wisdom, Milan Fust—all of whom represented the old culture of Budapest, and also, because of their age, were a kind of link between the 1910s under Franz-Joseph and a time full of postwar optimism in 1948. One year later, all these people had disappeared, forbidden to teach. One had fled abroad, and the curtain dropped on a chapter of Budapest's culture. It was decreed that psychology did not exist, and neither, of course, did psychoanalysis. They were nothing but products of the "false consciousness" of the bourgeoisie and weapons against the working class. More or less in secret one could still read David Rapaport's thesis of 1938, or typewritten works by Leopold Szondi and Laszlo Noszlopi, and precious printed copies of Ferenczi and Freud. Publishing was already becoming like the later "Samizdat" (private publication): produced on typewriters, bound by hand, but still obtainable. In a few years' time it would be dangerous to ask for such works in a public library, classified as they had been only a decade or so earlier as reflecting the spirit of the "Jewish plutocracy," and now, as that of the "decadent bourgeoisie." These were terrible times: the prisons—the same ones as during the German occupation—were full again, and methods of torture were if anything more refined than before. It would certainly be misleading to claim that this was a time for thinking about becoming a psychotherapist. All the same, it remains true that this period stirred a desire—very much in secret in myself and in others—to employ human powers to render relationships more bearable and free them from the sadism that, imported from abroad, had slowly taken possession of the country and led to the great trials of the Communists themselves, Rajk and others, and representatives of other types of thought, like Catholic Cardinal Mindszenty and the Jewish rabbis—all guilty of a single offense: thinking *differently*.

If politics and social conditions assume such importance in reminiscences about my motives for becoming a psychotherapist, it is, in addition, because I think that the work on fanaticism that I wrote in collaboration (Haynal et al. 1983) is ultimately the fruit of some important lines of research into social life, as well as being an expression of hope about the possibility of change in its degenerative manifestations.

All the same, I get the impression that, in the light of external, political events—discrimination, persecution—an inner project had been maturing in me for a long time. This was connected with the difficulties of having been an only child and of seeing my parents split up when I was 10 years old (I found my father again as an adolescent, and he came back to live with my mother and me when I was 16 years old). Oedipal conflict with this father was certainly very difficult, and I tried to resolve it by means of extravagant idealization. This was entirely conducted within the bounds of what seemed acceptable both to that patriarchal world and within a very family-minded family of the Transylvanian minority in Budapest. In that situation I had to fight against feelings of depression and loneliness that I first became aware of at 10 years of age (I can picture myself in my room, where I kept racking my brains to find out what to do with my life). These feelings resurfaced after I had emigrated to Switzerland, having lost, overnight, all my contacts, support systems, and relationships—in fact at that point they pushed me toward analysis. All the same, they are remnant in me from an earlier time of life, and have spurred me on to try to understand myself and above all to understand other people—both of my parents, so as to try to make peace between them, and others in my circle who seemed to make demands without my always understanding why, and without my being able to understand my own reactions of anxiety, timidity, and repulsion. Finally, it was this internal constellation that impelled me, very early in adolescence, to devour philosophy and characterology books, as they were then called, and novels that helped me to gain considerable nonprofessional knowledge—literature in many languages, since I had only to set eyes on print to plunge into it. Studying philosophy was, once again, an effort to find certainties in life. Besides psychology, my favorite discipline, before medicine, was the history of philosophy, where I could obtain—or at least I thought I could obtain—a condensed summary of ideas, of what others had thought about life and what an adolescent, inevitably, feels are the big questions in living, or weltanschauung. Choosing medicine was also choosing a job, an apparently realistic prospect of earning my living, even if there were of course other more hidden reparative aims behind which, in turn, lay identification with the other. At the end of the road, at the moment of truth, when it finally came to choosing a profession, it came down to a compromise—"medicine for the soul," as psychoanalysis struck me as being in light of my own very real need for analysis, connected with emigration from Budapest to Zurich and the losses I have already mentioned.

Looking back, another curious thing is that without the words to say it that analysis offered me, I had been so little aware of my depression, even though it had come back at several points in my life: at the point, as I have said, when my parents split up, and then after the war, when I realized how many of my friends from childhood had perished, above all through deportation in the Holocaust, in the early days after my emigration, and when I had had some setbacks in love. How little aware I was of being depressed, even though I sensed that I was living with a certain uneasiness, which I put down to the autumn weather, or damp from the Swiss lakes, or the uncertainties of existence, or—in neurological terms—to the excessive corticalization of the twentieth-century human being that I was. Reading, which during my final years in medicine once again came to the fore, from Sartre and Camus to Thomas Mann, from Luther's Bible, read in one go like a novel, to the existentialist philosophers, and once again, psychoanalytic texts—none of this reading helped me very much in itself.

What I did begin very slowly to understand through my first analysis is that it was dialogue, the presence and understanding of the other, that was actually helping me, and I, in turn, wanted to convey the benefits of that help to people who presented themselves to me. This was the point at which I began professional activity. However, although personal analysis opened up prospects in me for understanding through "saying," I must make it clear that supervision with people as different as Fritz Morgenthaler in Zurich and Raymond de Saussure in Geneva, then Germaine Guex and Marcelle Spira, and others whom circumstances only let me follow for a very short time, such as Gustav Bally or Michael Balint, sometimes afforded me thrilling new perspectives for understanding other people. Something curious also happened: Freud's works, a first reading of which had left me with an aftertaste of something complicated, tortuous, and ultimately irritating, seemed all of a sudden to tell the story of the tortuousness and complexities of my own internal workings and those of others to whom I listened. A certain sense of satisfaction and happiness began to set in—my personal equilibrium had changed; I had found myself in my professional work, especially when, thanks to the University of Geneva, I was able to devote part of my time to research and teaching, which seemed to provide a balance of complementary activities that suited me well. Besides analytic relationships, I could have more direct teaching relationships in a university setting, with people who wanted to study and know something about what can be known about mankind, passing on a taste for finding human beings and meeting humanity in all its complexity with the other. Companionable relations with people of my own age group formed a horizontal exchange. Mixing with a sort of sibling group that I had lacked in childhood rendered me serene and contented. Passing on this serenity and contentment remain to this day one of my greatest sources of satisfaction.

However, the history of my meeting with the human being in myself and in others—something that I have become increasingly aware of through my own experiences and history, especially the difficulties in this history and the contradictions and complications that fate and above all the fate of Europe, and Central Europe in particular, has partly imposed on me, and which in part I have sought out and manufactured for myself—all this must not give the impression of a slow ascent toward a happy ending, as in a cheap sentimental novel or the sort of history that, after describing a difficult life, ends with eternal salvation. It also gives access to human fragility in everyday life, under conditions that could in macrosociological terms be called "societal," which I experienced both in the university and in psychoanalytic institutions. The latter have been the subject of much discussion, especially since the 1970s, and it seems to me today that without understanding the institutional history of psychoanalysis one can understand neither one's own present nor one's future. I therefore turned myself into a historian of psychoanalysis—and, returning, as they say one always does, to one's first loves, I found in it a continuity with my passion for the history of philosophy and of ideas in general. In fact, it seems to me that without delving back into the atmosphere of Vienna and Budapest in 1900, whose last cultural and social throes I myself witnessed as a small child, one cannot understand the determinant past of our present-day institutions—the benevolent paternalism and fierce authoritarianism that held sway, the conflicts between Berlin and Vienna–Budapest, between the Berlin conception of a systematic, not to say Prussian, teaching institution, and the poetic and artistic liberalism and taste for improvisation and openness to cultural life that was especially characteristic of Vienna and Budapest.

I mention these particular dichotomies not because I think that the whole scene can be reduced exclusively to them, but because in present-day debate, Freud versus Ferenczi, it is the world of Berlin, which became the mainstream North American model, that is currently the center of interest. But I myself believe we will never reach an adequate understanding of all that has happened unless we look carefully into our own history. Psychoanalysts' difficulty in taking an interest in their own past very strongly suggests a ubiquitous resistance; how, otherwise, can we make sense of the fact that people who regard the present as determined by the past should take so little interest in their own past as a professional community and institution? In a line of work that subjects the identity of individuals to scrutiny and that on principle demands personal security so as to be truly accepting of other people struggling amidst their own contradictions and suffering, practitioners never seem quite ready to step aside from the identities they have acquired in the course of their education and personal development. This gives rise to internal strife that dares not speak its own name, because people are unwilling to reveal their professional motivations in public. Instead, there are exchanges of dogmas, positions, and convictions. What is more, it is so difficult to identify fact in the work we do that, in contrast with other scientific domains, it has proved almost impossible to hold exchanges supported by evidence. Conviction against conviction, and above all identity against identity and roots against roots—this makes dialogue difficult, rather as happened long ago when professional identity was apparently based upon divine revelation. Once again the merest "iota" can unleash everything we know of at the level of human murderous passions. The history of psychoanalysis is in no way exempt from this type of passion, as the Freud–

Klein controversy in London demonstrates, as well as other still darker chapters in the history of the psychoanalytic institutes, with their exclusions and anathemas, or even nonexclusions and nonanathemas, and where these passions are just as prevalent in relations between subgroupings as they are in larger, more theatrical, events.

What does all this imply? I am convinced—and, in my own case, this also comes from past experience and what I have made of it, and from my cultural roots and identifications, for example, with my father who, during the war, hung a picture of Erasmus over his bed—that one of the most important contributions psychoanalysis could make to the culture and community life of our lands is triggering a fresh burst of creativity in this fascinating twentieth-century way of thought and at the same time making one of its most important cultural impressions. This might become possible if, in a spirit of further development, such a review of the roots of its tensions could be conducted from inside, at a level of psychic workings that is not simply individual but is also more collective, in the sense of its historical and sociological aspects (especially sociology of institutions). This could release fresh creativity and make a truly seminal contribution. But in the meantime, the different linguistic and cultural blocs—almost in the nationalistic sense—wage war on one another, which turns into wars for financial resources and also for a following. These wars are being fought without awareness that they are a continuation of the wars between Freud and Ferenczi, Freud and Rank, Freud and Abraham, and I know not whom else, and between Berlin and Budapest, between London and Vienna. I think psychoanalytic thought, despite some local positive initiatives, is heading for a complete standstill, bogged down under an increasingly heavy institutional bureaucracy, and this in spite of all the good analysts who, in the hear-silence of their consulting rooms, go on thinking well, if less creatively than they might. And here, perhaps, once more, we meet humankind, which, even in psychoanalysis—itself interminable, as we know—can never rid itself of its fragilities and contradictions in a more definitive way.

André Haynal, M.D., is a Training and Supervising Analyst at the Swiss Psychoanalytical Society.

REFERENCE

Haynal, A., Molnar, M., and de Puymége, G. (1983). *Fanaticism*. New York: Schocken.

15

Decision or Destiny?

ALTHEA J. HORNER

My becoming a psychologist and a psychotherapist was in part a ser-
endipitous decision and in part destiny. I define destiny as where one
is at the present moment, the inevitable outcome of all that has gone
before. The multitudinous threads that enter into the fabric of our existence are greater, for example, than the dynamics of our family of
origin. The number of parentified children who have become psychotherapists is legion! Although this was not my role, striving to be special to a narcissistic father certainly honed my skills at empathic understanding.

My life course was probably atypical, but considering I was born
in 1926, not surprising. I married at the age of 19 at the end of my
sophomore year at the University of Chicago. It was 1945 and the
country was still at war, so for a brief interlude I was a Navy wife—
an interesting window into a very different world from that in which I
grew up. I was finally awarded my B.S. in psychology seven years later,
with two small daughters in tow. I settled down to the life of a suburban doctor's wife during which time my two sons entered the scene.

In spite of all I had to do, I found myself restless, bored with the
social routines and with the petty politics of women's organizations—

no worse, I later came to realize, than the politics of academia or psychoanalytic institutes.

Yearly I would accompany my obstetrician husband to the conference on infertility held in Palm Springs, sometimes sitting in on the sessions, sometimes basking in the February desert sun. One year he turned to me and said, "Why don't you go back to school for a Ph.D. in psychology and do your research on psychological aspects of infertility?" I was registered at the University of Southern California within weeks, and the rest is history. Serendipity? Most certainly! I had toyed with the idea of going to medical school when I entered the University of Chicago in 1943, but organic chemistry and the animal experiments in physiology did me in. I simply could not bear to pith the frog and let my lab partner do the dirty deed. So I married a doctor instead, the easy and honorable out for a girl in 1945.

But what of those other threads, invisible silver and gold perhaps, that contributed not only to my affinity for doing psychotherapy but also to my way of being a psychotherapist, to what I saw as a goal of psychological treatment, to the human values that go beyond theory?

My mother took my name from the poem by Sir Richard Lovelace—"To Althea, From Prison." I read it over many times as a child and the lines became part of an abiding philosophy of life.

> Stone walls to not a prison make,
>   Nor iron bars a cage;
> Minds innocent and quiet take
>   That for an hermitage.
>
> If I have freedom in my love,
>   And in my soul am free,
> Angels alone that soar above
>   Enjoy such liberty.

What better way to describe the escape from the walls we built between us and ourselves and between us and others in the unhappy years of childhood, with psychotherapy being the key that unlocks the gate of our internal prison? We rescue the true self from the imprisoning adaptations made early in life by the people with whom we work.

And certainly my sense of destiny early on was colored by the meaning of my name which was Greek in origin—"a healer."

As an adolescent, following the temperament I seemed to have been born with (what I call "the intrinsic self"), often choosing autonomy over security I seized on the lines from another poem, by Henley, as my watchword:

> I am the master of my fate;
> I am the captain of my soul.

At times I would lose the courage of that path, only to regret it later on.

And what of the literature I chose as a child and adolescent—mystery stories, following the clues to the ultimate revelations? I found the same excitement in doing the work of psychotherapy. No two stories are alike. The plots are intricate and complex, full of paradox and feedback loops. Doing crossword puzzles called on the ability to shift categories and to play with words—another thread in the process I have come to love.

Then there was the emphasis on ethics and good deeds in my early religious education. That too entered into the fabric of what would become my professional self. What better way to make the world at least in some small part a better place?

Of course, my studies and training in graduate school entered in, but in all truth my real learning began after my formal schooling was done. I found a veritable treasure trove in books and journals, particularly the psychoanalytic literature. I shied away from the political-ideological wars of that world and following the threads of my way of being in the world, came to my own synthesis and integration of the experience and wisdoms of others. In my opinion, one cannot and must not stagnate in this work. We must never stop our studying, learning from the insights of others, not as sychophants or as ideological dilettantes, but always integrating, enriching, deepening our own understanding of what it is to be human. In effect, I am still becoming a psychotherapist now at the age of 70, and anticipate the process will go on for as long as I do.

―――――――――――――――――

Althea J. Horner, Ph.D., is in the private practice of psychoanalysis in Pasadena, California.

16

Mentors in My Mind and Heart

VIRGINIA HUNTER

Friday I had left my position as the nonmedical director and chief psychiatric social worker of the Psychiatric Clinic for Children in Long Beach, California. Now, on the following Monday, in September 1967, as I drove into the parking lot of Los Angeles's internationally prestigious child therapy program, Reiss-Davis Child Study Center, I would begin a two-year full-time postgraduate fellowship. I felt I was ending one journey and beginning another. The names of the faculty at Reiss-Davis were recognized for their contributions to the psychoanalytic literature.

I knew I had a lot of energy and enthusiasm, and loved learning, but I was neither a writer nor a scholar. Knowing that I had struggled with dyslexia throughout my life and school career, I started to think and wonder—how had I gotten to Reiss-Davis?

I wanted to be a skilled therapist for children and their families. I had already explored the possibility of going to study at Hampstead in London but was advised that I had insufficient funds to begin that path. I am grateful to have been accepted by Reiss-Davis. I believe myself to usually be intuitive, curious, emotionally available, empathic, and sensitive to people. Many mentors had lifted me and carried me toward

Reiss-Davis. I have been extraordinarily lucky and blessed in the mentors that I found or that I was chosen by. I have had the good fortune to have people who cared about me. They enabled me and supported me to care about myself and about my work.

My first mentor was my loving father, Archie Deason, and his siblings. He was a chemistry professor who enjoyed debate about subjects as varied as the Bible and science. Many of my earliest memories are of being rocked in his arms or the arms of one of his nine older siblings on a porch on his family's modest farm in Northport, Alabama. They valued their college degrees and debated issues that they considered weighty. They had a humorous way of describing their own personalities, politics, and histories along with those of their friends and neighbors, and relating those histories to the person's current behavior or peculiarities. There was candor and acceptance in the way they explored personality. They were a family that enjoyed some high jinks. For example, at one point, as children, the brothers put a farm wagon on the top of their church's steeple. The scaffolding and paint the family regularly used to maintain the church was stored in their barn. They never revealed how they had gotten that wagon to the top of the steeple. They trusted I would figure it out eventually. They had humor and wit. They helped each other and supported each other, cared about each other's feelings and were loyal to the family. They had some rivalry that was usually, but not always, friendly. They seemed to have as much respect for the mind of a female as they did for the mind of a man, which in those days was pretty unusual. I do not recall any taboo subjects. I knew early that I was expected to be accountable for decisions I made and it was necessary that they made intellectual sense, not just emotional sense. They loved, nourished, and played with me as well as challenged me to figure out various riddles. I was the first female grandchild born of the family surname and, as such, enjoyed a special place.

My dear mother, who is a social worker, also valued and encouraged me. Her beginning, though surrounded by wealthier relatives, was less secure than my father's. On the day of her birth, her father, also a college professor, had gone away for a job interview and had never returned or been heard from again. Detectives found no trace of him.

My mother's mother and my mother's older brother, William Parker, were left struggling and often were taken care of by the Georgia Anthonys, the family of my mother's mother. My mother was proud of the merchants and ministers, some of whom had published, in her extended family. They helped my mother complete her college education at Huntington College, Montgomery, Alabama, where she earned a degree in literature. I felt the absence and loss of my mother's father affected all our lives, and this interested me.

May Parker, my mother's mother, was a pretty lady who, to me, seemed emotionally fragile and somewhat wispy. She had been raised to be a wife and mother, and a lady. She had few skills designed to enter the work world. After her husband's disappearance, she worked making hats, handmade garments, and my clothes and my doll's clothes. She eventually ended up as a housemother at a woman's university. She had to be hospitalized for depression on a number of occasions and had shock therapy. When I was in college she died in Louisiana State Hospital where she had been admitted because of Alzheimer's disease. My mother felt guilt and shame when she was unable to continue to care for her mother in our family residence.

I was consciously desired by both my parents, but my mother had an extremely difficult pregnancy with me, losing much weight and spending the last three months of her pregnancy in the hospital because of pernicious anemia and severe nausea. At some point, doctors recommended that she terminate her pregnancy in order to save her life because she was losing so much weight. She refused to do this, but by the time I was born she was exhausted and weighed only eighty-seven pounds.

I spent all the summers of my childhood at a now defunct resort, Louisiana's Magnolia Park, usually in the care of my maternal grandmother, May. The resort had a lake and also a wonderful, cool, freshwater river that was grand for swimming. The park itself had year-round and summer homes and many activities that were free to the dwellers, such as miniature golf. My father built our cabin. The family reports that I swam before I walked and it's possible that this is true. I cannot remember a time when I did not swim. I liked floating around in water then, just as I have liked being suspended, a blank screen or mirror for ideas from another's mind.

I was an only child for eight years until my sister, Beth, and then, two years later, my brother, Robert, were delivered after normal pregnancies. Our parents read to us, played with us, and took us places. When I was young, we lived on a small farm and my father had a large garden as well as numerous farm animals. My father and I were keen observers of animals and nature. My mother believed I should get to try almost anything I thought I'd enjoy such as ballet, gymnastics, tap dancing, having a horse and other pets, playing the piano, and so forth. The Methodist Church was part of our life.

Compared to today's children, I had tremendous freedom in my rural neighborhood. I had a black nanny and we were close. I remember visiting her church and loving the gospel music there. I felt safe and free in my neighborhood. Our watchful neighbors seemed to be friendly and they offered conversation, stories, or help with my horse's bridle or whatever might be needed. Many took the time to help me with my learning difficulties. My father loved to cook, and both my parents liked to play bridge and entertain. We enjoyed visitors and our home was often the center of activity, which included professors, study groups of students, and our friends. My father quietly and discreetly tutored black students who needed to complete a chemistry course to enter college and did not, in those days, have chemistry in their segregated schools.

It was said of me that I never met a stranger and that seems to have followed me all my life. I've always been interested in strangers and felt willing to seek or return their friendliness. My parents encouraged me to evaluate people and "run like the wind" if I got any uncomfortable feelings about a stranger. I was taught not to follow anyone, even an adult, if I thought they were out of order. This included, but was not limited to, those straddling a pulpit and waving the Bible, saying the Bible justified slavery, or someone wearing a white sheet with the eyes cut out, straddling a horse and cracking a whip.

Predicting people's behavior and possible feelings was a game played between my parents and myself. My pop, for example, might say, "Look how that waitress changed her ordinary walk to a seductive catwalk. Who is she trying to get to notice her?" My mother and

I would laugh and say, "She got you!" Pop would laugh and say, "And who else?" My mother and I would look around and find the person we felt was ogling the waitress the most. The question then was, "What will happen next?" Introspection, self-awareness, empathy, observation, creating stories, and projection were games that were encouraged. Later in life I became aware of and grateful for the tremendous intellectual freedom they encouraged and required. They were both pleased if I picked up on something "going on" that they had not observed. They were amused if I created an ending to a story that was a surprise. No observation or subject was forbidden by Pop, though my mother did have some reservations about the freedom my father encouraged. I have had a feeling of surprise when others, whom I admired and trusted, had different needs or values. Both of my parents valued and created silence. They believed in taking care of things and people. They both felt intelligence and good health carried with it some responsibility for those less fortunate. My father was skeptical and inquiring. My mother wanted people's approval and worked to deserve it.

My maternal grandmother was afraid of lots of things—snakes, spiders, people—and pretty early I felt more that I was looking after her than that she was taking care of me. At Magnolia Park I had a series of symbolic older brothers who teased and protected me. Since my grandmother was a very quiet person, who spent most of her time reading the Bible and prayer books, I quickly learned which cottages had occupants who might be friendly and who might play games or tell stories or even who might be drinking and ugly on a certain day and so forth. Many, both children and adults, were available to help me or look after me. I earned pennies and nickels by doing small chores for people at a pretty early age, and I observed people and studied them. My grandmother, who had been in the mental hospital, was of particular interest to me. She seemed so much less of a person than many of the people I knew and yet she was a noncritical, nonjudgmental, gentle person who would usually play board games or cards with me. She was also insistent that each day I collect three groups of flowers or leaves and arrange them in our cabin. Beauty was important to her.

My mother, Theo, loves to read and, being a social worker, was interested in people's histories and behaviors. She was a keen observer of how relationships were conducted between people. My mother liked high society and manners. She and my father sometimes stood in sharp relief—my father, a scientist, country farmer, and fisherman, and my mother, an educated, high-brow, emotional lady. My mother enjoyed making clothes and shopping for me. She admired and respected my choices, but I believe she was a little threatened by me until I was an adult.

I had a terrible time being still as a young child and probably today would have been diagnosed as a hyperactive child with an attention deficit disorder and dyslexia. But in the days of my childhood there were no such diagnoses. Both my parents were impatient with my learning difficulties. I had the good luck, however, that they were determined that one way or another I was going to use my mind, whether I could spell and memorize or not. My teachers wrestled with my problems, too, twice skipping me a grade to try to retain my interest since it was clear from intelligence tests and learning tests that I had learned the content of the lessons, even though I had difficulty pronouncing the phonetics, spelling, or writing. I also had a problem with organization of written material. I was really good, though, at hearing a story and being able to remember what was important. I learned early that if I could get someone to let me tell them orally what I had learned, I would do okay. But if I were confined to the written or memorized word, I would perform much less adequately. I had wonderful, patient tutors throughout my school years. I had a special ability to do commonsense planning. Listening, despite my problems with phonics, was my favorite way to learn and relate to the world. My tutors all seemed kind and I felt they were on my side. They were all, with one exception, supportive. I did have a piano teacher whom I really hated; she would sharply hit my fingers with a ruler, leaving red marks, when I didn't keep to the metronome just right. I was not with her long! I was always a protestor when I felt there was injustice.

It seems to me now, when I hear the stories of many children with learning difficulties and the struggles of their parents, that I was very fortunate to have survived feeling mentally competent, considering the handicaps I did have. I don't remember hearing anyone, other than myself, ever calling me dumb or stupid. Nor do I remember being humiliated by others. I, myself, was frustrated and embarrassed with my difficulties. Of course, it was known that both my parents were my advocates and that they were not likely to put up with much deprecation of their child. I was also encouraged to advocate for myself. Both my parents were quite firm that if I had done a wrong, I had to figure out how to make it right. They believed in reparation. There was a strong requirement that I keep trying at things like word pronunciation until I got them correct or nearly correct. That's been a struggle all my life. Both my parents felt that right and wrong should be carefully considered and debated by both parent and child. They shared a belief that after around age 4, if an adult needed to physically discipline a child, something had gone amiss in someone's communication or understanding. There was a strong sense of protection of the family name. I could be checkmated against making careless decisions by the question, "What would Pop's students or your mother's friends say about us if you make that decision?" Both considered decision making to be something that should occupy a considerable part of one's mind. Keeping your word and being responsible was essential. Introspection was constantly required of me as the eldest child. "Have you done unto others as you would have them do unto you?" was asked as often as "What do you feel?" or "What do you think?" or "What do you want?"

Both parents were mentors of my thinking. Even when they had a theory about something, they encouraged me to find the flaw in their thinking and come up with a different way of thinking about something. Both were fond of making a game out of thinking what people using theories, research, statistics, advertisements, goodness, or scripture to influence your mind or checkbook might have to gain for themselves. They taught me to value my mind. Their philosophy would also get me into difficulty with authority figures who wanted to teach me to think in only their way. All my life I was to be a grateful learner from many but a disciple of none. Of course, it's rather difficult to be a good follower when you may not be sure how to spell key words in the leader's theories.

My mental abilities are uneven. I completed college with a degree in education. During high school and college, I was on a college swimming team, and was a Girl Scout leader and a waterfront counselor at camp. During that period of my life, I had mentors who admired my creativity, energy, sensitivity, and patience with children. The late Julia Hope Hall, director of the Memphis YWCA and the summer camp, Camp Merimechee, was especially supportive of my leadership abilities. My name would be suggested as a possible helper for any child having emotional difficulties or problems in their relationship with others. The Boy Scout counselors, up the river from our camp, taught me Indian dancing and I became efficient at Indian lore. Then, and now, I loved white-water canoeing and kayaking. Even then I had great interest in and respect for the spiritual and aesthetic experience of nature, including human nature. Part of my work had to do with trying to facilitate moving and creative experiences in the human mind and heart. In addition to waterfront activities, I was often in charge of church services, evening vespers, and campfire ceremonies. All of these involved singing or chanting. I did not know anyone then who believed playing about in the spiritual world might connect you to the devil. The world did not seem nearly as severely "splitting" as it is today. Dualism and a feeling of guarded alertness toward those who need to subjugate or devalue other's feelings, beliefs, or values seem to have always been a part of my character. My parents were quick to question themselves and me regarding unconscious and conscious motivations or gains. All this helped prepare me to be a psychotherapist.

After college, I taught briefly but knew being a teacher was not a good life choice for me. My difficulty with phonics and spelling has influenced me in finding simple words to express myself. I feel the ability to make an idea simple has helped me as a psychoanalyst and psychotherapist. I became a welfare worker and then a child welfare trainee. I began graduate school, eventually completing my master's in social work at Louisiana State University. After a year of graduate school, I returned to work in child welfare. I had become puzzled by and interested in the relationship between the welfare rules, which did not require or help recipients to "move," and the recipient's dependent and often hopeless lifestyle. When I was thinking about my master's thesis, my mother shared my interest and told me that as a welfare supervisor, she and her workers could identify a scattered group of families who were third-generation welfare recipients. These clients were not trapped in the inner city, but they were trapped. I was curious. What could help enable them to create their own freedom? I liked challenges and have usually approached new work with optimism. How could we understand their lifestyles? By a series of efforts on my part and sponsorship by mentors, particularly Josephine Gandelman of the Bureau of Child Welfare of Louisiana, I was allowed to work with ten third-generation welfare recipient families for several years. During those years, I had a weekly psychiatric consultant. He was housed on the grounds of the same hospital my grandmother had died in. The psychiatrist seemed to enjoy my grass-roots exploration of what connected to or made inroads into these backwoods families. He evaluated members of my research families and helped secure psychological testing when it was indicated. He shared his mind and knowledge with me and encouraged me. He also lent me articles from the psychiatric literature.

My master's thesis was related to my work and findings with those ten families. I became convinced that some members of these families were treatable. It was exciting to me to explore what transformations they could make, but I had become very aware of defenses, family myths, hopelessness, and resistance. I loved my work. I worked several years in child welfare between completing my certificate in social work and my master's degree.

When I went back to complete my master's, I had secured a Veterans Administration fellowship and spent six months working and living in the Shreveport VA Hospital. I believe I created the first psychotherapy group on a tuberculosis ward. Some loosely held mystical beliefs about the healing effects of sunshine and my response to the patient's feelings of being caged led me to go to great lengths to secure the support or indulgence of the doctors in psychosomatic medicine and contagious diseases. They helped me arrange to take my contagious group down the freight elevator and out into the hospital grounds where I was allowed to remove my protective face mask while leading their group. I became very interested in the immune system and its relationship to affects and object relationships, both conscious and unconscious. I became sensitive to these patients' breathing and its effect on me (Hunter 1993). Around the same time, a pathologist encouraged me to watch him perform autopsies. Among other things, he wanted me to see what smoking cigarettes could do to the lungs. Later, I stopped smoking. I was impressed with many things, but what I remember the most was his love of teaching and his respect for the dead person. He showed me a great deal about body systems and the brain. I was fascinated in his theories about the relationship between affects, object relationships, lifestyle, genetics, diet, exercise, and physical illnesses. The doctors at the VA were like my father's personal friends—scientists who were open to discussion and debate, particularly after five o'clock.

After completing graduate school, I returned to child welfare but knew I wanted to become a psychotherapist. Jo Gandelman supported my therapeutic work with children in foster care and encouraged me to seek further training. I then joined the staff of the first outpatient mental health clinic in Arkansas, at Fort Smith, where I was mentored by a group of very talented, energetic, older, mental health professionals, mostly men. We mirrored and supported each other. We had to prove our value to legislators, schools, families, police, radio stations, newspapers, and community leaders. We were innovative in many ways. The Rockefellers contributed to our expenses while we were trying to get the state legislature to appoint a centered mental health authority so the state could receive federal funds and grants. We worked long hours. I studied and I did a lot of public speaking about subjects related to mental health. I also had a radio talk show. I left that position somewhat reluctantly to go to Long Beach, California to become the nonmedical director of the Psychiatric Clinic for Children.

I was accepted for a fellowship at Reiss-Davis Child Study Center the second time I applied. From the day I arrived at Reiss-Davis, psychoanalysis became a focal point in my life. Reiss-Davis was a powerful influence on my thinking. There I had unusually gifted mentors, lecturers, and supervisors. We lived and breathed psychoanalysis. The commitment to keep my mind open and ready to discover new understanding was a strong value for me and my teachers. Those of us in training were unaware that the future of such intensive training was already in danger. Child analysts, including Anna Freud, and child development specialists from all over the world visited and lectured. Reiss-Davis was dedicated to a team approach that included social workers, psychologists, and psychiatrists. Every case had an intensive psychosocial evaluation, psychological testing, a psychiatric evaluation, and a team consensus as to the treatment plan that required the parents to be involved in weekly treatment and the child to be seen two to four times a week if a case was to be accepted for treatment. Whether we were the therapist seeing the parents or the therapist seeing the child, we had separate weekly individual supervision. Today, when I think of the intensity of the experience, it seems almost unbelievable. Each member of a team was required, at least once, to be able to do the work of another discipline. The clinic also provided medical insurance that helped pay for our own personal analysis. To my knowledge, all of the fellows and most of their spouses entered analysis. We were all learning. The fellows were a dependable group to be training cases for the two psychoanalytic institutes that existed in the 1960s in the Los Angeles area. My first four-times-a-week didactic analysis with the late William Brooks, of the Southern California Psychoanalytic Institute, lasted over six years.

Reiss-Davis encouraged contributions to the literature. I realized I would not feel I had shown my gratitude until I could contribute something myself. I remember the freedom to allow a patient's material to develop. Psychoanalytic theories and interpretations were not jumped to or insisted on by staff. There were many research projects going on, for example, in autism, childhood psychosis, and child development. Lillian Weitzner, who was a graduate of Hampstead, was one of my child therapy supervisors. She was extraordinarily generous; and even after the fellowship was completed, she and Reiss-Davis allowed me to continue two ongoing cases at Reiss-Davis with free supervision. Morton Shane and Rudolf Ekstein both influenced and encouraged me to find my own psychoanalytic style. I have written elsewhere (Hunter 1994) that Ruth Bro, my social work supervisor, contained my negative transferences. She struggled with me to improve my poor writing skills. I experienced the staff's strong commitment to me as a student, and I hope I have continued that with my own students and patients.

I had planned to return to directing another outpatient clinic when I completed Reiss-Davis, but I was still in my first analysis and was committed to successfully completing it. I didn't really enjoy the politics necessary to support and run a clinic. I had already begun a private practice. I decided to risk continuing a private practice without a secondary income. In the 1960s this was a rather unusual decision for a psychoanalytic social worker to make. I liked that my patients and I could be independent, and free to do intensive and long-term work where we felt it was indicated. I believed then and now that deep changes take time, trust, and the security of "going on being."

After I left Reiss-Davis, I continued studying with various therapists. Some, like Virginia Satir and Carl Rogers, were not psychoanalytic. Periodically, I had supervision or treatment with Fritz Perls, and I studied with Allen Watts. Eventually when one of the patients I was seeing four times a week developed a tenacious, erotic transference, I entered supervision with my former analyst, William Brooks. I felt since he knew me he would be able to help me sort out what was going on better than anyone. He was very helpful. I have learned a great deal from those I've been supervised by and those I have supervised. Psychoanalysis was the method of treatment I most understood and valued, but I have also enjoyed being a marriage counselor, a family therapist, a group therapist, and doing brief goal-directed psychotherapy. I've had a special interest in learning difficulties, blocks to creativity, psychosomatic illness, affect regulation, attachment, and problems related to self-esteem, assertion, and independence.

Soon after I left Reiss-Davis, Arthur Nickerson, a Menninger-trained child psychiatrist who had been my consultant at the Psychiatric Clinic for Children, invited me to share his suite in Long Beach. Our ongoing collaboration has continued from 1969 to the present. He encouraged my research and writing. Through all these years, we have spent thousands of hours discussing case dynamics and sharing our knowledge and readings. He has been a constant mentor and friend throughout much of my adult life. The psychological testing done by Marvin Beitner informed our work until managed care destroyed easy access to good mental health evaluation and treatment for many. All my career, my analysts and my supervisors have referred cases to me.

I continued leading groups in my private practice and I became a patient in one of the late Martin Grotjahn's psychoanalytic groups for professionals. Later, he also supervised my groups, including a couples group that he visited. He was a mentor to me for the rest of his life. His active use of countertransference, interpretation, and his willingness to share his cartoons, as well as images that developed in his mind with patients, was one of the most meaningful and freeing experiences of all my training. He was not afraid of his infantalized, sexual, or aggressive thoughts, associations, or fantasies. After my supervision sessions, we would often stroll around Beverly Hills during his lunch hour. We visited and corresponded until two days before his death. His use and understanding of the importance of play and humor in the treatment relationship contributed to my own analytic style. He knew and understood my distress regarding my inability, in those days as a social worker, to enter institutionalized training that would allow me to become eligible for membership in the American Psychoanalytic Association or the International Psychoanalytical Association. He was generous and did many symbolic things that touched my heart and my treatment techniques (Hunter 1996). He was an artist at creating symbolic and meaningful exchanges between himself and his patients. He trusted himself and he trusted others to narrate their way with openness and freedom through whatever reactions were created.

In the 1980s Lawrence Hedges, who had also been a student at Reiss-Davis, began a Freud study group that I attended in Orange County, California. The Newport Psychoanalytic Institute was created from that study group. I was a founding member, later a student and graduate, and I am now a training and supervising analyst. I had more supervision with Louis Gottschalk and Robert Stolorow. Both have been valuable mentors.

Gottschalk has presented a model of respect, human responsiveness, and attachment. Very recently, during lunch at his Balboa Bay Club, he learned from me that I did not know how to work the computer at the library. His response? "I have time, if you do, too. We could go to the library right now and I'll teach you." And he did teach me that very day!

The editing and publishing of my book *Psychoanalysts Talk*

(Hunter 1994), which was part of my dissertation, was invaluable to me. My journey of psychoanalytic interviews and case discussions began with Hanna Segal and John Bowlby, both of whom I paid for their time. After those two interviews, it occurred to me that others might be interested in my analytic adventure—that it was a form of research, and I stopped offering to pay for the time of the subjects of my book. The Newport Psychoanalytic Institute had been granted the right to issue Ph.D.s and I wanted to do research to complete my Ph.D. My second analyst, Jay Martin, helped me and supported me in my first publishing efforts. Like my first analyst, he, too, is a graduate of the Southern California Institute. Gottschalk was his training analyst. My work with him freed me to try to use written language to communicate with others. I hope I pass his generosity and his freedom to allow a unique dyad to develop to others trying to free their creativity and their lives.

Martin Schulman, the editor of *The Psychoanalytic Review*, was generous to me and published my work. He, too, helped open up the world of publishing and correspondence. My book was also published in Italy in Italian. The book has been surprisingly well reviewed and received. Joseph Reppen also has affirmed my work. It is very interesting to me that having been helped to run the gauntlet of trying to publish, despite my dyslexia, I am now able to light the way for my own students and patients. My life seems to have been a continuous process of releasing my creativity and finding others whom I could help release also.

Currently, in 1996 and 1997, I have added a new commitment, to the inner city, to my work as a psychotherapist. I am the analytic consultant to a national after school tutoring program for at risk children called S.A.Y. YES. The board and staff, with which I participate weekly, are housed and sponsored by the Calvary Baptist Church in the inner city of Compton, California. This is, for me, a new, interesting, and challenging analytic experience. We are creating a history, new understanding, and a cautious, respectful dialogue between scientific theories of child development, learning difficulties, family dynamics, and biblical and religious thought. My journey into this world has been sponsored and mentored by the prayerful Reverend Robert Smith,

Wanda Parker, and the S.A.Y. (Save America's Youth) YES staff, which is dedicated, in its own unique biblical way, to lifting up and saving the human spirit, exploration of misattunements, race relations, introspection, literacy, and freeing creativity.

Now as I look back I see I have been mentored in various ways by my family, teachers, friends, associates, and those who trained me who have helped release me in becoming my own self, as a psychotherapist and as a mentor for others.

Virginia Hunter, Ph.D., is a Training and Supervising Analyst at the Newport Psychoanalytic Institute.

REFERENCES

Hunter, V. (1993). Clinical issues in the breathing behaviors of patient and therapist. *Clinical Social Work Journal* 21:161–178.

——— (1994). *Psychoanalysts Talk.* New York: Guilford.

——— (1996). Symbolic enactments in countertransference. In *Strategic Emotional Involvement*, ed. L. Hedges, pp. 25–37. Northvale, NJ: Jason Aronson.

17

What Made Me Want to Become a Psychoanalyst

HANNA E. KAPIT

Early on, life seemed dismal and frightening to me. My mother cried a good deal and the lullabies she sang to my brother and me were filled with melancholy. The rare times my father was present and talked to us, he would talk about germs, sickness, contamination, pogroms, death, and war. When he sang specifically to me, it was from "Hobellied," the death song by Raimund: "Death takes his plane and levels every-one." Or: "Berlin, Berlin, that's where the crazy people are/That's where you belong." Sometimes he would sing a song that made a pun on our family name, Elias: "All Eliases, all Eliases were once great prophets. Only little Hanni, only little Hanni, a rhinoceros." These songs seemed to epitomize my early life and hung over me like a threat of my life to come.

I was depressed and remember my wish to make my mother and father smile. I wanted to drive away the dark cloud that hung over our home by being determinedly cheerful.

VIENNA

I grew up in the heart of Vienna, a city of contradictions. It was a beautiful place with lush gardens and impressive baroque and gothic buildings. When I was growing up, the formerly powerful Austro-Hungarian Empire was reduced to the small defeated and partitioned country of Austria. Having lost its emperor—the father, and therefore its power and self-confidence—it had trouble adjusting to a new government, a truncated life, and very real starvation. It was a poor, weak, crippled, angry, and envious country that—on the surface and as a defense—was dancing, cheerful, and gay. But "gay Vienna" and the blue Danube were an illusion; the Viennese were not gay, and the Danube was not blue. It is no coincidence that psychoanalysis was born in Vienna. The Viennese needed help.

Anti-Semitism was everywhere—at family gatherings where cousins could make anti-Semitic comments, in school where Jewish and Christian girls sat at opposite sides of the classroom, and between "friends" who were kept apart. Although some teachers in my school were Jewish, the principal hated Jews. I believe that the contradictions of my family situation—with the Christian mother active in school activities and the Jewish father being rarely seen—also confused my teachers. The antagonism toward Jews was flagrant and filled me with anxiety.

A positive memory of my high-school days, however, was of Dr. Emmy Sachs (divorced wife of Freud's Hans Sachs), who used her psychoanalytic sensitivity to enrich her teaching of literature. It seems that every step of my way provided another brick in the road toward psychoanalysis.

MY FAMILY

Some of my childhood memories are as clear as if they had occurred yesterday, whereas others are a bit fuzzy. It is hard to know how they have been modified by the passage of time and by emotional elements. My stepmother and my mother's sister, witnesses to my early life, have straightened out or confirmed many of them. Others were unearthed, clarified, and corrected by my own work in analysis.

My family life was also filled with contradictions and conflicts that were hard to understand or integrate. My parents came from different backgrounds and religions and had conflicting values and antagonistic attitudes toward most things. As far as analysis was concerned, for example, my father disbelieved and my mother was attracted to Jung's theories.

My father was Jewish, an utterly cerebral man of science who was rarely home. My mother was the overemotional daughter of an aristocratic Lutheran family, who left the upbringing of her children to a maid and an English and French nanny. The marriage was restless and stormy from the beginning, with the respective families disliking each other and avoiding contact. I was born at the end of World War I when my father was still at the Russian front, and my mother was alone in Vienna, faced with real and emotional difficulties. My father's return, of course, presented her with new problems. They rarely agreed on the issues of daily life—food, children's education, friendships, and so on. Heinz Hartmann, a close friend of the family, told me once, when he referred me to my first analyst, "Your mother could have been analyzed. Your father, never. He was much too rigid."

When I was 15 months old, my brother was born, which confused and upset me. Why did my mother need another child? And why was her love for him so passionate and exclusive? The answer to the second question was clearly that he looked like my father. I had to believe that I was unacceptable to my mother because I was female and, as my father indicated in his songs, unacceptable to him in general. I remember and was often told that I soon turned my envy into maternal feelings and took care of my brother. Today we are good friends and I always look forward to our regular visits.

While my mother neglected me in favor of my brother, I looked more and more toward my father. My view of him was always conflicted. I saw his dedication to healing but also his cruelty. On Sundays, I both loved and dreaded his taking me to the hospital and telling me about his research and his sick and dying patients. During his rounds, I sat in his laboratory with little dogs, electrodes in their heads, bats with opened heads—all parts of my father's experiments. I was proud that he was the first to discover how radar makes bats able to fly at night. I was also frightened and pitied the animals my father tortured. I asked myself why such cruel research was worth the results my father so strongly believed in. I identified with the little animals, promised myself never to be like my father—physician or otherwise—and strove never to hurt anybody.

My father also talked for years about the glorious days of the war. He was a "Generalstabs Arzt" of the Austrian Medical Corps, in charge of epidemic hospitals on the eastern front. He would travel on horseback with a servant behind him, saving sick and dying soldiers. Listening to all this when I was too young to understand—5 or 6—only frightened me. My admiration for my powerful, important, elegant, tall (six-foot two-inch) father mixed with trepidation and left me anxious in general and as far as medical issues were concerned in particular. Once, when I returned from a school excursion with an open wound on my heel, he put iodine on it, turned to me with piercing eyes and a threatening voice and said, "If you had been in the army, you would have been called a malingerer and been shot!"

When I walked with him on the streets of Vienna, he paid great attention to the returning soldiers with amputated limbs and empty eye sockets. I, of course, found them frightening but thought that my father, who explained it all to me, could cure them. In my mind, he could destroy, kill, and resurrect anyone he wished. I never wanted to take care of the veterans, though, whom I saw as victims of my father. Rather, I wanted to heal their emotional and mental wounds.

Sunday mornings, he would come home, newspaper in hand, to read us the names of women and men who had died that week. That was frightening enough, but he also often added, "Ich habe diesen Mann zu Tode behandelt" (I treated this man to death). Today I know he meant to indicate that he had been this person's physician until the end. But in my child's mind, I thought he had killed these poor people. I knew who Semmelweiss and Pasteur and Ehrlich were, before I heard of Cinderella. I similarly knew what Napoleon had died of and what had caused Konrad Ferdinand Meyer's depression, before I heard of Little Red Riding Hood. Although I had no idea what made these famous people important or what the diseases meant, I was frightened and fascinated, determined to understand the mysteries behind them.

During the early years of my life, my parents' marriage deteriorated steadily, and when I was 5 or 6, my father moved into his own room. They then decided I should no longer share a room with my brother and moved me into the bed next to my mother's. Leaving my brother felt like a serious loss. Gone were the comforting fairy tales he used to tell me to help me sleep. This was made all the more painful by my mother's frequent crying into the night. I was also depressed, but I remember that quite early (3–5?) I felt that I had a right to my feelings of depression (a well-known social democratic song of the day said: "Die Gedanken sind frei"—thoughts are free!) but no right to impose them on others. The others, I thought, I had to help.

Added to this sadness came fear caused by the obstinate presence of a shiny skull that looked out at me from atop a cabinet across from my bed. It terrified me! It came from my father's medical school days, and his explanation that it couldn't hurt me never managed to reassure me. My fantasies continued about the identity of that person: Who had he been, why was he dead, and how was my father connected? (It remained there until I was 17 when my father moved out and I got my own bed back in his room where, finally, I was by myself.)

This must have been a sad and difficult time for my mother. She became aware that her husband was having a long-term affair. Divorce was not easily accepted in Vienna, though infidelity was.

His mistress played an important role in my early life. Dr. Ada Hirsch had returned from the war at about the same time he had— shortly after I was born. Her presence was freely accepted in our house; she was my mother's friend whom I loved and became very attached to. Other times, my mother would not allow her to visit us, so that I lost her and missed her badly.

Around this time, my mother, in her desperation, tried to kill herself twice. When my father discovered her body, he revived her and, when she was ambulatory, he sent her to her parents to recuperate. This left us children without a mother, lost and confused.

When I was around 6, the mistress must have been permanently banished. She disappeared from my life until I was 17, when my father told me that he had divorced my mother and married Ada while we children were away on summer vacation.

The revelation of my parents' divorce and my father's remarriage was a shock. As a result, I was too angry and hurt to talk to my father's new wife for years. But I suddenly understood something that had mystified me for years: my father had often seemed omniscient, knowing things I thought he could not know about my school behavior and me. The reason, now clear, was that his mistress and then wife had been our school doctor! She would stand in front of her office and watch me arrive at my classroom every morning. She'd also go to teachers' meetings and then report my behavior to my father. This new understanding made me angry, but anger at my father felt very uncomfortable. Questioning him was a hazardous undertaking, and nobody was allowed to contradict him.

At that time, my brother and I were old enough to be out of the house often, frequently leaving my mother alone. Though she had the support of many friends and her parents, she must have been lonely and humiliated at being left. I don't think that the many years of misery had prepared her or had made it any easier. According to my memories of that time, with my father gone, my mother moved closer to her parents. In any case, the divorce was never mentioned in any way. It was ignored by everybody and clearly unacceptable to our family and the whole of Viennese society. I got the message and never talked about it. Much later, in my analysis, I explored my conflicting feelings of abandonment and rage.

I lost the old comfort I had found in the thought that even though my mother preferred my brother, my father preferred me. My father's departure, therefore, left me depressed and doubtful that life was worthwhile. I no longer had anyone to answer my questions, more than just why the sky was blue, but also why did he leave not only my mother but also me? What was wrong between him and my mother? Wouldn't he miss me? The suffering around me and in myself, the secret lies and contradictions I sensed in my family plagued me. I had to find explanations!

I had been told early on—with intensity—that honesty and decency were essential to life. Dishonesty, lying, and a spot on the tablecloth were crimes that had to be seriously punished. I earnestly believed that these traits were reprehensible. But I was slowly learning to see that my father was dishonest, at the very time he was trying to control me and make me believe he was a hero—my hero. He even

secretly followed me home from school to listen to my private conversations! And he acted as if his long affair was honorable! But when
he saw me kissing my boyfriend at age 17, he challenged him to a duel!

It was clear quite early that what we were told was not true. But
finding my father so unexpectedly devious and dishonest was a trauma
that took years of analysis to integrate and understand.

Of course, it must also be said that losing my father first to my
mother and then to Ada was a double blow and might explain the
opinion of Phyllis Greenacre, my highly respected senior mentor, that
I had the worst Oedipus complex she'd ever seen. A general depression did not help the situation or my own sadness when I felt I had
lost my father and could not understand or control my life.

Throughout these difficult years, my grandmother was the one I
loved most and admired. I internalized her emphasis on togetherness,
love, and goodness and wanted to be like her. Her warmth, acceptance,
and generosity toward me seemed to make up for my mother's neglect.
She read Greek and Latin and taught me things I still enjoy today—
knitting, crocheting, and sewing. As a token of her love, she made me
a vase on which she painted the words: "Nicht mitzuhassen, mitzulieben
bin ich da" (I exist to share love, not hate).

She was not immune to the anti-Semitism rampant in Vienna,
however. I still shiver when I remember her advising my mother before the divorce, "Give him the children; then you'll be rid of the Jewish breed." Knowing this, I was puzzled by her warmth toward me,
one of the breed. How come she seemed to love me, the Jewish grand-
daughter, as much as my Aryan cousins?

This issue of religious identity perturbed much of my childhood.
If I were Jewish, my maternal grandparents would think I was bad like
my father; if I were Christian, they would see me as good like them,
but my Jewish family would ostracize me. My resolution was not to
accept any religion at all.

My brother and I were brought up without any formal religion,
but in reality both parents pulled in their own direction. My elementary school had mostly Jewish children, but I spent the next two years
in a Catholic school where I was terrified by the big Christ on the cross
at the front of the room, blood dripping from his wounds. The ques-

tions of identity, belonging, and loyalty could never be fully resolved. I still today have a Christmas tree and a menorah every December. Christmas was always a special time for me, the only time my father joined the extended Christian family and I hoped that peace had been made. The external harmony, however, didn't alleviate the internal discord that I always sensed.

FREUD, VIENNA, AND PERSONAL INFLUENCES

A similar discord existed between Freud, psychoanalysis, and the Viennese. Over time, and starting when I was around 5 or 6, I became intrigued by the ideas of psychoanalysis. I often heard friends and acquaintances of my parents vehemently discuss the new science. By the 1920s it had become a definite presence in Vienna—very controversial and discussed with passion. It is not surprising, of course, that the Viennese with their psychological problems did not welcome psychoanalysis. On top of it all, it was a science proposed by a Jew.

The circles of both my parents consisted of doctors, psychiatrists, psychoanalysts, and academics. In my memories, in addition to my childhood pain and confusion, I had the opportunity to be in the presence of these men—often with long beards—who had so much to say and who said it with such authority. I remember listening intently to whatever they said and believing that they were like gods. Their beards proved it! Their opinions had to be correct, and I wanted some of their wisdom!

To know how things worked, especially the mind, would free me of the dangers in my life and give me security. There were so many things I didn't understand! I was disconsolate, for example, when I couldn't understand how magicians performed their tricks. And I was frustrated when crossing Vienna's intersections, because I was always trying to figure out the diagonal from knowing the two sides—long before hearing about Pythagoras.

Vienna was a hotbed of gossip. Everybody talked about everybody, and sexual affairs were the order of the day. I was already primed to be curious, to understand my parents' and Ada's behavior. The concerns of the adults around me fascinated me, even if it was only my dentist's; he also treated Freud, and, while drilling my teeth, shared his opinions about "the professor" with my father or mother.

I heard much that I only half understood, of course, or that I considered fantasies. But all of it supported my wish to understand more. My earliest memories are walking around the Ring, the most elegant street in Vienna, with my father. He would stop, flourish his wide-brimmed medical hat to greet this or that doctor or professor. Sometimes it was Freud, sometimes Koenigstein or Erdheim. They would then stand and talk a few minutes about events of the day, medicine, psychoanalysis, or gossip. I stood nearby, sometimes impatient, but always listening and piling up in my brain the puzzle pieces that would answer my questions.

Dr. Jakob Erdheim, a close friend of my parents and frequent dinner guest, was very friendly to us children and one of the first puzzle pieces I met. He was a pathologist who had written a report on Freud's medical condition that Max Schur called "a masterpiece of pathological examination." Though I don't remember the details, I do recall "Uncle" Erdheim and my father discussing Freud's medical condition as well as his theories, while we children were only allowed to listen, not talk.

I remember a beautiful, sunny Sunday, visiting the Koenigsteins, friends of my father and Freud in Gumpoldskirchen, near Vienna. The Freud family was there. I listened eagerly to the adults talk—but I also greatly enjoyed riding a bicycle. All these and many similar experiences presented a contradictory image of a man who was both condemned and admired by different people. But what I saw was a courageous man with brilliant ideas, who struggled and fought valiantly against his jaw cancer.

The few times I met him personally, he was already an old man with a full beard. In my little girl's mind, I saw him as God-like, omniscient and unjustly maligned, especially by my chronically critical father. I clearly idealized the wise man and wanted someday to do what he was doing. It hurt me to see my father humiliate him, which seemed, somehow, as if he were humiliating me. How could he do that to this wise man who was so human and accepting of feelings? Perhaps Freud could even accept me, which my father in his moralistic attitude certainly didn't. Maybe I could defend him the way I wanted to defend myself but could not. Freud seemed a better father than my own. I then rooted for the underdog—a tendency I still have today. I remember my analyst asking me once, "Why do you think you have to defend Freud?" I also remember a dream I had during my own analysis; I was Anna Freud, so I managed to make Freud my father.

As a result of this idealization, I gave special value to all my experiences that were somehow connected to Freud. A very early pleasure for me was the visits with my mother to her friend Elise Gomperz, "Tante" Gomperz. The widow of Theodor Gomperz, a philosopher and analyst as well as a friend of Freud, she always dressed in black and was very friendly to me. She had always prepared cookies for us, so she and my mother could talk in peace about their concerns. Since Freud had treated Elise Gomperz with hypnosis in 1892 and my mother was a Jungian, they certainly had reason to argue. In 1900, Gomperz tried to use her influence to gain Freud's promotion to the rank of Professor Extraordinarius.

Another impressive colleague of my father was Professor Julius von Wagner-Jauregg. He was the director of the psychiatric clinic of the Vienna General Hospital and won the Nobel Prize in 1927 for the discovery of the treatment for syphilis. With his piercing eyes that seemed to look through me, frightening me, he was decidedly not friendly to children. But in his relationship with my father, he was collegial and supportive. When, for example, my father was concerned about his children and asked Jauregg what he thought would happen to the children of two "schizoid" parents, Jauregg's answer was, "Don't worry, Herr Professor, the Christian and Jewish elements in your children will enhance each other." I think he was right. With or without analysis, my brother and I both became good healthy neurotics, well-functioning individuals.

Dr. Ada Hirsch also played an important role in my childhood and later became a good friend and advisor until the end of her life. In her early medical days in Vienna, she had a brief analysis with Freud and also participated in his Wednesday meetings. Those experiences gave her a tolerance and knowledge about human behavior that I often appreciated and found helpful. Kurt Eissler interviewed both Ada and my father for the Freud archives, and I hope to be able to read them in the year 2000 when they open to the public. Although I know the interviews will focus on their memories of Freud, I'm hoping that some more personal elements will be revealed. I might read some details about my own family romance!

As for my own first love, it coalesced my personal need for life's answers with my fascination by this field. Martin Deutsch is the brilliant, charming son of the pioneer analysts, Helene and Felix Deutsch. At 17, we were both sent, independently, to London to perfect our English. Soon the language of love seemed more important than the language of the country. Martin reminded me of my father in both his dark and gaunt looks and his intelligence. I idealized him, thinking he knew and understood everything. Also like my father, he was willing and eager to answer the questions I was overflowing with. But, unlike my father, he did it with warmth and words I could understand and even allowed me to ask for more.

Being Helene and Felix's son, he had listened to and absorbed the ideas around him. And even if he listened with skepticism and didn't necessarily agree with what he heard, he listened with the wish to understand and make sense of life. This gave him a deep understanding of the complexities of the human psyche. His insight also covered familial, social, and political topics. I was completely open to him, eager to listen and absorb what I saw as his wisdom.

The days in England went by quickly and we were soon back in Vienna where we remained close. Sometimes I was present at meetings or parties at the Deutsch's and could listen to the adult conversations. These grown-ups talked about famous people in Vienna whom they knew from the couch whose psychological and sexual problems fascinated my rather naïve mind. They talked about things that would not have been allowed in my home. I was finally getting answers to some of my questions: What was suicide? What was depression? How did men and women relate to each other? How were they different? And how about the unconscious, sexuality, and aggression?

Sometimes Helene would interpret what I said or did. I didn't always understand what she meant, but I wanted to find out. Martin would interpret the interpretations of Helene for me. I was intrigued with Helene's thinking. I started to read Freud and audited a few lectures by Anna Freud and August Aichhorn at the Vienna Psychoanalytic Institute. This convinced me all the more that I wanted to study psychology and psychoanalysis.

When I faced my father with this wish, he countered with, "You'll never make a living with psychology. You have to learn something practical." Besides, he had played tennis with Helene and, though she was a beautiful women, she was aggressive as well. He didn't want me to become like her. Needless to say, this reinforced my determination to become an analyst, but my father forbade it. I took a course in nursing, learned to sew professionally, and enrolled, in spite of my father, at the University of Vienna with a major in psychology. Today I make my living as a psychoanalyst and knit and sew for the pleasure it gives me.

Unfortunately, Martin had to leave Vienna for America that year for political reasons. We kept in loose contact, but it took Hitler to bring us together again. The day after the Germans marched into Vienna, I received a cable from Martin: "Do you want to come to America?" I responded with enthusiasm and gratitude: "Yes!"

Martin saved my life in a very real way. He also brought me closer to my goal of becoming an analyst, by arranging an affidavit for me, without which I couldn't enter the country. A patient of his mother, Hildegard Plehn, gave me the necessary entrance papers. Now I could live in the country where Helene Deutsch, Helen Ross, Richard Sterba, and Fritz Redl—all writers I had known and read—were practicing psychoanalysis.

During my one and a half years in Litchfield, Connecticut, I worked for Hildegard as a governess, taking care of her little boy, and got adjusted to America. I was fortunate because she was knowledgeable about psychoanalysis, having been analyzed by Helene Deutsch and having translated *Wayward Youth*, Aichhorn's book on delinquency. She had learned the theory of psychoanalysis and taught me child psychology, personality development, and the theory of psychoanalysis, while referring to the behavior of her little boy. She also told me about her own treatment and insights. How lucky to have such an immediate model!

Another eighteen months at the University of Michigan brought me a bachelor's degree, again in psychology, and close contact with two Viennese analysts: Fritz Redl and Otto Spranger. Every contact provided me with further knowledge and understanding. My marriage to a Viennese physician, who accepted my wish to continue my education, a daughter whom I tried to bring up with psychological insight, and my husband's death delayed my professional goals. I taught school in Detroit and then New York and was satisfied with my life with my daughter until Martin reappeared. Again he changed my life. This time he did so by telling me I had to do more than just teach school. I took this seriously and, while teaching school, enrolled in a Ph.D. program in psychology at Columbia University. Then, I got psychoanalytic training and finally, in 1956, opened a private practice that I have enjoyed ever since. Supervision, teaching, consultation, and training analyses offer me contact with young people that brings me great joy and satisfaction. How fortunate I am that my profession—listening, understanding, and analyzing—represents my early fascination.

> Freut Euch des Lebens
> Weil noch das Lämpchen glüht
> Pflücket die Rose eh sie verblüht
> Man schafft so gern Sich Sorg und Müh
> Sucht Dornen auf und findet sie
> Und Lasst das Veilchen unbemerkt
> Das uns am Wege blüht!

Or, in English:

> Enjoy life as long as the little lamp glows,
> Pick the rose before it wilts
> We make our own worries and troubles
> Looking for thorns and finding them
> And ignoring the little violet on the road
> That grows for us on our path.

Perhaps it is not a coincidence that my favorite song, which I sang to myself whenever life seemed difficult, begins with the word *Freut*, a word that sounds like *Freud*, the name of the man I admired—and the German word for "joy."

Hanna E. Kapit, Ph.D., is a Training and Supervising Analyst at the New York Freudian Society and the Institute for Psychoanalytic Training and Research (IPTAR).

18

On Becoming a Psychoanalytic Myth Maker

ROBERT LANGS

There were two pivotal moments in my becoming a psychoanalyst and psychotherapist (terms I use interchangeably). The first involved my selecting psychiatry as my medical specialty and then psychoanalysis as my preferred approach to understanding the human mind and the therapy process. The second followed later on and entailed the unexpected creation of a new paradigm of psychoanalysis (Raney 1984, Smith 1991) which I call the adaptive-interactional or communicative approach (Langs 1976, 1978, 1982, 1992a, 1993). It is this unusual event that I explore in this chapter.

For present purposes, I define psychoanalysis, in all of its present incarnations, as a theory and form of therapy that is in substance a myth rather than science. In this context, I propose that the communicative approach originally was a new myth of psychoanalysis and is now best seen as a mythical science. I will clarify these propositions by comparing the features of the communicative myth with the currently dominant mythologies of the field—those of Freud and his followers, and Jung.

By myth I mean an effort to deal with the fundamental problems and anxieties of life and death, origins and fates, through a conglomeration of highly selected and ill-defined observations, beliefs, and fantasies that have no essential support in quantitatively based, formal science. As individual creations that obtain cultural acceptance without incisive or unbiased examination, myths are unconsciously designed to relieve basic human anxieties in lieu of adaptive efforts based on verifiable truths.

Myths are belief systems that are consciously and unconsciously prejudiced, but they are eagerly sought after because they falsify and obliterate painful truths and realities, and offer denial-based forms of emotional defense and reassurance. The relief they offer, however, is very costly because their prominent denial elements interfere with sound adaptive responses, and with personal growth and a deepening understanding and mastery of nature (Langs 1995, 1997).

Myths are on a continuum with, but essentially distinctive from, *science*, a word I use to refer to investigations of nature that are based on quantitative measures and mathematically based efforts that reveal deep, universal laws—so-called formal science (Langs and Badalamenti 1992). There are in addition theories that are established on the basis of repeated and verified measurements without the realization of quantitatively based laws of nature (for example, the fundamental biological theory of evolution) or on the beginnings of a formal science (as I will show for the communicative approach). I call these mythical sciences because the use of statistical and stochastic measures and the initial applications of quantified variables are a step up from qualitatively based mythology and yet still vulnerable to error and myth making.

It is understood that validated formal scientific results may eventually prove to be incomplete, but they seldom are the basis for myth making. In addition, given the insubstantial basis of myths, we should acknowledge that the choice between competing myths is almost entirely subjective and driven by deep unconscious needs. In contrast, scientific debates are open to arguments built on the basis of quantitative empirical evidence—and its validation or the absence of falsifications. Even so, they too tend to be biased emotionally, under strong cultural and mythical influence, and prejudiced by the position taken by revered leaders. In this light, my creation of the communicative approach can be seen as an effort to redress the prevailing but misleading myths of psychoanalysis and to move the field closer to becoming a mythical science and to achieving status as a formal science.

SOURCES OF THIS VIEWPOINT

The idea that current psychoanalytic theories are essentially mythical in nature arises from two sources. First, this realization was an outgrowth of the newly formed communicative paradigm itself, which provided a fresh vantage point that offered unprecedented perspectives on prevailing psychoanalytic ideas and techniques, perspectives that are quite foreign and almost unfathomable to therapists who have embraced these ideas and their mythical foundations. The unique manner in which the adaptation-oriented communicative approach organized and understood clinical material—its listening and formulating processes (Langs 1978)—led to new ways of conceptualizing the modes of relief underlying the various versions of classical psychoanalysis.

This fresh clinical vantage point soon was expanded to include other advantageous ways of looking into these domains. Included were the creation of a new mode of therapy that provided a novel field of, and method for, clinical observation (Langs 1993); a formal science of psychoanalysis (Langs and Badalamenti 1994a,b, Langs et al. 1996); an understanding of the architecture and evolution of the emotion-processing mind (Langs 1995, 1996); and insights into the role of death anxiety in emotional life and psychotherapy (Langs 1997). The results of the many investigations based on these explorations failed to support Freudian and Jungian theories and practices, and served mainly to further highlight their mythical qualities.

The second stimulus for this discussion came from a fascinating book by Hogenson (1983), who explored Jung's struggle with Freud in terms of the competing and incompatible myths that characterize the theories proffered by the two leading figures in the field of psychoanalysis. Hogenson proposed a sequence of events that begins with aspects of the personal life of the myth maker, followed by a statement of general principles based on those experiences, and concluding with a series of statements that provide (supposed) insights into the emotional experiences of others that then find general acceptance.

According to Hogenson, Freud and Jung had gone through very different emotional experiences, had then generated distinctive theories of the mind, and had arrived at sharply contrasting views of the emotional experiences of others. Hogenson offered several characterizations of the basic explanatory myth of each writer. In the main, he saw Freud's myth as emphasizing power and violence, the killing of the father and the oedipal possession of the mother, and the need to resolve the subsequent experience of guilt—a myth that afforded authority precedence over meaning.

Freud's myth was said to also involve personal and collective regression, which is needed in order to facilitate the reworking of ancient oedipal issues, while repression was identified as the primary psychological defense. Freud's emphasis on inherited guilt and the use of repression was viewed as a way of fixating humans on repetitions of past conflicts, without adequate room for future growth and development.

Hogenson conceptualized the Jungian myth as a rebellion against Freud's authoritarian narrative, and as a Gnostic countermyth that saw projection as the essential mental defense. Jung's myth was understood to allow for multiple interpretations of personal conflict in ways that free individuals from the past by enabling them to deal openly with the past and present so as to look toward the future.

As is true of all myth-based assessments of myths, Hogenson was biased by his Jungian commitment; his ideas would arouse considerable disagreement from the Freudian camp. There are, indeed, no fair and neutral ways to resolve the truth value of competing myths—the choice is culturally grounded and made personally on the basis of deep unconscious needs and forces.

A myth can be assessed on the basis of other myths, mythical sciences, and formal sciences—each approach rendering its own conclusions. Dissatisfaction with a prevalent myth is generally based on qualitative and/or quantitative empirical counterobservations and on deep unconscious needs, healthy or pathological, that render a widely accepted myth unserviceable to the dissenter. Seemingly innovative my-thologies may actually be new variations on an existing myth, as is true of Jung and contemporary psychoanalysts who have moved the Freudian myth from its exclusive intrapsychic and sexual focus to an interpersonal and self-psychological concentration. On the other hand, a novel myth may entail a radical departure from present mythology and constitute a genuinely innovative mythological system, such as the status I claim for the communicative approach.

COMPARING THE MYTHS

From the outset, the myth I generated had two central distinguishing features: first, the propositions that humans, including psychotherapy patients and their therapists, are first and foremost adaptive organisms whose primary task is to negotiate immediate environmental events, communications, and interactions; and second, that definitive forms of deep unconscious perception, experience, and processing play a criti-cal role in emotional life, adaptation, and psychotherapy. These fun-damentals initially were directed against the prevailing Freudian myth that gave inner mental fantasies and memories primacy over real, ex-ternal events, and only later were used to challenge the Jungian myth because it shares key features with the Freudian position.

FREUD AND THE NEO-FREUDIANS

In essence, the Freudian myth proposes that patients' efforts to cope with their inner mental lives—intrapsychic fantasies, memories, and conflicts—are the primary source of neuroses or emotional maladap-tations (terms I use to allude to all forms of nonpsychotic psychopa-thology, whether mental, affective, interpersonal, or physical in their manifestations). The initial version of the Freudian myth argued for a relatively isolated intrapsychic source of neuroses in which unresolved memories and fantasies in the minds of patients create conscious and unconscious conflicts that are the basis for their emotional symptoms. In keeping with this position, the analyst in the analytic situation was seen mainly as a relatively detached observer and interpreter (Freud 1915–1916).

The more recent versions of this theory (Langs 1998b) are interactionally framed in that patients' intrapsychic fantasies, memories, and conflicts are understood to be played out in some ill-defined manner in their relationships with their therapists. These relationships are, however, considered in broad terms, reflecting a weak adaptive position (Langs 1996), rather than in light of patients' adaptations to the particular conscious and unconscious meanings of their therapists' specific, moment-to-moment interventions. Furthermore, listening and formulating tend to be limited to manifest contents that are, at times, afforded ill-defined unconscious implications. There is an absence of definitive trigger decoding of the kind carried out with the communicative approach (see below).

Misapplying the subjective aspect of perception—that perceptions are in part created from within—this myth also promulgates the idea that patients and therapists are able consciously to determine the nature and meanings of reality events, as if unconscious implications can be directly articulated without the use of a decoding process. The myth also implies their joint assessments determine what has transpired because there are no universal aspects to reality and environmental events. This approach fails to recognize that first, there is a consensual core to reality events around which individual assessments, both conscious and deep unconscious, are selectively made; second, that conscious appraisals of reality are exceedingly defensive in nature; and third, that deep unconscious appraisals of the meanings of reality events are far more incisive and reliable than those carried out consciously (Langs 1997).

Freud supplemented his basic position by affording etiological primacy to sexual needs and conflicts—oedipal and incestuous; aggressive wishes were added later on. Present-day analysts have stressed issues of personal identity, self-regulation, self-actualization, narcissistic needs, and reactive aggressive fantasies. Inner needs are stressed far more than traumatic external impingements such as inappropriate seductions and acts of violence, and psychological assaults and hurts, by parents and others, especially therapists themselves. And most importantly, existential death anxiety, a universal dread and root cause of neuroses, is all but overlooked. The wish to kill or have sex is substituted for the fear of being killed and the ultimate, existential realization that each of us must die.

In contrast, central to the communicative approach is the recognition of two forms of death anxiety that lie at the heart of every neurosis (Langs 1997). The first, termed predatory death anxiety, stems from threats and actual moments of uncalled-for violence, seduction, and emotional trauma caused by other individuals and natural disasters. The second, referred to as existential death anxiety, pertains to realizations of personal mortality, a much neglected but universally critical adaptive issue that is a root cause of all neurotic symptoms (and, if soundly adapted to, of emotional health).

The inevitability of death, and its conscious and especially deep unconscious ramifications, involves a most unique and influential adaptation-evoking trigger that, first, is both an external and internal reality, and second, cannot in any conceivable way be fully mastered. In this light, we can appreciate the intense need in all humans, including both patients and therapists, for denial-based myths like the Freudian and Jungian constructions—the truth of the matter is quite unbearable (Becker 1973, Langs 1997).

There is considerable evidence that Freud was personally conflicted about his own death (Schur 1972). He made several predictions of his date of death (Schur 1972), he denied that death could be represented in the unconscious (Freud 1923), and he turned the fear of death into a wish for death and a death instinct (Freud 1920). In terms of personal experience, when Freud was 18 months of age he suffered a significant death-related trauma—the death at age 7 months of his brother Julius. In addition, a more general concern about death probably occupied the young Freud in that his father, Jacob, was 41 years of age when Freud was born—a rather advanced age for the father of a newborn and young child. We may take these as the core personal experiences that led Freud to create a death-denying myth that met the needs of many psychoanalysts and their patients, and of people the world over.

JUNG'S MYTH

In brief, Jung's myth was a turning against Freud on several accounts. Jung objected to Freud's excessive concern with sexuality and oedipal wishes, which he criticized as a restrictive view of the causes of human emotional behaviors and neuroses (he is known to have had affairs with patients and former patients). In creating his own myth, Jung correctly understood that myths are always mixtures of truth and falsification, and that the unconscious mind is capable of subliminal perception, cognitive processing, attitudes that compensate for biased conscious positions, the expression of complex needs and wishes, and much more. On the whole, however, Jung misapplied these innovative insights in developing his theory and techniques (Jung 1954).

In an evidently defensive manner, Jung stressed the manifest contents of dreams and treated them as if they directly and without disguise reflected unconscious thoughts and ideas, some of them supposedly important breakthroughs from the unconscious realm. He had little use for Freud's ideas about latent dream contents and he failed to realize that manifest images are stimulus-evoked, encoded reflections of unconscious perceptions and their deep unconscious adaptive processing. In addition, as did Freud, Jung shied away from death themes and converted death-related imagery from his patients into far more neutral interests. He also found a unique way of denying death and human mortality by proposing the existence of modes of expression that were said to reflect an inherited set of collective unconscious forms and specific memories—a concept with a grain of truth that was used to turn mortality into immortality.

Jung's primary early family trauma was the hospitalization of his mother for psychiatric reasons when he was 3 years of age. The death-related meanings of this temporary loss, and possibly of actual losses through death in Jung's wider family, are reflected in his well-known earliest dream, which was dreamt between ages 3 and 4. In the dream, Jung enters a hole in the ground (associated with the idea of a grave) and comes upon a terrifying, man-eating monster (Jung 1961).

This core experience, along with Jung's religious upbringing (his father was a minister and his mother a believer), helps to account for the central feature of Jung's denial-based mythological system—a turning to religion and transcendental experiences that speak for the existence of God, telepathy, precognition, mediums, dialogues with the dead, life after death, and the like. The essence of Jung's myth, then, was a religiously based denial of death and personal mortality. Jung evidently was unable to use Freud's sexually based denial of death (though oddly enough, he probably did just that in his real life), so he substituted a denial through religion and the immortality of the human soul.

THE COMMUNICATIVE MYTH

My personal doubts about the validity of the Freudian myth began intellectually with an inability to grasp how aspects of fantasy life could outweigh the impact of real traumas in the etiology of neuroses. In retrospect, it's no coincidence that my first clinical psychoanalytic paper explored the interplay between reality and fantasy in emotional life and psychotherapy (Langs 1971). That particular concern announced the basic theme of much of what would follow in my work.

The need for a secured frame precludes personal self-revelations, so it must be left to the reader to assume some distinctive aspect to my own early death-related trauma history in order to account for my need for a healing myth of psychoanalysis that stressed reality far more than fantasy. I can, however, speak in general of my first experience with therapy, my classically oriented training analysis, in that, as is typical of such analyses, it was fraught with unrecognized frame-breaking, traumatic interventions of the kind that are commonly accepted without question or exploration in the context of the Freudian and Jungian myths. My reactions to these events were either ignored because my primary responses were on the deep unconscious level and encoded (trigger decoding is not a feature of the Freudian myth) or explored in terms of my fantasy/memory life on the basis of conscious reactions without appreciation for the deeper and more powerful meanings of the evocative triggers.

When the analysis, which was helpful in many ways, was terminated and fresh problems arose, I had to make a choice. I could (1) seek further analysis with my training analyst, though now without his reporting to an education committee; (2) find another Freudian analyst; (3) turn to another type of analysis or therapy; or (4) do some self-analysis. Without my knowing it at the time, these choices implied (1) returning to the version of the Freudian myth that I had already experienced with mixed results, (2) finding another version of that same myth (the choice made by most of the patients I interviewed in a study of psychotherapy experiences—they kept searching for answers within their chosen mythical system [Langs 1985]), (3) seeking a different myth, or (4) trying on my own to use the Freudian myth that I had experienced in my analysis and had been trained to use.

I chose the last of these possibilities. The unrecognized reason for this selection turned out to be the need for a new healing myth, in that the prevailing credos were unsuited for the healing process I needed. Although I began with the myth I had been taught, I ended by somehow creating a new myth—the adaptational-interactional approach. It proved to be personally healing, and I believe it also possesses understanding that has the potential for generalization and broad acceptance.

The key realization that sponsored the development of the communicative myth and its far reaches was that patients' fantasies and memories, conscious and unconscious, do not materialize spontaneously from within their minds. Instead, they are activated by, and are responses to, what I called specific adaptation-evoking contexts and currently refer to as emotionally charged triggering events or triggers (Langs 1973, 1992a, 1993).

The earliest version of this myth stated that transferences (patients' experiences of the therapist) were evoked by the interventions of their therapists—essentially that unconscious fantasy is prompted by definitive immediate realities (Langs 1973). Once articulated, this idea seemed self-evident and it was elaborated by realizing that patients' transferences are not primarily distortions, but involve valid, personally (intrapsychically) selected, deep unconscious perceptions that are encoded in the narrative tales they tell in the course of free associating. Unconscious perception was afforded primacy over unconscious fantasy—each entailing a very different basic characterization of the worlds of emotional experience and mental adaptation, and of psycho-therapy.

These fundamental ideas never caught on. As I later realized, they were the key elements of an alien and forbidding myth that, if accepted, would overthrow the prized, denial-based defenses offered by the two existing mythologies. Instead, the development of these ideas quickly isolated me from my colleagues and from book and journal editors who were committed to the Freudian myth. Without my knowing it, the competition between myths had begun.

Nevertheless, once my new perspectives had been established, I garnered more and more evidence and support for their basic proposi-tions. The new myth opened a creative vein that kept transporting me into new domains and insights, as it does to this very day—the latest realm being a comparative study of the two protective systems of the human organism— the emotion-processing mind and the immune sys-tem. Indeed, the expanding explanatory powers of this myth, and its creation of new and seemingly more effective forms of therapy, spoke strongly for its vitality and validity. This impression was reinforced by the observation that most of these critical areas have been all but ignored by those invested in the Freudian and Jungian myths—the need to buttress denial-based myths greatly limits insight, growth, and cre-ativity.

Clinically, the communicative myth is based on trigger decoding and unconscious/encoded validation. These efforts essentially involve deciphering the deep unconscious, encoded meanings in patients' nar-ratives about outside events in light of the immediate and recent inter-ventions of their therapists—interpretations made on this basis are the only interventions that obtain encoded, unconscious confirmation.

In time, this basic methodology led to an understanding of the evolved design of the emotion-processing mind as a two-system adap-tive entity, with a conscious system committed to survival functions and a deep, unconscious system operating via unconscious perception and possessing a strong processing capability for the unconscious as-pects of human experiences (Langs 1995, 1996). This latter system is able to communicate the results of its adaptive efforts solely through encoded narratives because the meanings of the environmental impingements with which it deals are so utterly terrifying. The conscious system is thereby protected by denial-based and other defenses; without these barriers to awareness, the conscious mind and each individual would be overwhelmed with death and other forms of anxiety and rendered nonfunctional.

The Freudian and Jungian myths provide theories and clinical practices that support these costly, denial-based unconscious defenses, including the means by which the flaws in each myth are rendered invisible to its adherents. In contrast, the communicative myth recognizes and deals analytically with these defenses and the death anxieties they are intended to obliterate, doing so because of the enormous harm, suffering, and limitations caused by denial mechanisms.

The two adaptive systems of the emotion processing mind each have their own values, needs, executive functions, perceptive capabilities, self-observing faculties, and such. Importantly, the most influential realm of experience differs for the two systems. Because the conscious system is a basic survival system, it has a wide and diversified view of the world. In contrast, the deep unconscious system is a stabilizing system that is focused almost entirely on rules, frames, and boundaries—a most critical dimension of nature and an enormous influence on every aspect of human and therapeutic interactions (Langs 1992a, 1993, 1998a). The Freudian and Jungian myths are conscious system myths that are relatively insensitive to frame issues and their deep unconscious aspects, while the communicative approach is a deep unconscious system myth with a strong appreciation for frame-related encoded communications and the pervasive effects of ground-rule interventions on both patients and therapists.

Through communicative listening and formulating, it was found that patients' deep unconscious needs—as reflected in encoded responses to ground rule interventions—universally are for an ideally secured framework of psychotherapy. On the other hand, modified frames—any departure from the ideal, unconsciously sought, and validated ground rules—are persecutory and harmful. They are, however, favored by the conscious mind because they are a major, however maladaptive and costly, means of defending against and denying existential death anxieties. Every rule break creates the deep unconscious illusion and delusion that the frame breaker is an exception to the rules, especially the fundamental existential rule that death follows life.

Secured frames are deeply healing but entrapping (Langs 1998a). They arouse unbearable secured frame anxieties that are linked intimately and unconsciously to existential death anxieties. By avoiding trigger decoding and the deep unconscious meanings of frame-related interventions, the Freudian and Jungian myths support the loose management of the ground rules of therapy and frame-breaking, and through these actions the avoidance of secured frames and the death anxieties they arouse as well as encoded expressions related to these issues. The communicative approach recognizes these powerful concerns and anxieties, and endeavors to bring them into the patient's awareness to facilitate the adaptive working through of the related conflicts and maladaptations. It is the wide chasm that lies between denying death and confronting it in an interpretative manner that renders the classical analytic and communicative myths nonnegotiable.

THE COMMUNICATIVE MYTHICAL SCIENCE

The beginnings of the transformation of the communicative approach from a myth to a mythical science can be found in the use of encoded, unconscious validation to substantiate all interventions and formulations. While not infallible, this safeguard is less open to bias and myth making than the relatively arbitrary methods of confirmation used in the Freudian and Jungian approaches. Further progress in this direction was made when, with the aid of a gifted mathematician, Anthony Badalamenti, I was able to create a formal science of psychoanalysis by quantifying the amount of narrative (versus nonnarrative) expressions in the communications of patients and therapists, and in lay people as well (Langs 1992b, Langs and Badalamenti 1994a,b, Langs et al. 1996).

The research included a comparative study of the therapeutic interactions conducted by five classical and two communicative psychoanalysts, and the results strongly favored the communicative paradigm and its techniques. In addition, the fact that the communicative approach was the basis for the development of the first formal science of psychoanalysis, and the discovery of true laws of communication and the mind, supported the truth value of its myth and gave strong reason for seeing it as a mythical science.

The discovery of universal laws of communication that distinguish patients and therapists within their therapeutic interactions—that is, universal laws individually obeyed—also was evidence for the existence of a species-specific mental module that accounts for emotional adaptations, the aforementioned emotion-processing mind. The classical myths have sustained themselves by arguing for the distinctive features of each patient, therapist, and therapeutic interaction so as to deny universal features and lawfulness—aspects that challenge their mythical positions. On the other hand, the communicative mythical science acknowledges the existence of universal laws and mental structures, and sees individual differences as engrafted on these species-specific attributes.

Still, beyond these divergences, the approach to the problem of existential death anxiety appears to be most critical (Langs 1997). This fear is a new problem for living species—it's a language-based realization that is only 150,000 years old. Natural selection has evolved only the most rudimentary mental capabilities for adapting to this remarkable threat, and defense, especially in the form of denial and knowledge reduction, has been its almost exclusive survival enhancing solution. It is for this reason that the Freudian and Jungian myths are widely embraced, and the communicative (the Langsian) myth is either ignored or attacked without sound basis.

A nondenial, emotionally adaptive system is difficult to embrace, but it is far less costly than the expedient but obliterating and growth-preventing denial myths. Until now, nature and we as humans have preferred emotionally related defenses over illumination and active coping. It will take, I suspect, a great deal of time—perhaps millennia—before we evolve more effective and realistic and less costly means of adapting to emotionally charged events and realizations. In this light, only a major change in our fundamental myths and understanding of emotional life of a kind that structurally we as yet are quite unprepared to effect can save the day. As for myself, I stand relatively isolated and alone waiting to be called to the cause, knowing full well the quality of our individual lives, the effectiveness of psychotherapy, and the very survival of our planet and species is at stake.

Robert Langs, M.D., is a Visiting Professor of Psychiatry at the Mount Sinai School of Medicine and a member of the American Psychoanalytic Association.

REFERENCES

Becker, E. (1973). *The Denial of Death.* New York: The Free Press.
Freud, S. (1915–1916). Introductory lectures on psycho-analysis. *Standard Edition,* 15/16.
——— (1920). Beyond the pleasure principle. *Standard Edition* 19:3–64.
——— (1923). The ego and the id. *Standard Edition* 19:1–66.
Hogenson, G. (1983). *Jung's Struggle with Freud.* Wilmette, IL: Chiron, 1994.
Jung, C. (1954). *The Practice of Psychotherapy.* Princeton, NJ: Princeton University Press, 1985.
——— (1961). *Memories, Dreams, Reflections.* New York: Vintage, 1989.
Langs, R. (1971). Day residues, recall residues and dreams: reality and the psyche. *Journal of the American Psychoanalytic Association* 19:499–523.
——— (1973). The patient's view of the therapist: reality or fantasy? *International Journal of Psychoanalytic Psychotherapy* 2:411–431.
——— (1976). *The Bipersonal Field.* New York: Jason Aronson.
——— (1978). *The Listening Process.* New York: Jason Aronson.
——— (1982). *Psychotherapy: A Basic Text.* New York: Jason Aronson.
——— (1985). *Madness and Cure.* Lake Worth, FL: Gardner.
——— (1992a). *A Clinical Workbook for Psychotherapists.* London: Karnac.
——— (1992b). *Science, Systems, and Psychoanalysis.* London: Karnac.
——— (1993). *Empowered Psychotherapy.* London: Karnac.
——— (1995). *Clinical Practice and the Architecture of the Mind.* London: Karnac.
——— (1996). *The Evolution of the Emotion Processing Mind: With an Introduction to Mental Darwinism.* London: Karnac.
——— (1997). *Death Anxiety and Clinical Practice.* London: Karnac.
——— (1998a). *Rules, Frames and Boundaries in Psychotherapy and Counselling.* London: Karnac.
———, ed. (1998b). *Current Theories of Psychoanalysis.* Madison, CT: International Universities Press.
Langs, R., and Badalamenti, A. (1992). The three modes of the science of psychoanalysis. *American Journal of Psychotherapy* 46:163–182.

———— (1994a). A formal science for psychoanalysis. *British Journal of Psychotherapy* 11:92–104.

———— (1994b). Psychotherapy: the search for chaos, the discovery of determinism. *Australian and New Zealand Journal of Psychiatry* 28:68–81.

Langs, R., Badalamenti, A., and Thomson, L. (1996). *The Cosmic Circle: The Unification of Mind, Matter and Energy.* Brooklyn, NY: Alliance.

Raney, J. (1984). Narcissistic defensiveness and the communicative approach. In *Listening and Interpreting: The Challenge of the Work of Robert Langs*, ed. J. Raney, pp. 465–490. New York: Jason Aronson.

Schur, M. (1972). *Freud: Living and Dying.* Madison, CT: International Universities Press.

Smith, D. (1991). *Hidden Conversations: An Introduction to Communicative Psychoanalysis.* London: Tavistock/Routledge.

19

The Roots and the Journey

RUTH F. LAX

Our autobiographical memory is in constant flux, is constantly being reorganized, and is constantly being subject to changes which the tensions of the present tend to impose.

Kris (1950, p. 679)

A process of thematic self-analysis started when I undertook to write how it came about that I became an analyst. I had a year's time. The apparent lack of pressure resulted in occasional musings and snatches of rememberings. This introspective curiosity led to a reflective awareness of material different from the unconscious issues examined and worked through when the choice of vocation was the topic of my lengthy, in-depth training analysis. I consciously recognized for the first time that the apparent disparate facets of my life did indeed fit together, and that all these aspects converged to form the path I chose. I enjoyed the pleasant discovery that it all started before I knew it had started.

Having been an only child and grandchild for years, I was told many anecdotes about myself. A theme that bound most of these stories together was my incessant curiosity. My unending whys, supposedly an essential ingredient of my earliest vocabulary, were both amusing and exasperating to my elders. My attempts to find out led to simple discoveries of how things fit together, to mishaps, and eventually to fantasies I created to provide answers that were not forthcoming. Raised on Grimms' and Andersen's fairy tales, my father's version of the Old Testament, and my nursemaid's versions of the New Testament, with

saints, devils, witches, sorcerers, elves, wizards, and fairies abound-
ing, the multiple choices for answers were unending. I believed as a
child that everything I did not understand and no one could explain
was due, in phantasmagoric ways, to the constant presence and action
of those from the unseen world. The personages from this omnipresent unseen world who became the actors, heroes, and villains of my
fantasies, stories, and dreams depended, I now understand, on the nature of the unconscious intrapsychic questions and conflicts that pressed
for resolution. In the bygone days of my childhood, fantasy and reality intermingled and the personages of the unseen world were a constant presence in my life.

To amuse myself during long and solitary walks with my gov-
ernesses, I created a fantasy world contained in an imaginary box,
which became real when I opened the lid. In it, princesses and princes,
kings and queens, witches, sorcerers, and fairies played out the dra-
mas I directed. Good children, after many tribulations, were rewarded
and the bad were always punished. The conflict of good and evil, justice and injustice, in its many disguises, became resolved in terms of
how it should be. The princess, in spite of the wicked stepmother or
malevolent sorcerer, in the end always found the perfect prince. The
young ones departed for distant lands, leaving the king and queen. Thus
the many variations of the oedipal drama ended in a happy resolution.
The fairy tale with its many variations was my creation.

Father, during our walks together, told me stories about his childhood. He was the oldest and grew up with responsibility for his siblings. His mother ran a little store to support the family and his father
spent the days studying the scriptures. I found it difficult to imagine
my righteous aunts and uncles as unruly children, but I could imagine
my autocratic father as being in charge. He felt sufficiently secure to
tell stories about his own naughtiness and how he got away with it. I
never thought of him as saintly but rather as a tyrant with a soft side
I knew how to bring out. He was proud to be a Kohen; the Kohanim
were the priestly ruling caste in the days of Israel's glory when the
Temple stood in Jerusalem. In fantasy I descended from princes. I
experienced when I went to synagogue and saw my grandfather, father, and uncles with closed eyes, the tallitot (prayer shawls) over their

heads, bless the congregation, the mysterious power of their blessings spread over all alike. There were, I believed, no preferences, and therefore no injustice. My father spoke about the Kohanim as learned and wise. They were the judges. He told stories exalting knowledge, depicting it as the greatest treasure. My father, whose education was limited, instilled in me the love of knowing. I learned to read at an early age because of my wish to find out for myself the secrets of the books.

I sat in the synagogue with my father, proud to be next to him. As I grew older, I began to wonder why so few girls sat with their fathers and why the mothers sat upstairs, separated from the religious activities. I also wondered whether the blessings of the Kohanim could reach the women upstairs with the same strength as they did the men and the boys. I was 6 or 7 when my father announced I must sit with my mother upstairs. I objected strenuously but he insisted: it was the rule. My questions and my crying were to no avail. According to the rule, girls had to sit with their mothers upstairs, far from the *bima* (dais). I was shocked! It then suddenly became strikingly clear and apparent to me that only men and boys participated in the service and that only boys had bar mitzvahs. I was terribly upset. I could not comprehend why girls were excluded from doing these things. Why were girls sent upstairs when they grew older? Why were boys so special? I concluded that God and the rabbis were unfair to girls.

A male cousin was born and I heard a lot of talk that "finally there is a boy to carry the family name." I did not understand what the fuss was about and asked my grandmother. She looked surprised and said, "Don't you know? When a girl gets married she takes her husband's name and she then becomes part of his family." I told her, "I'll never do that, I want to be in my family." She patted me on the head and said, "Wait till you grow up." I decided not to wait and to announce my decision to my parents immediately. When I returned home, at dinner I told my parents, "I will never change my name. It is unfair that boys can keep their name and girls have to change theirs." My mother shook her head and said, "That's how it is." I told her it was horrible and she said, "That's the difference between boys and girls."

Pondering boys' advantages and finding they had many convinced me girls were treated unfairly. I wanted to know the causes of these injustices and wished to make it right for girls.

Questions without answers multiplied. Observations and stories heard increased my perception and awareness of the things girls were barred from and boys were permitted to do. I found this incomprehensible since I knew I could do the things for which boys were chosen just as well as they did. I read Hebrew and I was sufficiently strong to carry the Torah. I could even climb over fences, which I did many times, but did not tell my mother about it.

When I accepted that I could not become a boy, my fantasy world changed. I now created stories about girls who had the same opportunities and privileges as boys. They did not have to change their names, they could sit together with men and boys and they had bat mitzvahs. They could jump and run and climb. My aunts and uncles became the witches and sorcerers who criticized me for not being ladylike.

I discovered the Princess Dzawacha books probably when I was 8. I do not recall how it happened. I do not remember the author, though I think it was someone named Montgomery. The books were translations from English. As I considered the writing of this essay, I tried in vain to find the books in libraries and through searches. I wanted to check the accuracy of my remembrance of the stories. Frustrated, I finally realized that the veracity of the narrative was actually irrelevant. The story of Princess Dzawacha was my tale. I constructed and reconstructed it over the years into a composite in accordance with the vicissitudes of my conscious and unconscious motivations. The story I wove, as I remembered it, probably is my creation. It has significance because of its effect on me, and the shape it gave to my life. Only now, since I am delving into the roots of the many threads that resulted in my choice to become an analyst, do I understand the importance of the story for me.

Princess Dzawacha lived with her father in a remote castle. Her mother was probably dead. I do not recall her presence in any way. The father, a shadow, was both present and absent. He disappeared while Princess Dzawacha was growing up lonely, not too happy, seeking . . . I do not know what. She was always described as very courageous and very just, neither playful nor surrounded by friends. The princess next appears in my memory as a physician utterly and completely dedicated to alleviating pain, finding solutions for impossible situations, still solitary but greatly admired and sought after. The event that left an everlasting imprint dealt with Princess Dzawacha's confrontation with a young woman patient whom no one could understand or help. The patient did not speak. She looked at everyone who approached her, then turned her gaze and wept. She'd wring her hands but made no sound. She hardly ate or moved. She was an enigma.

Princess Dzawacha was puzzled and curious. She spent hours sitting with the patient in silence, sometimes stroking her hand. The patient did not move or make a sound. Princess Dzawacha sent her emissaries to find out who the patient was, her life story. She wanted to know everything about the patient up to the moment when an unknown woman brought her to the hospital and left her sitting on a bench. I do not recall what Dr. Dzawacha found out. I think it was a story of some terrible disaster in which the patient lost all her loved ones. The patient was the only survivor. As I recall, Princess Dzawacha believed that if she could re-create the elements of the disaster, she could make the patient relive it and free herself of a sense of having been abandoned, perhaps of a sense of guilt.

The image of a darkened room comes to mind. Princess Dzawacha is talking intensely, the patient is screaming, then crying for a long time in her doctor's arms. I recall rereading the scene of the "cure" many times, yet I remember it only in this very sketchy way. I was moved and amazed by Princess Dzawacha's power to break the spell, to set the patient free. She found and provided the link that once again connected the patient to life. Princess Dzawacha depicted for me at that time the power and magic of the healer whose curiosity, persistence, and devotion leads to the curing solution.

Looking back at it now, it is as if this tale from my childhood presaged some techniques with which I became familiar during my studies: the work of Alpert (1959), Rosen (1963, 1964), Kubie and Hyman's (1955) "Say You're Sorry," certain aspects of Searles's (1965) methods, and the work of Sechehaye (1951a,b).

The story of Princess Dzawacha, who became a doctor devoted to curing, became my childhood inspiration and model. It fueled my fantasies and provided the answer to, "When I grow up, I want to become . . ."

The details of the story of Princess Dzawacha receded under the pressure of adolescence, the vicissitudes of growing, and frequently not fitting in. My adolescent years were filled with Sturm und Drang and the emotional oscillation my parents described as "*Himmelhoch jauchzend zu Tode betrubt*" (from blissful ecstasy, to sadness onto death).[1] The phrase became a suitable cliché description, which gave grown-ups preexisting slots in which to place adolescent tumult. My tumult was great.

During these years I became a tutor, and also a leader of a group of youngsters in a quasi-political organization. I learned to listen to their trials and tribulations and sometimes to soothe. Consciously, but probably more often unconsciously, the power of Princess Dzawacha's "cure" remained a source of puzzlement and stimulated my wish to possess this kind of knowledge and power.

Decisive events took place the year I became 15. Browsing through the recent-acquisitions section of the library I came upon "The Psychopathology of Everyday Life" (Freud 1901). The title fascinated me even though I did not know what it meant. I can't recall whether I had ever heard of Freud. In those days psychology was not taught in the gymnasium, and mine was a nonintellectual family.

A new world opened: the unconscious. A revelation, a discovery of unknown territory, which held the key to the secrets of the mind. Finally the omnipresent unseen world of my childhood fantasies became comprehensible; the personages, the strivings, the wishes, the tragedies—everything fell into place. In the unconscious was the repository of motives, of conflicts, of the given, of the repressed, of the wishes of the forbidden: the bubbling, pushing, pulling cauldron that affected conscious feelings, ideas, motives, thoughts, decisions. If one only knew and understood this unconscious, one would have control of one's life. All the questions, all the whys and wherefores could find answers. The anxiety of the unknown would come to an end once the technique of analyzing the unconscious was mastered. I was convinced that a method for the discovery of solutions to the puzzles with which I struggled existed. Aladdin's story came true. If one knew the magic

---

1. From Goethe's *Egmont* (my translation).

formula, the secret door opened and then . . . the discovery.

I was enamored, enthralled, ecstatic, and wished to be analyzed immediately. My parents thought I was crazy and wanted to confiscate the book. I told them that my unconscious would not stop existing if they took the book, the book just "told about it." They thought I was more off my rocker than usual, and wondered whether to consult our family physician. Fortunately, some important business took my father abroad and my mother was happy to forget my latest eccentricity. I learned once again to keep my own counsel.

I felt very lonely with no one to talk to. I turned, as usual, again to my diary, "analyzed" my thoughts and behavior and those of others, and wrote various "self-exposés."

The everlasting question regarding the differences with which boys and girls were treated once again came to the fore. I did not like the rules for girls, the limitations, the curtailment of freedom, the privileges boys had, the deference always shown to men and frequently boys. Even in the Bible boys were privileged. I had a quarrel with God about these matters and stopped going to synagogue. I furiously filled pages of my diary with essays on this subject. I hoped that I would eventually find the answers to all my questions in my analyses and in the study of Freud.

Serendipitously, after the discovery of Freud, I came upon two other books that also had a profound effect on my life: Jacob Wasserman's *The Maurizius Case* (1929) and *Kerkoven's Third Existence* (1934). The heroes of these two books, their characterological development, and the vicissitudes of their lives provided an emotional experience that contributed to the consolidation of my earlier model of Princess Dzawacha. Etzel Andergest, the lonely 16-year-old adolescent boy who lived in his mind, propelled by curiosity and a conviction that injustice must be righted, appealed to me. I admired and envied his courage, his independence, his brilliant capacity to solve the puzzles his life presented to him. I wished I had his qualities. Now, half a century later, in my memory Etzel's story is a search for truth fueled by ambition and a wish for power. It is unconsciously motivated by the oedipal struggle with a gigantic, emotionless father who deprived the boy of his mother.

Dr. Kerkoven embodied the ideal healer. He was aware of his limitations as man and physician, yet persisted in his search for answers and method. I experienced him as a wise man, a mender of broken hearts and soother of aching souls, a pathfinder for those lost in the struggles between reality and their inner world.

By the end of my fifteenth year, my mind was made up. I wanted to be a special kind of doctor, one like Princess Dzawacha and Dr. Kerkoven: a healer of that inner ache no x-ray can expose.

From the time the war broke out, and during our wanderings, the sense of pain and displacement was repressed by the need to survive and to find solutions. In 1941, however, when I was fortunate to become a permanent refugee in New York City, the pent-up feelings of estrangement and loneliness took over. Everything was unfamiliar even though my family was with me. I didn't like my surroundings. I didn't think New York was beautiful. We were impoverished and any thought of further education appeared out of the question. I knew I was at an end of a road, and as yet could see no side paths that might lead to the destination I dreamed of. I was unqualified and untrained and so felt grateful to find a job working in a factory. A lucky break came when, after a year, I was able, through family connections, to become a salesperson for a product much sought during the war years. It enabled me to earn enough money to go to college. I got my B.A. in two and half years.

I was fortunate during my years at New York University to be befriended by two of my professors: Sidney Hook, and Professor Stout, the head of the psychology department. I finally found mentors and friends with whom I could share my dreams, my doubts, and my ambitions. Sidney Hook spoke on my behalf to Ernst Kris (a Ph.D. and former art curator). It was to no avail; not even an interview was granted. I'd have to become an M.D. to qualify for psychoanalytic training. For a Jewish woman refugee in New York City without money and connections, this was impossible. I was bitter and disappointed. My fantasies were sorely tested. Professor Stout, who did not share my still very simple Freudian views but who knew my work and hopes, offered a choice between a fellowship and scholarship. I made the mistake of choosing the latter, thus depriving myself of a possibility of an academic position.

My university years did not gratify my quest for psychoanalytic training. The grounding I obtained, however, in psychological diagnostic testing, epistemology, and research techniques was and is of great value as a background. It endures and in many ways deepens my understanding.

My first analysis started following a traumatic loss, probably magnified by the many losses of the war.

I became a candidate at the National Psychological Association for Psychoanalysis, founded by Theodor Reik, concomitantly with graduate work at NYU. In those days the institute was strictly Freudian. I met new teachers, new colleagues, and made new friendships. As usually is the case, some instructors were wonderful, others terrible, and some courses inspiring, others varied. It was a heady time. My friends and I were excited and completely involved. For a while, analysis, one's own and the learning of it, became the most important aspect of our lives. We'd go after class to a little café nearby and spend time arguing, gossiping, trying to find answers, and remaining puzzled. These meetings eventuated into the formation of study groups in which we learned a lot.

Since the courses and seminars at our institute were very uneven, my close group of colleagues and I arranged for private seminars. John Herma, a psychologist trained in Vienna, met with us weekly and conducted a seminar on the theory of the neurosis. I was able through his suggestion to organize Martin Bergmann's first seminar. It lasted for ten years and was devoted to a reading of Freud's writings and corresponding papers by current analysts. This seminar gave us an excellent grounding in psychoanalytic theory. I began at this time also to really learn about the politics of the medical psychoanalytic institutes in New York City, the discrimination toward lay analysis, and the broken promises to nonmedical analysts trained in Vienna.

A lot of my training was bootlegged and underground. Being a refugee, I somehow became acquainted with a group of refugee M.D. analysts, members of medical institutes in New York, who, however, were not biased against lay analysts. They were willing to teach psychologists. I was very fortunate. My analytic training was enriched by some of the most stimulating minds of the analytic profession. Gustaf Bychowski, William Niederland, and Otto Kernberg agreed to lead private seminars. I was fortunate to have among my control analysts Berta Bornstein, Bychowski, Edith Jacobson, Esther Menaker, Theodor Reik, and Andrew Peto. Esther, a psychologist trained at the Vienna Institute, was my first control analyst. She stimulated my curiosity and independent thinking and was an exacting, excellent teacher. Esther remained bitter and angry toward the New York Psychoanalytic Institute, which broke its promise to her. I believe that her becoming a Rankian was in part stimulated by this experience.

In my days becoming an analyst was not an easy journey. Only a burning desire to become a Freudian analyst made it possible to overcome the difficulties, feelings of injustice, and humiliations.

Psychologists were not welcome at scientific meetings of the Freudian psychoanalytic medical institutes.[2] They were made to sit in the back rows, which always reminded me of the Orthodox synagogue, the anti-Semitic regulations at the Polish universities, the Nuremberg laws, and antiblack discrimination in the South. To attend the American Psychoanalytic Association midwinter meetings, International Psychoanalytic Association (IPA) meetings, and others, permission had to be obtained via intercession of friendly M.D. analysts. One had to ask for favors to be able to learn. I was appalled. Was this an expression of the antibias ideals of psychoanalysis? What were the secrets the medical analytic establishment so strenuously tried to guard? Freud's (1926) ideals seemed disregarded and his acceptance and recognition of nonmedical analysts ignored. It seemed to me at that time that for the most part American medical psychoanalysts were imbued with the spirit of the closed shop trade unionism. I was told in recent years that these rules existed to make analysis acceptable to the American Medical Association. How this acceptance helped the spread of the true spirit of psychoanalysis I never understood.

My first job was at the Child Development Center, an enriching environment of a therapeutic nursery and ongoing child analysis. I

---

2. In contrast, the William Alanson White Institute as well as the Post Graduate Center gave full training and privileges to psychologists.

worked as a child observer in nursery classroom settings, and did literature searches for Dr. Peter Neubauer, the director. Augusta Alpert, Ph.D., the associate director, became my mentor, controlled my first child analytic case, and befriended me. She shared with me her ideas about corrective object relations (1954), a technique to ameliorate, and perhaps even undo or reverse, the effects of early maternal deprivation in young children. This hypothesis and treatment plan struck me as familiar. I recalled in my analysis once again the story of Princess Dzawacha and recognized congruent elements. The significance of a therapeutic regression combined with a reliving of relevant emotional elements continued to preoccupy me. I was influenced by the work of Sechehaye (1951a,b) and wrote a proposal for the treatment of schizophrenic children combining Alpert's and Sechehaye's ideas with my own, but could not obtain funding.

The analysts who trained and helped me were Europeans raised in the spirit of Freud's endeavor to teach and spread psychoanalytic findings and have them understood and accepted. They were analysts unafraid to oppose the policies of their institutes regarding the training of the psychologist. I became, at the suggestion and with the help of Dr. Margaret Mahler, a member of the Psychoanalytic Child Association. This was my first link with the official psychoanalytic movement since the child association was recognized by the IPA.

Though I was grateful and appreciated my good fortune, I felt it was demeaning to have to ask for the opportunity to learn as a special favor. I felt "second class." Being a girl, a girl from an Orthodox Jewish home, a Jewess in Poland, and a refugee in America accounted for the long history of many narcissistic hurts, which contributed to my vulnerability. I did not play psychoanalytic politics well. I maintained for many years the naive illusion that analysts, since they had been analyzed, would hold to the lofty ideals of analytic principles and build on them. I was disappointed to learn, the hard way, that in their drive for political power the narcissistic component among analysts is very strong though multiply determined and with many different aims. For many analysts, to be in, to be seen, to belong, becomes an aim in itself. Endowed with a superior ability to rationalize, analysts find many guises for their power drive.

Though the "compact majority" (Ibsen 1928) of analytic journals rejected all my papers for many years, *The International Journal of Psycho-Analysis* offered a forum for the expression of my ideas. The fact that each of my rejected papers was published reassured me and encouraged me to continue in the exploration of the multifaceted canvas encountered in analytic work, and in the quest for answers to the many puzzlements. The lack of bias against nonmedical analysts, and the *Journal's* openness to new ideas, which they were willing to publish, assured me that in some quarters Freud's ideals did prevail.

I was pleased by and supported the lawsuit that broke the monopoly of the American Psychoanalytic Association and gave nonmedical analysts the possibility to qualify and join the IPA. We thus were no longer excluded from the worldwide psychoanalytic community. The Rome congress was a memorable occasion. In the United States those candidates who wanted to could now train in the Institutes of the American Psychoanalytic Association, which were previously closed or highly restricted.

I hope a time will come when the nonmedical analysts will forget the narcissistic injuries they suffered, and the welcome of the American Psychoanalytic Association will become more than a token gesture. I hope the institutes belonging to the Independent Psychoanalytic Societies will be invited and welcomed to join the American Psychoanalytic Association.

Because the usual combination of unconscious motives and fantasies that lead to the choice of our profession are well known and apply to most of us, I feel it is superfluous to dwell on them. I also firmly believe that truly intimate revelations of impulses and fantasies stemming from the unconscious are only possible, if at all, in the manifold different forms of communication with one's chosen analyst. The more sublimated autobiographical material can sometimes be found in the discussion of patients, and in papers in which cases and therapy are presented. As is well known, this method was used by Freud and many others.

I thank Dr. Joseph Reppen for his invitation to contribute to this volume. It stimulated reminiscences previously never fully examined. I had almost forgotten about Princess Dzawacha. The books by

Wasserman were more clearly in my mind. However, what I recall is not an equivalent to the actual content of these novels, but rather memories arranged and determined by the motives of the past formed and reformed in accordance with the conscious and unconscious needs of the passing years. Yet these three books contributed most significantly to the formation of a vocational/professional ego ideal I pursued since adolescence. Deprived of specific models and mentors in my early environment, and having the conscious/unconscious need to "right an injustice" fueled my quest. Margaret Mahler spoke about the capacity of some infants to evoke in those available to them a response to their needs. Provided a variety of choices and no direction, I found, by good fortune, during early adolescence, the fictional characters who resonated with my needs. My childhood dream came true via circuitous paths, and with the help of mentors found in early adulthood, I became a psychoanalyst. I continue to be extremely curious and find each patient unique. I am still enthusiastic about the intricate psychic texture encountered in analytic work, and I still would not want to pursue a different vocation.

Ruth F. Lax, Ph.D., is a Fellow of the Institute for Psychoanalytic Training and Research (IPTAR) and a Training and Supervising Analyst at the New York Freudian Society.

REFERENCES

Alpert, A. (1954). Observations on the treatment of emotionally disturbed children in a therapeutic center. *Psychoanalytic Study of the Child* 9:334–343. New York: International Universities Press.
——— (1959). Reversibility of pathological fixations associated with maternal deprivation in infancy. *Psychoanalytic Study of the Child* 14:169–185. New York: International Universities Press.
Freud, S. (1901). The psychopathology of everyday life. *Standard Edition* 6.
——— (1926). The question of lay analysis. *Standard Edition* 20:183–250.
Ibsen, H. (1928). *An Enemy of the People.* In *The Works of Henrik Ibsen.* New York: Blue Ribbon.
Kris, E. (1950). The personal myth: a problem in psychoanalytic technique. *Journal of the American Psychoanalytic Association* 4:653–681.
Kubie, L. S., and Hyman I. A. (1955). Say you're sorry. *Psychoanalytic Study of the Child* 10:289–299. New York: International Universities Press.

Rosen, J. M. S. (1963). *The Concept of Early Maternal Environment in Direct Psychoanalysis*. Doylestown, PA: Doylestown Foundation.

———— (1964). *Psychoanalysis Direct and Indirect*. Doylestown, PA: Doylestown Foundation.

Searles, H. (1965). *Collected Papers on Schizophrenia and Related Subjects*. New York: International Universities Press.

Sechehaye, M. (1951a). *Autobiography of a Schizophrenic Girl*. New York: Grune & Stratton.

———— (1951b). *Symbolic Realization. A New Method of Psychotherapy Applied to a Case of Schizophrenia*. New York: International Universities Press.

Wasserman, J. (1929). *The Maurizius Case*. New York: Liveright.

———— (1934). *Kerkoven's Third Existence*. New York: Liveright.

20

An Interpersonal Therapist

EDGAR A. LEVENSON

Gregory Bateson (1979) said that the point of the probe is always in the heart of the explorer; that is, every voyage of discovery leads back to the self. As I understand it, this is the theme of this book, namely, how the therapist's own life experience inhabits and defines his or her theoretical and clinical understandings.

In the process of thinking about this issue, an iconic memory popped into my mind. Iconic memories are those highly stylized and persistent accounts we have of our lives, memories that loom like monoliths through the mists of the past. Their tangibility is deceptive, however, inasmuch as they seem very clear to us until they are stressed, and then they fracture and deconstruct in very odd ways.

My iconic memory, par excellence, is of being in a synagogue with my father. I was, I suppose, about 8 years old. My father was not a religious man. He was, rather, a sort of diffident Marxist, unlike several of my uncles who were really rabid and unregenerate Stalinists. We were in synagogue because my mother—who did not entirely believe in God, but was afraid of Him—thought that my father should do his paternal duty and take me there. It was an Orthodox synagogue with the women upstairs, the entire service in Hebrew, and notably

lacking any of the choral effects, organ music, or other chic, "reformed," *goyish* elaborations that would have sent my grandfather
spinning in his grave.

At any rate, there came a point in the service when the doors of
the Ark, which contains the sacred scrolls, were opened, and the members of the congregation covered their bowed heads with their prayer
shawls, and looked fixedly at the floor. "Don't look," said my father.
"Why not?" I asked (already a troublemaker). "Because you'll die on
the spot," he said. That's like telling a kid not to touch wet paint. So,
I glued my eyes to the floor, dreading their inexorable upward drift. I
would look! I would see! And that would be the end of little Edgar.

I did, however, sneak a sidelong look at my father, and to my absolute horror, he was staring straight ahead, totally unperturbed! I can—
to this day—still see with total clarity the tiny red capillaries in his
eyes. Now, that's where the iconic memory ends. I don't know whether
I then looked, or if I expected him to drop dead, or if I decided that he
must be immune to God's vengeance. I don't know why he constrained
me in such a draconian fashion (a variant of the Old Testament story
of the Hebrew who rushed forward to steady the unbalanced Ark and
was killed on the spot for his troubles). Was he exasperated with my
endless whys? Was he kidding? In his Freudian unconscious (not a
concept either of us was cognizant of at that time) did he hope I'd drop
dead? Did I hope he'd drop dead? The more I think about the incident, the less clear it becomes. As I said, this heavy overdetermination
is a cardinal characteristic of iconic memories.

So I became a skeptic. Or, maybe I became a disenchanted kid,
and later a skeptic. The ancient Greek skeptics were defined by their
belief that the truth of all knowledge must always be in question, and
that true inquiry was a process of doubting. There is no absolute truth,
and inquiry into the premises of belief is more fruitful than belief itself. This is, I think, not the same as Jewish skepticism, wherein truth
is not given by authority, but must be arrived at individually.[1] I suspect, but I am not sure, that the classic skepticism is more austere. Truth
remains always elusive and in question.

---

1. See Handelman (1982) for an interesting exegesis of rabbinic thought in psychoanalysis.

Somewhat later, I found myself sympathetic to the anthropologist Kluckhohn's (Kluckhohn and Murray 1953) claim that every culture is defined by pervasive and profoundly unexamined premises about the nature of time, space, and reality. This led me quite naturally to the cultural relativism current in the 1940s and 1950s, when anthropologists Benedict, Mead, Whorf, Lee, and Sapir were questioning the ethnocentricity of Western man and his view of "primitive" cultures.

Ethnology seemed to me to be a very attractive career, but I'd already gone through medical school, the usual route for bright, but uninspired, Jewish boys in a world that did not, in 1943, permit very many other options. I might add that my father was a physician, which certainly influenced my choice. I really did not have much ambition beyond getting into a medical school, which seemed nigh on impossible, and, when to my surprise, I found myself to be a newly minted M.D., I didn't quite know what to do with it. I was too prone to panic to make a good surgeon and internal medicine seemed like a depressing and overly intellectualized business.

After my internship, a residency in neurology became available, so I took it. I then spent two years (1948–1950) in the Army Medical Corps, mostly in Berlin. The army, in its inimitable fashion, had no category for neurologists, so I was designated a neuropsychiatrist, and a neuropsychiatrist I became. On my return to the States, I entered psychoanalytic training, quite possibly my first entirely proactive career move, a decision that seemed to me then, and seems to me now, an enterprising and creative way to do what I wished without admitting that after all those years of unremitting and agonistic striving, medicine was not what I really wanted to do. Nor was I about to go live in a straw hut and eat witchetty grubs (for all I know, Margaret Mead lived on tinned foie gras, but that's not what I'd been led to believe). Oh—and also I needed a personal analysis rather badly, although I didn't quite admit that to myself. Undergoing a "training analysis" seemed like a face-saving way to get therapy, since psychoanalytic treatment, in those presumably less enlightened days, was not considered an entirely acceptable undertaking. Being an analyst was somewhat like being a syphilologist—treating and disease was OK, having it was not.

I applied to the William Alanson White Institute because of its strongly cultural orientation, particularly manifest in Erich Fromm's teaching. I was not as aware of Harry Stack Sullivan's teachings, nor of Clara Thompson's. The White Institute's position was a heady amalgam of the views of these three innovators—Fromm's social (Marxist) psychology; Thompson's Ferenczi-derived, democratized psychoanalysis; and Sullivan's interpersonal psychiatry (note, *not* psychoanalysis), which was heavily influenced by Adolf Meyer's institutional psychiatry. Moreover, White was decidedly different from the New York Psychoanalytic Institute. Candidates were considered colleagues, dissension and challenge were appreciated, and psychologists were accepted for training.[2] I must confess that, although apprised of it, I had no real interest in the intense political struggle taking place between White and the American Psychoanalytic Association.[3]

I wish I could claim that becoming an analyst was the culmination of a sequence of focused experiences, but I think I fell into it, through a congeries of converging needs, and corrections of errors made in my life choices. Is it chance or destiny? Actually, I suspect it is how many people arrive at their destinations. This echoes the theme of my first book, *The Fallacy of Understanding,* that therapy consists of just such a series of falling into enactments with the patient (transformations) and then creative extrications (Levenson 1972). That is, therapy consists of a backward reaching process: getting into messes, recognizing and delineating them, and then working one's way through and out—not so dissimilar to how one arrives at one's life. Regardless of metapsychological differences, all analysts meticulously monitor their deviation from the standardized technique, their lapses from ideal participation, be it neutrality or authentic interaction. Therapy is a series of lapses and corrections. Isn't that what countertranference is all about? I do not believe that a therapist stays ahead of the patient, leading him or her to the promised land. Sullivan would certainly agree;

---

2. At that time, 1952, on a somewhat compromised basis, but shortly thereafter on full parity.
3. Times have, indeed, changed. In 1994 I was made an honorary member of the American Psychoanalytic Association.

wasn't it what he had in mind when he said, "God keep me from a clever psychoanalyst."

It would appear, again in retrospect, that it was not incidental that I gave so much space in *The Ambiguity of Change* to Freud's dream the night before his father's funeral (Levenson 1983). According to Krüll (1979), it was quite possibly the key to Freud's critical abandoning of his seduction theory. In the dream he reads on a board the following message: "It is requested to close the eyes." As I pointed out, it is intriguing that the priestesses of the Eleusian mysteries were called *mystes* and were bound to secrecy. "Mystery" is from the Greek *myein*—to close the eyes! It was nothing short of a blessing for me to discover a community of psychoanalysts who thought, *pace* little Edgar, that opening one's eyes was desirable, and moreover, that raising one's eyes—subjecting authority to a good, hard look—was not a likely invitation to instant death.

Were I to be in a Freudian institute—assuming I'd survived—I would still remain a skeptic. One can no more change one's characterological style than a leopard can change its spots. Even the White Institute has its share of constitutional conservatives, crypto-Freudians. But I suppose that had I been in the New York Psychoanalytic in the fifties, they would have wished I'd looked up at the wrong time in the service.

It is consistent with my avowed skepticism to be skeptical of the usual explanations of how one becomes anything. So I have elided life experiences which helped shape my path: teachers, books, experiential epiphanies. I like to think that I have become what I always was. My historical tradition is a variety of Jewish freethinking, with an outsider's sense of irony and play, a lack of conviction about authority, and a traditional entitlement to question what I am told. The post—World War II explosion of interest in cultural perspectivism, the foment of intellectual activity that takes place occasionally in the world (Renaissance Italy, Berlin in the twenties, Paris in the thirties, and New York in the post—World War II diaspora) was current when I returned from the Army after a two-year breather, an involuntary yet very welcome interlude in a lifetime of dogged study. It was, as I have indicated, an easy step into psychoanalysis, which was then an honored and, believe it or not, relatively well-remunerated profession. Philip Lehrman, who was an early Freudian and a close friend of my father, told me that in the early days of psychoanalysis, he paid patients twenty-five cents a session to come to be analyzed. No such sacrifices were required of me. I was paid fifteen dollars a session, which was ample recompense in those halcyon days.

Sometimes, though, in the hour of the wolf, I wonder if indeed I became what I was or whether I became what I am. Is adult personality an evocation of a unique core self, or are there, as Sullivan suspected, many selves, many outcomes? Would I have become the same person had I done something else? Is there, in a parallel universe, another me, the successful cosmetic surgeon or scriptwriter, driving a Mercedes and wearing gold chains? It is certainly more comforting to stick to my original conceit—that there is a core personality, which is, one hopes, approximated, however inchoately, over time—even if I sound a bit like the parrot in Woody Allen's movie who sings, "I've Got to Be Me."

Edgar A. Levenson, M.D., is a Training and Supervising Analyst at the William Alanson White Institute.

REFERENCES

Bateson, G. (1979). *Mind and Nature: A Necessary Unity.* New York: Dutton.
Handelman, S. (1982). *The Slayers of Moses: The Emergence of Rabbinic Interpretation in Modern Literary Theory.* Albany: State University of New York Press.
Kluckhohn, C., and Murray, H. A. (1953). Personality formation: the determinants. In *Personality in Nature, Society and Culture*, pp. 53–67. New York: Knopf.
Krüll, M. (1979). *Freud und sein Vater.* Munich: C. H. Beck.
Levenson, E. (1972). *The Fallacy of Understanding.* New York: Basic Books.
——— (1983). *The Ambiguity of Change: An Inquiry into the Nature of Psychoanalytic Reality.* New York: Basic Books.

21

Sex, Lies, and Psychoanalysis

KAREN J. MARODA

Writing about why I became a psychotherapist is harder than I thought. I want to say something personal because I am a firm believer in the theory that we all become therapists for deeply personal reasons. Yet confessional writing is distinctly unappealing to me. What can I say that is personal enough to be informative while maintaining a measure of privacy and dignity? That is my dilemma.

I suppose the easiest place to start is somewhere I've already been. In my book, *The Power of Countertransference* (1994), I wrote extensively about the need for transformation, not only for the patient but also for the therapist. I said we become therapists so that we might transform ourselves through transforming others. But the implication is that there is something wrong with us, or with our parents, that transcends the everyday. Otherwise, we would choose some other vocation. Here is where I sidestep the confessional in favor of saying that I felt both alike and different from other children. I also demonstrated a unique empathic ability from an early age that was rewarded and reinforced by my mother, my teachers, and my peers.

When I was 13 years old I went to the public library to look up the works of Sigmund Freud. I did so because I was having dreams that mystified me and I had read in a magazine that he was a great genius who understood people's dreams. I muddled my way through *The Interpretation of Dreams* (1900), understanding only parts of what I read. But I took enough away to start analyzing my own dreams, and soon started showing off this talent to others. Naturally I was not the only adolescent who craved an understanding of what was going on in her mind and body. Soon all my friends were bringing their dreams to me, and we would discuss them and analyze them in a group, like a primitive tribe I read about once that started each new day with this ritual.

As my prowess grew I returned to the library to read more. I spent hours in the psychology section, and browsed through dozens of volumes. But nothing spoke to me the way Freud did. The other books seemed too scientific, or too superficial, or just too unreadable. Freud talked about the ubiquitousness of sex and aggression, about the striving for life and the striving for death. He was dark, primitive, and sexual. He was a precocious adolescent's dream.

Most of my reading was not psychoanalysis. What I read mostly was literature. But that was something Freud and I had in common. He loved Shakespeare. So did I. He loved philosophy. So did I. He saw the heart of darkness in the human soul. So did I. When I read the typical novels of female adolescence like *Madame Bovary* or *Wuthering Heights* or, on a less lofty note, *Of Human Bondage*, Freud was there with me. He talked about the aspects of human nature known so well to me and so ignored by my parents and teachers. When a friend brought out an unexpected treasure from her mother's bureau drawer, our surreptitious reading of *Lady Chatterley's Lover* was viewed from beyond not by God but by Freud. My guilt was minimal, my curiosity unbounded. And Freud gave me permission to search and know everything, not just the good things. Not just the easy things. He taught me there was no love without hate, no ecstasy without angst, no wisdom without suffering. I was hooked.

Amateur psychoanalysis became a central part of my life and filled a need I had to be needed. My parents weren't good at giving their children responsibilities and then rewarding them for doing well. As a child I had no responsibilities whatsoever. I was the only girl I knew who *asked* to do the dishes—and was refused. I acquired a burning need to feel competent—to feel that I was making a contribution to the family. In my mind, the only thing I seemed to offer that was valued and accepted was my ability to quickly understand others' feelings and be comforting. My mother also enjoyed my sense of humor and took great joy in my teasing, playfulness, and ease in imitating others. Suffering as she was at times from agoraphobia, I brought the world to her through my active social life and skills as a storyteller.

I had the potential for a number of different vocations. And at different periods of my life I considered many alternatives. My teachers wanted me to be a teacher. And my idealization of them, and of the learning process, influenced me very much. I also liked the idea of bringing knowledge to others, knowing how much it meant to me to learn.

At times I thought of being a stand-up comedian because I was so good at making people laugh, and because the gift of laughter seemed magical. But when I considered this option I realized quickly that the reality of making people laugh meant working late at night in sleazy bars. So much for the magic.

Naturally, I also thought of becoming a psychoanalyst, but rarely told anyone this. Racine, Wisconsin, was not exactly a hotbed of intellectual activity and most people either didn't know what a psychoanalyst was or thought it odd that a young girl would even consider such a thing. When I was in the ninth grade we were all assigned a "career paper." The object, of course, was to choose a potential career path, find out everything we could about it, and then write a report. Toward this end, the school librarian had books, pamphlets, magazine articles, and government reports to aid us in our search.

On the day we were to do our research the librarian had spread out all of these materials on the counters and library tables, with little stenciled signs indicating which pile belonged to what occupation. ARCHITECT, TEACHER, SOCIAL WORKER, BUILDING TRADES, and dozens of others were in plain view. I asked the librarian where I might find out something about being a psychoanalyst. He chuckled with obvious amusement, then asked why I wanted to know about that.

I informed him that I had been reading Freud and wanted to become a psychoanalyst. The librarian laughed out loud this time, but stopped when he saw the hurt and anger on my face. He turned serious and said he didn't think he had any materials on psychoanalysis, but he would see what he could dig up for me. He said it might take some time and asked if there was anything else I was interested in. I reluctantly admitted that I was interested in teaching, thinking he was simply distracting me. He directed me to the table with the information on secondary-school teaching, suggesting I write that up as a career in case the materials on psychoanalysis didn't arrive in time for me to meet my deadline. If they did, he said, I could simply have two career papers.

I said all right because I didn't think I had much choice. At this point I didn't have a lot of faith in the school librarian. He found the whole notion far too amusing for me to believe he was really going to help me. But the next week I received a note telling me to come to the library. And, sure enough, he had pamphlets from two psychoanalytic institutes outlining the requirements. When he gave them to me I was overjoyed. I pored over them immediately, my heart racing. Then, just as suddenly, my joy hit the library floor with a thud. Although I was prepared to see stiff educational requirements—I knew that just anyone couldn't be a psychoanalyst; that was part of the appeal—my disappointment was beyond expression when I read the word *physician*. I looked again to make sure there wasn't some alternative. There wasn't. So I threw that pamphlet on the table and rushed to the next one. Once again I saw that word. *Physician*. It said more, of course. It talked about a residency in psychiatry. About the courses that were to be taken over a period of years. The "control cases." But none of that mattered. I hated science. I was lousy at it. I hated hospitals. And the thought of blood and cutting into a living human being made me nauseous. In that moment I knew that if I had to be a physician, I would never be a psychoanalyst.

I wrote it all up for my career paper anyway, with the faint hope that something might change by the time I went to college. But it didn't. Psychology wasn't a good option because psychologists at my school were mostly doing cognition experiments and running rats through mazes. When I thought of doing that, stand-up comedy started looking good. So, teaching it was.

But as the Buddhists say, when the student is ready the teacher appears. Not only did Freud make an appearance during my adolescence, Rogers, Laing, May, and Maslow made their reputations while I was in college, giving me something more philosophical to read and think about. And the English department in the small liberal arts college I attended turned out to be heavily into psychoanalytic literary criticism and character study. Film study was required and was also approached psychoanalytically. I dropped my math major and graduated in English and secondary education.

I lasted two years in the public school system. And, once again, what I discovered was that I loved talking to my students and helping them find out about themselves. I had them write journals and gave theme assignments that steered them toward integrating what they read with their own life experience. Soon many of them were asking to talk to me on their lunch hour or after school and my colleagues were encouraging me to become a school counselor.

I left teaching and went for a master's in counseling. But I quickly realized I was never to return to the public school system. When I was halfway through I knew I wanted to get my Ph.D. and become a psychologist. I didn't go on immediately because I didn't have the money. I worked at Marquette University Counseling Center for two years, then went on to Michigan State because they taught psychoanalysis there.

I completed my doctorate and returned to Milwaukee. Soon I began a five-year commute from Milwaukee to Chicago for my psychoanalysis, and bootlegged training from analysts in Chicago and Milwaukee. By the time the landmark lawsuit was passed and Ph.D.s could be admitted to the analytic institutes, I was already approaching two-person analysis and middle age. I wanted to write and the two-person viewpoint was distinctly unpopular at that time. Getting published in the journals was almost impossible. Hiding what I believed in so I could get through an analytic training program was unthinkable. Besides, I didn't have that much free time, and more than anything I wanted to write.

So I have pursued my private practice and my writing in my own way. People often ask me how I am able to be creative working in Milwaukee. And I answer that I enjoy fewer demands to earn a great deal of money, and am free from any influence. Here I am able to think on my own. Nothing is really in vogue here. Nothing is de rigueur. I continue on the path that I started as an adolescent. Independent and rebellious, I make my own way and find that if I follow my heart most of what comes along is right for me.

As I reflect on the title of this essay, I note that I have spoken briefly of sex and much of psychoanalysis, but not at all of lies. So, where are my lies, I ask myself. Did I not choose this title because I knew I would lie? I knew that for everything I said about myself and my becoming a psychotherapist, there would be something I was hiding.

If I look deep inside myself I know what I have hidden. I have hidden the details of just how unhappy my mother was at different periods in my life and how heartbreaking this was for me. I have hidden how I would have done anything to make her life happier. I have hidden how guilty I've always felt for being more successful than anyone else in my family.

I have not mentioned the specifics regarding my feeling different from other children, in spite of being accepted and liked. Most well-adjusted children would not have the need to search out Freud at such a young age. I wanted and needed to know how I was different. After an agonizing late adolescence and early adulthood, I finally came to the realization that I was gay. I was different in a way that was permanent.

If this were not enough, there are more lies, more secrets, more things left unsaid. I have mentioned my absolute joy in the pursuit of learning psychoanalysis. I have hinted at, but not said, that this joy extended to the work of doing therapy. I have been a therapist for twenty years and, like most good marriages, the first ten years were filled with discovery and a growing self-efficacy. I loved being a therapist and loved doing it well.

But as I approach my fiftieth year I find that I have grown weary of the struggle. I think that I have been altered by the repeated engagements with my patients—that I truly have been transformed in many ways as I helped them to transform themselves. But after a certain point in life, it is enough. Perhaps this is a normal developmental stage. Perhaps it reflects the extent to which I have succeeded in my personal odyssey. Perhaps I am less tolerant than I once was. The most likely answer involves all these things. As a result, I am less enthusiastic about treating difficult patients.

Every time a troubled person regresses and moves into the inevitable state of ambivalent attachment to me, I sigh with the knowledge of what this will mean. I am tired of being accused of unfairness, lack of understanding, lack of love, and falling pitifully short of the longed-for "good mother." Never mind that the patient is simply expressing what she felt toward her own mother. Never mind that this is something she needs to work through. Never mind that I fully understand that this is what a good treatment is all about. It's a lousy way to spend a day.

These days my favorite patients are the ones with enough ego strength to tell me when they feel hurt or angry or disappointed, but who do so within the boundaries of normal behavior. They don't yell. They don't make unreasonable demands. They attend religiously and pay their bills. And they inspire me to help them through their pain and struggle to find themselves. When I feel for them and even weep with them, they feel loved, and sometimes unworthy, but not suspicious.

Yes, I know. Everyone wants to treat patients like this. And they are increasingly hard to come by. We are more likely to treat those who cannot go on without intensive psychotherapy. With no more insurance benefits, the less troubled go without, unless they are very rich. So we see a greater percentage of the walking wounded and the pressures of outpatient practice increase incrementally.

I don't mean to make myself sound old and without energy. I am neither. I love working with the patients who have a decent prognosis. I enjoy teaching and supervision. And I am ecstatic when I have the time to write. I work very hard and take pleasure in being productive. But my priorities have changed. My main interest in life is not the lives of others. It is my own. I don't want there to be a day, let alone weeks, when I have no time to look at what *I'm* thinking or what *I'm* feeling, or what *I* want to do next with my life. I don't want the focus of every day to be what other people are thinking and feeling. And I don't want to feel like a dispenser or a life support system.

Toward this end, I keep developing techniques for a two-person psychology, which frees me up as well as freeing up my patients. To the extent that I can be honest and forthcoming with my patients while facilitating their growth, I have less need to escape them. More mutual relationships are better for them and better for me. Yet we all know that the therapeutic relationship is an essentially asymmetrical one. Consistent freedom of thought and expression for the therapist is not possible. This is a luxury that belongs only to the patient.

So I continue to work as a therapist, knowing that most of my motivations for becoming one have diminished. I understand myself fairly well and have came to terms with my homosexuality and the subsequent limitations of my life. I care deeply about my patients and look forward to seeing many of them. I am proud of my skills and what I have learned. I feel very good when others tell me that my writing about psychotherapy has helped them to do it better. And I look forward to many more years of doing psychotherapy and writing about it. But if I had children, I would not want them to be therapists. I would wish something easier for them.

At times I have thought of doing something else. Something easier. But whenever I consider other careers I know they are not for me. There is something wrong with everything else. Other jobs either focus too much on money, or don't pay enough. They are either too intellectual or not intellectual enough. Mostly, everything else seems unbearably superficial in one way or another.

One need of mine that is met by being a psychoanalytic psychotherapist is the need to address what is really important to me, and to do it every day of my life. Although I consider myself skilled at small talk, my appreciation of it is limited. My colleagues seem to feel the same way. At a recent analytic meeting some of us were sitting around talking, and all agreed that we were intimacy junkies. We never get tired of making that deep connection to our patients and our own primitive emotions.

For me, psychoanalysis is not a job. In some ways it seems to have much in common with my sexual orientation. That is, it often seems equally unchosen. It is not something I do six or eight hours a day. It is who I am. When I am not doing analysis, I am writing about it, or I am reading a novel from a psychoanalytic perspective. This same perspective informs everything I observe in the world, be it something within my own personal sphere or a *New York Times* headline. It permeates everything I do. It is my philosophy and my religion. It is a lens through which everything must pass. It is my life.

Karen J. Maroda, Ph.D., is Assistant Clinical Professor of Psychiatry, Medical College of Wisconsin.

REFERENCES

Freud, S. (1990). The interpretation of dreams. *Standard Edition* 5:339–627.
Maroda, K. J. (1994). *The Power of Countertransference: Innovations in Analytic Technique.* New York: Jason Aronson.

22

A Psychotherapist in France

AGNÈS OPPENHEIMER

As far as I can remember, I have always been curious, in search of the truth. But truth is more of an adolescent concept; the childhood equivalent is fairness or justice.

True and false pertained to religious beliefs for me. Born of a mixed Jewish and Catholic origin, I was raised a Catholic. I questioned the very existence of God at the time of my confirmation, the first year in secondary school. It was also the first year without my governess, and the marriage and departure of my sister, twelve years older than me. Solitude and loneliness led to distrust, pain, and intellectual inhibition. I was sent to a Catholic school and to psychotherapy with Serge Lebovici. Looking back, I can trace my vocation as a psychoanalyst to that experience.

The double Jewish–Catholic origin was linked for me to some contradictions I observed in my environment and discovered in myself. My mother, a prominent literary figure, a novelist and the founder-editor of a high-brow review, thought herself to be modern and liberated. She put me in a Montessori school where I was unhappy and did not improve. I resented the requirement of going to a school where there were no requirements. You could either work or play; there was no structure.

Once I was a pupil, for a short period of time, at a school in a small village where we had a country house. My father was a congressman and this was his district. I have good memories of this school and my sister told me later that I was so happy to have to raise my hand to be called on, to feel the authority of the teacher.

My mother sent me to a private primary school and then, when she thought I needed it, to psychotherapy. She always said there was equality between the sexes, but she would not allow me to do the same things as my male friends. She was very much involved in intellectual pursuits and stressed that money was not important, but she would not allow me to play in the streets with poorer girls. I was revolted by her attitude and made no attempt to hide it.

I went three times a week to therapy. I said I did not like it. I complained, but I was interested in and, in fact, committed to my analysis. Lebovici was a classical Freudian analyst who specialized in children; at that time, he was already very well known and I knew it. This may have helped the paternal transference since my father was also very well known: a lawyer, a politician, and a statesman, twice prime minister, sent to China by De Gaulle. Lebovici and my father were both a little bald. Lebovici was probably ten years his junior, but what 10½-year-old would make that kind of distinction? I felt proud to go to see him. I complained to my school friends, probably out of guilt: I had to deny being interested in an older man. His interpretations made me sometimes ill at ease, but not those pertaining to my Oedipus or castration complex: I just laughed and denied them. I was, however, put off by those references to me as a young girl or an adolescent. Lebovici, like Freud, was matter-of-fact and called a spade a spade.

At the same time—I can say it now—he was very respectful of narcissism and even made a contribution to it. For instance, his office and apartment were on the third floor and I would take the elevator. Once, the concierge, a woman, told me I was not allowed to take the elevator alone because I was not 14, the required age for solos in elevators in France at that time. I complained to Lebovici and he replied that if the concierge mentioned it again, I was to tell her that it was OK for me to take the elevator alone and that she could check with him. I felt recognized for what I was, a very precocious girl. This experience may also have confirmed that I was special: it conferred a sense of entitlement because I was Lebovici's patient as I was Edgar Faure's daughter.

The second example of narcissistic bliss is the following: I had a girlfriend who also went to Lebovici and he asked her to undergo some testing. I asked him why he did not require me to take those tests. He replied that he was sure I was intelligent but he was not so sure about her!

He sometimes told me to let go and cry if I needed to. That suggestion was often appropriate but I would never allow myself to cry in front of him.

I benefited greatly from this treatment, which helped me a lot with my studies and anxieties. More than that, it fed my curiosity and I continued to read not only novels, as before, but essays, philosophy, and even some of Freud's writings.

The end of therapy was strange. As I remember, after three years, I said to Lebovici that I felt much better and mature enough to stop. At that time, I was going once or twice a week. He agreed with me and we stopped. Years later during my analysis, I reconstructed that I had been devastated by what I felt unconsciously as abandonment.

Two years later, I went with my parents to a cocktail party I knew Lebovici would attend and I looked forward to seeing him again. He was pleasant enough but did not pay as much attention to me as I thought he would and I was disappointed, a vestige of paternal transference or a displacement of the little interest my father would show in me. My father's interest would wane if our conversation was a bit long or if it did not address a topic of relevance to him.

What followed was like a latency period regarding analysis. Although I was still interested in psychoanalysis, I thought of going to law school. I ended up registering, at my mother's suggestion, for a college-level curriculum. I developed a passion for philosophy although I did not neglect psychoanalysis, which also became part of my studies. At that time, my sister was finishing medical school and soon after decided to specialize in psychiatry and psychoanalysis.

Preparing for my M.A. in philosophy during the student protests of May 1968, I attended Lacan's seminars. I had some difficulties studying and decided to undergo psychoanalysis. Two years before, my mother had advised me to do that; she had even sent me to an analyst, but I was not ready. This thoughtful analyst understood my reluctance and said that I was doing quite well in spite of my parents, an assessment I repeated to my bewildered mother.

When I was ready, I asked my mother for advice. She was a friend of Sacha Nacht, the director of the Institute of the Paris Psychoanalytic Society. He gave me a referral and I began. Even if I was fascinated by Lacan, I felt suspicious not only because of all that was said about him—the short sessions, among other things—but also because of this very fascination I felt. Also, I did not want another famous person like my father in my life.

Nineteen-sixty-eight was a special year for students in France, a time of revolt and protest. With my adolescent crisis well behind me and my interest in continental philosophy (especially Kant and Heidegger), I was not exactly in the mainstream of the student movement.

Moreover my parents were actors in this movement in different ways: my father as a politician was very closely involved while my mother endorsed it. I felt that they were involved in my place and this caused me to ignore the whole scene.

After the crisis, my father was appointed Minister of Education. It was really unpleasant being a student at the same time. Anyway, I invested a lot in my analysis, and the transference neurosis along with studies, friendship, and love relationships must have taken all my energy and helped me to put some distance between me and my father's role.

This analysis, which lasted six and a half years, repeated something of the therapy as a deferred action. My vocation as an analyst was renewed. Contrary to the opinion of some, analysis was not a cold and totally silent business. My analyst was certainly neutral, but I felt a sense of warmth and interest.

Another word about my vocation and passion for psychoanalysis rather than psychotherapy: the desire to become a psychotherapist emphasizes the desire to help, to cure. I think that desire still exists even if one has to distance oneself in order to be an analyst. I have always thought there were two kinds of therapists, according to their own background: those who try to cure their dysfunctional parents and those who try to cure themselves. The two tendencies are sometimes hard to distinguish.

Whenever I tried to help friends, I would try to find solutions for them. I always treated friends as I treat myself, fortifying them more than empathizing. Psychoanalysis goes beyond helping in a specific way. The neutral stance means not being involved with one particular aspect of the patient, but being concerned, allowing some latitude in searching for the truth, discovering unconscious processes through transference. Psychoanalysis, then, departs profoundly from reparative or restoring tendencies, which therapists nevertheless have also to analyze and work through.

I decided I wanted to be a psychoanalyst, to transmit what I had received and discovered. At first, I was afraid to tell my analyst but finally I did; it took time to analyze this desire. To test it, I decided to undergo psychological studies involving internships to monitor my feelings.

I called Lebovici who ran the best mental health center in town, organizing seminars, consultations, psychotherapy training. I was able to attend consultations, and two years later I had an interview with him—a reparation for what happened at the cocktail party. He said, "You want to become a child analyst. OK. You'll have to become a training candidate at the institute and ask for selection interviews. Meanwhile, you can train here for child therapy." I thanked him and accepted. I knew I would not be a child analyst for life, but I was interested in the training.

This acknowledgment felt too good to be true; it was too much and I had to work on it in my analysis. Later on, Lebovici offered to supervise me, if I felt comfortable with him "since," he said, "we have had a long relationship together." I was very grateful. He supervised two of my cases, helping me in one case discover the hidden elements of transference neurosis in a child. The second case was more complicated, involving pregenital and bisexual tendencies. Meanwhile, I attended a collective supervision of psychotic and borderline cases with other supervisors.

When I became a candidate, it was Lebovici who told me I had been accepted. At the same time, I obtained a real job in the same center but in other psychoanalysts' teams. My sister was already a member of the Paris Psychoanalytic Society where I was a candidate. We had long discussions about our common vocation and the different routes we took to get there.

Training in France has been a very good experience. The supervisors were very different from one another and very helpful. André Green, who supervised me in a collective group, was very generous and committed, and offered a great deal of understanding and interpretation. He was and still is a charismatic figure.

An early case was a very silent and difficult borderline woman. I was lucky to have a supervisor who was not only imaginative and helpful but who also encouraged my freedom of spirit.

During my training, I obtained a Ph.D.; my dissertation, under the direction of Jean Laplanche, was a discussion of Robert Stoller's theories on gender identity, an example of my everlasting curiosity with extraordinary phenomena like transsexualism, reviving the old issues of true and false and double identity. My book on gender identity came out at the same time that I became an associate member of the Paris Psychoanalytic Society in 1980. I continued to attend some Lacanian conferences out of curiosity and to avoid getting into a rut.

The confluence of my interest in exploring the study of identity and the treatment of difficult patients led me to read a lot of psychoanalytic writings: Bion, Searles, Bleger, Kernberg, Kohut, and so on.

Since I wanted to obtain a more permanent position at the university where I was a lecturer, I decided to study the notion of identity, which was the foundation of the notion of gender identity. Reading Lichtenstein, I had to go back to ego psychology to understand American trends in psychoanalysis and I began to read analytic philosophers as well.

In France, the psychoanalytic approach is different from ego psychology; it is more of a classical return to Freud, influenced by Lacan. One does need to choose between a natural science or hermeneutic approach, a drive or an object-relations perspective. Some authors like Green and Laplanche each in their own way have offered a way of conceiving the dialectic relation between intrapsychic reality and intersubjective stance.

I never thought difficult patients were just resisting; I questioned my own listening, technique, and theories. Reading Kernberg was helpful and gave me a pleasant, even narcissistic, impression of mastery; he could be a model of identification.

Reading Kohut gave me a totally different experience, a kind of discovery. Intellectually speaking, I agreed about the patient's being right, the Popperian idea, as I see it, that psychoanalysis is eliminating false theories by trial and error. But emotionally speaking, empathy was a talent I had to develop in myself.

I still teach a lot of Kernberg because, in my opinion, Kernberg and Kohut's cases are not the same and both approaches are helpful. I attended self psychology conferences for years in order to deepen my empathic understanding, and I wrote a book on Kohut and self psychology. If I do not identify myself as Kohutian—and even less as a self psychologist—I agree with his idea of an everlasting method as opposed to transitory theories. Being a self psychologist seems to me anti-Kohutian.

I have my own interpretation of empathy, the ongoing search for eliminating inappropriate understanding. The use of empathy is only negative like the philosophy of pure reason in Kant's *Critique of Pure Reason*, "a discipline for the limitations" which "instead of discovering truth, has only the modest merit of guarding against error." The experience of empathy, being understood or being told by the other that he or she feels understood, has been a real discovery. Even if I had experienced it, I never articulated its importance in treatment and in life before I read Kohut.

I think that an analyst does not adhere at random to theories, and this chapter for me is an opportunity to try to articulate my thoughts and feelings. Theories stem from unconscious and conscious fantasies—pathogenesis; they have to be questioned. One can choose a theory because one feels an affinity for it or because one feels alien to it. I have never chosen any particular post-Freudian theory as a unique framework. I think that each theory is Janus-faced, a discovery and a resistance, showing one side of the coin to the exclusion of the other.

The history of theories is like analysis—an opening and closing of unconscious processes. Observing the evolution is part of self-analysis. I study some authors in depth, take what seems useful and integrate it, constructing my own metapsychology, which may not be without contradictions, like the human mind and the unconscious. I have my own reading of Freud, enriched especially by Jean Laplanche.

My practice is mainly psychoanalysis and psychotherapy of adolescents and adults, some depressed and narcissistic disorders besides classical neurosis. I still work with transsexuals and I do supervision as well. Being conversant with lots of theories, I became aware of their potential. But I have also discovered my own style. This broad interest shows my continuing curiosity. Accepting contradictions, trying to deal dialectically with them, is a political stance that may parallel my father's Popperian view of history. My double origin, which could be assimilated to the processing of bisexuality, may have something to do with the apparent paradoxes it contains; the principle of complementarity could legitimize such a position, which is not eclectic but an open-ended search.

Agnès Oppenheimer, Ph.D., was a Training and Supervising Analyst at the Paris Psychoanalytical Society. She died, unexpectedly, in 1997.

23

How I Solved the Problem of Not Lying about Becoming a Psychotherapist

GAIL S. REED

I have never thought of myself as a psychotherapist. When I do psychotherapy, something I do when psychotherapy is the treatment most beneficial to someone, I think of myself as a psychoanalyst who has decided on psychoanalytic grounds to work in psychotherapy with another person. But in my deepest professional identity, to myself, I am always a psychoanalyst.

Not only that. I think of myself as a contemporary Freudian psychoanalyst. Today, that's like declaring oneself to be a Communist in the 1950s, an invitation to the blacklist. So you could say that I make my living standing up for something unpopular.

How did I become an analyst? Whoever knows one's unconscious completely? My first psychoanalytic paper was on a novel by the eighteenth-century French philosopher Denis Diderot who defied the monarchy to publish an encyclopedia. I'd loved Diderot for years, particularly this novel, *James the Fatalist*, as it is called in English. In it, Diderot made the reader conscious, again and again, of the latter's tendency to believe in illusion. He described two men, a master and his servant, traveling together talking, a common picaresque convention. But he wouldn't divulge the destination as was usually done. Instead, he had the narrator respond as if the reader had asked him where the two protagonists were going. The narrator would then answer as I did, "Who knows? Does a person ever know where he is going?" Diderot caught readers off guard by undermining the fictional conventions earlier novels had conditioned them to expect.

Diderot was actually putting into practice, more brusquely and provocatively, of course, a process between author and reader similar in certain respects to that between analyst and patient. I enjoyed the disequilibration and the self-revelation about expectation that followed. Cervantes was doing the same thing, more gently and complexly, a century earlier. So you could say that the great writers were my first psychoanalytic teachers. Diderot knew a great deal about the mechanisms of our psyches. And, as Freud later discovered, he already knew many of the basic truths of the unconscious. If a child were given complete liberty, he once wrote, he would murder his father and sleep with his mother.

The particular unconscious of each of us, with its fantasies of incest, ghosts returned from the dead to extract vengeance, cannibalism, and more, is the most individual and defining thing about each of us. But besides the internal nightmare these unconscious thoughts can create in us, we are currently living a real nightmare: a tank with a sign "for profit only" rolls over people, one at a time, inexorably. It won't stop. It is corporate downsizing, managed-care regulations on mental health treatment, and the systematic attack on culture and the individual.

In grade school we heard that the Hungarian people had risen up against Russian Communism, that "other" inexorable force that supposedly crushed individuality. The Hungarians made hand grenades and threw them at those tanks. It seemed a glorious, heroic moment. When the tanks came on anyway, the moment died. Nothing, it seemed, as the United States stood by, could stop that inexorable progress that would crush us all.

And yet, and yet. We didn't know that the Hungarian Psychoanalytic Society existed and was working underground, literally saving souls. In Czechoslovakia, too, underground training in psychoanalysis was going on. Underground training went on in the United States, too, when physicians attempted to shut out others wanting to become psychoanalysts. Nothing to splash on tabloid headlines, or profit sheets. More like drips of a faucet eroding authoritarianism, drips that refused to be shut off. Of course, like everything, it can be grossly misused, as recent history in Brazil shows. There the student of a former Nazi from the Goering Institute took on a torturer as a candidate. But misuse, even gross institutional misuse, cannot obscure the power psychoanalysis has to liberate the individual. There is always a chance psychoanalysis will have to go underground in our profit-fixated times. It would be nice if we could exchange our despair at being misunderstood by the times and feel honored to have the knowledge to carry forth that flickering torch.

Psychoanalysis comes from extremely revolutionary roots. The help it can give is real. The hope it holds out is likewise real. Nothing is more irrepressible than the truth that the unconscious exists. The responsibility we have to future generations is to keep knowledge of it alive so that there is the slim shred of a chance that somewhere the forces that drive it and us will not *only* be acted out.

I was working on a doctorate in comparative literature and was teaching English. I discovered that the students and their minds interested me much more than writing another obscure interpretation of a piece of the Western canon. So many of the students seemed mysteriously trapped by their minds, inhibited from using their gifts. If you hear a rescue fantasy in all this, you would, of course, not be mistaken.

But that would leave out the pleasure and passion of the work. Once I discovered my passion and discovered, personally, the power of psychoanalysis to free me from inhibitions and knots and suffering, becoming a psychoanalyst was the easy part. It only took perseverance and lots of hard work. If you feel passionate about something, obstacles of the sort that confronted me as someone with no previous clinical training in the climate set by the medically dominated official psychoanalysis from which I was excluded did not seem insuperable. They weren't. Partly that was because others had come before me and alternate systems of training were in place. Partly that was because things were already changing. Mostly it was because I had found what I wanted to do.

But as any psychoanalyst knows, accounts of external motivations are half truths, at best. The psychoanalyst particularly has a responsibility to herself and to patients—past, present, and potential—not to engage in a spiritual striptease. I can, but shall not, tell you more about why I became an analyst. The answer would be irrelevant in any case. What is relevant is that each of us has his or her own motives. None is pure. None is self-effacing. In the best of cases, we subordinate them to the task of helping people understand themselves.

Gail S. Reed, Ph.D., is a Training and Supervising Analyst at the New York Freudian Society and the National Psychological Association of Psychoanalysis (NPAP) and a member of the Institute for Psychoanalytic Training and Research (IPTAR).

24

Cycles in the Life of One Psychotherapist

SEBASTIANO SANTOSTEFANO

Initially, my familial and cultural background, an immigrant Sicilian family with deep roots in a mountainous village, struck me as an unlikely source of my becoming a psychotherapist. But over the years I have reflected on various experiences that gradually guided me into careers in psychotherapy and psychoanalysis, while simultaneously maintaining a commitment to clinical research. Paraphrasing Thomas Wolf and Sigmund Freud, a person is the sum of all the moments of her/his life; all that is in the individual is in them. In what follows, I share some of these moments.

INFANCY AND CHILDHOOD

Solutions to the Storms of Life

It was a late, summer afternoon. I was 5 years old. Dark clouds rolled in the sky as a torrential rain pounded against the small patch of ground, trash cans, and fence that stood just outside the open door of our apartment, located at the rear of a tenement building. My siblings and I were huddled around the radio listening to the latest episode of "*Jack Armstrong*." My mother was busy preparing dinner. Taking a breath of fresh air, and silhouetted by the silver-gray sky, my father stood at the doorway. Suddenly, in our native Sicilian dialect, he called out to us to come quickly, so we could see a marvel of nature at work. As we huddled around the doorway, he directed our attention to an area of tall grass and weeds in the corner of the fence. There stood a large cat, and from her mouth dangled a very small kitten by the back of its neck. With one paw raised, the cat turned its head from side to side, frantically looking for a safe haven from the downpour. Suddenly the cat raced across the patch of ground through the rain and into a barrel that had tipped over. The cat emerged from the barrel without the kitten, ran to the corner of the fence, picked up another kitten buried in the tall weeds, and again raced to the barrel. She repeated this several times. As we marveled, my father commented that there were always solutions to the storms of life if we took time to find them.

Solving a Puzzle—the Tangle of Conflict

We were all seated at the kitchen table, after one of our typical meals, debating, laughing, and sharing stories. My oldest sister, reminding my mother that she had been wondering what we were learning in school, announced that she had something to show us. With this, she dramatically set down a puzzle she had obtained at the school's toy-lending library: two long nails twisted together as pretzels. Challenging my mother, my sister noted that if the two nails were manipulated in the right way, they could be untangled. My mother studied the tangle for what seemed a long time. Then she picked up the nails, and after several twists and turns of her wrists, held up the pretzeled nails, each freed from the tangle. As we burst into cheers, my father noted that there is a solution for every "imbroglio," or tangle.

An Office in the Home

Apparently my father was good at finding solutions to tangles. Our street, and the neighboring streets, were populated by immigrants from two neighboring villages in Sicily. Each Sunday afternoon neighbors visited our apartment: sometimes a husband and wife, sometimes a father and son or daughter, sometimes a group of relatives. Sometimes they came holding documents. These visitors took turns sitting in our small parlor, usually talking softly, and at times engaging in intense arguments. My father, I learned later, continued providing a community service that his father had provided in the village: negotiating disputes and solving family problems. Many years later, while engaged in my personal psychoanalytic treatment and training, I became very interested in arranging an office in my home where I could conduct therapy. While it was customary for some psychoanalysts to have offices in their homes, my interest in this arrangement was intense and overdetermined. My analyst helped me realize the roots of this interest—that I would continue from my father as he had from his.

Victor, My First Therapy Patient

I was in second grade. My brothers and I were leaping about playfully with our cousin Victor on the third story of an outdoor fire escape. Exactly what happened is a blur, but suddenly Victor tumbled over the railing, striking his head on the sidewalk below. He lay there limp, blood oozing from his curly hair, ears, and nose. We ran to get his parents and ours. They wrapped Victor's head in a towel and raced off. We did not see Victor for a long time. When we asked about him, we were told that doctors were helping him get better. Then one day Victor returned, but he was not the same. He could not talk, but grunted and waved his arms, and he seemed tuned out and far away. Each day when I returned from school, I went to Victor's apartment. Soon he began to recognize me, greeting me with excited grunts and hand flapping. I sat next to him on the floor, day after day, and showed him pictures from my schoolbooks or from magazines, explaining what they were or making up stories. I have no doubt Victor enjoyed our meetings. As the years passed, Victor became more difficult to manage. When he turned 11 years old, he was placed in a state facility. My parents explained that there Victor would receive the care he needed. We visited him on occasion, and I always took a book with me to show him.

EARLY ADOLESCENCE

More than Restraint as a Solution to Personal Difficulties

After completing high school, I enlisted in the United States Army because the draft was still active, although World War II had already ended. I was trained to be a medic and assigned to a station hospital, eventually working on a unit reserved for those who had developed severe emotional problems. Of the many experiences that exerted an influence, two should be mentioned. The unit was a barracks-like building surrounded by a barbed-wire fence so that patients could walk about without wandering off. That they were caged in this way always troubled me. One day I asked eight or so of the soldiers if they wanted to take a walk. They responded with excitement, and we took a walk to the laundry unit. When I came out carrying a bundle of bed sheets, I learned that one of the soldiers had run off. After I called the MPs, we returned to our unit. Soon I was informed that the colonel wanted to see me. Standing before him with considerable anxiety, I tried to explain that I thought it would help the patients if they could do something other than receive medication and mill about outdoors, surrounded by barbed wire. Fortunately, this colonel was understanding. He gave me permission to organize work details but cautioned me to keep the groups small.

The Power of the Unconscious

In the second episode, a young man was brought in on a stretcher because he could not walk. The psychiatrist informed me that nothing neurological had been discovered to account for the soldier's immobility and asked me to prepare a syringe with sodium amytal, which he slowly injected into a vein in the soldier's arm. Then he conducted an interview. I stood there transfixed with fascination. Under the influence of the drug, the soldier revealed that he was soon to be discharged and married, but he realized that he did not want to go through with it. When told by the psychiatrist that his legs were fine, the man stood up, took several steps, and then lay down again. When the sodium amytol wore off, he woke up but could not move his legs. The psychiatrist, a very pleasant person who enjoyed teaching us, explained to me how an unconscious conflict could affect a person's behaviors, a notion I had not to that point articulated intellectually.

Action as Insight

From my military service I entered the pre-med program at the University of Connecticut. Discovering I was interested more in psychology and philosophy than anatomy and chemistry, I switched to a major in psychology. In that program at the time, behaviorism and animal research were emphasized, leaving me with the nagging feeling that the dilemmas of life, some of which I had experienced in my own childhood and later in the military, were not being addressed. Yet I was fascinated by experiments of Gestalt psychology. Familiar to some, one classic experiment went something like this: a monkey was placed in a cage, along with a stick and chair. A banana hung out of reach on a string from the ceiling. Running about and leaping, the monkey swung the stick at the banana but to no avail. The monkey also stood on the chair and reached up but still could not retrieve the banana. After many such efforts, the "sacred moment" of insight came. The monkey stood on the chair, stick in hand, reached up and easily obtained the banana. Experiments such as these stirred up what were then vague notions about the relation between action and insight and the importance of coordinating actions, and their meanings, with cognitive activity, notions that would surface in graduate school and eventually find their way into my views concerning psychotherapy with children.

LATE ADOLESCENCE

In 1953 I enrolled in the doctoral program in clinical psychology at Pennsylvania State University. Of many experiences, one in particular forged the initial shape of my formal interest in psychotherapy. Professor William Snyder, in collaboration with the University Health Service, assigned each student four treatment cases, undergraduates who had applied for psychotherapy. He requested that we conduct therapy with two cases following the guidelines of Carl Rogers's nondirected approach, which was a dominant method at the time. With the other cases, we were to conduct "more directed and interpretive" psychodynamic therapy, another approach that was dominant at the time. We submitted typed transcripts of each session (a few recorded and most reconstructed). Professor Snyder meticulously wrote notes in the margin of our transcripts, pointing out whether we were conducting therapy within the assigned approach or deviating from it. Comparing experiences conducting different psychotherapies influenced my interest not only in becoming a therapist but also in learning more about psychodynamics and unconscious meanings that influenced a person's difficulties.

My course work and supervision with Professor Snyder elaborated a related interest that stemmed from my cultural roots, which, in addition to attending to what a person said, also focused on actions and gestures and the meanings underlying them, an interest that was first piqued by the monkey experiments I learned about in my undergraduate studies. One of my cases, a member of the varsity wrestling team, from time to time asked to walk about outside or sit on the steps. I noticed that thoughts and feelings that he experienced when walking about were different from those he experienced when sitting in the office. And I noticed that particular memories about his mother occurred to him when he repeatedly rubbed the palm of his hand against the cement steps. In our supervision, Professor Snyder, representing the prevailing view (still maintained in many quarters) that therapy should take place only in an office, advised me to explore why I went outside. But he did listen to my wondering whether there was more to what happens in therapy than the reflections and interpretations of a therapist. Influenced by such questions, I conducted research for my doctoral dissertation on the topic of actions as measures of personality (Santostefano 1960, 1962). This line of inquiry led to a number of studies exploring the role of actions/situations in the meanings a person experienced (e.g., Santostefano 1965a, 1968a) and the relation between action, fantasy, and spoken language (e.g., Santostefano 1965b, 1968a,b, 1977). I will have more to say about these initial research projects later.

By the time I received my doctorate, my interests had centered on learning about development and psychodynamic psychotherapy with children, in part, I believe, because of my childhood experiences with Victor. In addition, I had been impressed by the developmentalist, G. Stanley Hall, who proposed in 1889 that research should address questions suggested by clinical problems, and by Shepherd Ivory Franz, who launched one of the first psychology laboratories devoted to the study of clinical problems (Santostefano 1976). To pursue a career as a child therapist and researcher, I enrolled in 1957 in a two-year postdoctoral program in clinical child psychology at the University of Colorado Medical Center. There I studied with a number of psychoanalysts who were also developmental researchers: John Benjamin, Gaston Blom, John Conger, David Metcalf, and René Spitz. Participating in several research projects, I had the opportunity to continue my interest in the meanings of actions and gestures. As one example, in a study of monozygotic twin children, I asked each twin (with the other absent) to stand on one of two wooden boxes that were identical with the exception that one box was half the height of the other. The actions the children took predicted which twin was dominant and which deferent in their twin relationship as determined later by treatment sessions.

In addition, with the benefit of a National Institute of Mental Health (NIMH) Career Teacher Award, I spent time with George Klein and David Rapaport, two psychologist-psychoanalysts. These tutorials sparked my interest in understanding cognitive functioning within personality and development, an interest that also led to a series of preliminary studies (e.g., Santostefano 1964a,b).

At the same time I was receiving intensive supervision in child psychotherapy. However, my studies of the relations among action, cognition, meaning, and development continually impacted what I did in treatment sessions, which, in one sense, continued what I had been wondering in graduate school when discussing my treatment of the university wrestler with Professor Snyder. As one example, I began twice-weekly sessions with Albert in the best way I knew at the time and within the psychoanalytic tradition to which I had already made a commitment. I entered each session sustained by the conviction that if I could help this boy successfully resolve his unconscious conflicts, he would perform better in the classroom and at home. However, as treatment progressed, I noticed behaviors that suggested to me that whatever else troubled this boy, he simply was not experiencing stimulation around him, stimulation that I took for granted he was taking for granted. For example, when he touched surfaces of different textures, he did not spontaneously show signs that he was aware of the differences. In another instance, when we entered the playroom one day, he did not react to the fact that furniture and play material had been completely rearranged by housekeeping staff since our last session. I found myself wondering whether what I was observing was related to the fact that his mother was hospitalized for six months before he reached his second birthday. At that time, in the psychoanalytic camp, little attention was paid to the significance for psychotherapy of the first two years of life, since the focus was on the years beyond age 4 and how a child resolved her/his oedipal conflict. A radical change has occurred since that time in how psychoanalytic workers view infancy (e.g., Lichtenberg 1983, Stern 1985).

Now and then I interrupted my nondirected format and asked Albert to join me in various activities. For example, we went outside to have a "feeling contest." I closed my eyes and Albert placed my fingers on one of the bricks that made up the wall surrounding the clinic. Then he lifted my hand away and again placed my fingers on a brick. My job was to decide whether I was feeling the same or a different brick. Then Albert took a turn. And whenever Albert stepped out of his robotic mode, I took him outside and set up a series of contests, each requiring a different degree of assertiveness and delay (e.g., hurling tennis balls at a tree trunk and lobbing them into a wastebasket).

When I reviewed these sessions with my supervisor, he became puzzled and annoyed. I will never forget one of his comments: "I don't know what you're doing; but I *do* know that what you're doing is not psychotherapy." I asked to review my therapeutic work with other supervisors. Fortunately, these psychoanalysts were involved in developmental research and understood what I was groping to understand.

EARLY ADULTHOOD

Stimulated by these clinical and research experiences, I enrolled in the

Boston Psychoanalytic Institute in 1964 for training in psychoanalysis and simultaneously assumed a position on the faculty at Clark University, the home of Heinz Werner. There I learned a great deal from Seymour Wapner and other colleagues about the organismic-developmental viewpoint, which conceptualized relations among body experiences, cognition, and levels of development. In 1967 I joined the faculty of the Boston University School of Medicine. Holding discussions with two colleagues, Louis Sander and Gerald Stechler, were particularly meaningful because they were integrating psychoanalysis and infant research.

Experiences with the organismic-developmental viewpoint, psychoanalytically oriented infant research, and my own training in psychoanalysis converged, elaborating how I conceptualized the relations among body/action, cognition, and emotion (Santostefano 1977, 1986). These efforts influenced my initial proposals concerning treatment with children: clinicians should move beyond nosology and diagnose from the viewpoint of development (Santostefano 1971); principles of infant development could be a useful guide in conducting psychotherapy with children (Santostefano and Berkowitz 1976); and therapists should address cognitive functioning within personality (Santostefano 1980). By 1973, I completed my training in adult and child psychoanalysis and assumed a position as director of the Department of Child and Adolescent Psychology at McLean Hospital/Harvard Medical School. In the years that followed I continued conducting psychotherapy and psychoanalysis with children and adults and, at the same time, continued research on the relations among action, cognition, meanings, and emotion (Santostefano 1985b, Santostefano and Moncata 1989, Santostefano and Rieder 1984).

MIDDLE AGE

As my experiences conducting therapy continued to converge with research activities, I focused on constructing an integrative approach to psychotherapy with children. With my first attempts (Santostefano 1978, 1985a,b), I described a set of treatment guidelines and methods that integrated cognitive development and psychodynamic psychotherapy. To aid in planning treatment, I developed diagnostic test methods that assessed cognition and emotion as one (Santostefano 1986, 1988). While intended for practicing clinicians, I also reported studies of mothers using the methods at home with their retarded children, studies that had their roots in my childhood experiences with my cousin Victor (Santostefano and Stayton 1967). I elaborated this approach (Santostefano and Calicchia 1992), emphasizing the relationship and enactments between child and therapist as the main catalysts for change, rather than interpretation and self-talk. I also reported a series of studies that illustrated the importance for psychotherapy of integrating, as one domain, embodied meanings, overt behavior, cognition, and emotion (Santostefano 1995). Most recently I have completed another revision (Santostefano 1998) that attempts to dissolve the boundaries that have been maintained for decades between psychodynamic, cognitive-behavioral, and developmental viewpoints. Child therapy techniques are described that integrate surface and deep behaviors and operationalize a treatment process between child and therapist as analogous to that which occurs between infant/child and caregiver.

I believe the roots of this integrative approach were formed by my earliest, personal experiences and subsequent professional training. These roots gave rise to branches that have articulated several issues concerning psychotherapy: that how a person thinks is as important as what a person thinks; that the relations among what a person does, fantasizes, and says, need to be understood, as well as relations between "deep" (unconscious) and "surface" (conscious) meanings; and that the main catalysts for change are dialectical interactions that occur between a therapist and patient, as they coauthor and share an intersubjective world within which discoveries are made, and each forges revisions in how he/she functions.

Sebastiano Santostefano, Ph.D., teaches at the Boston Psychoanalytic Institute and is Director of The Institute for Child and Adolescent Development.

REFERENCES

Lichtenberg, J. D. (1983). *Psychoanalysis and Infant Research*. Hillsdale, NJ: Erlbaum.

Santostefano, S. (1960). An explanation of performance measures of personality. *Journal of Clinical Psychology* 6:373–377.

———— (1962). Performance testing of personality. *Merrill-Palmer Quarterly of Behavior and Development* 8:83–97.

———— (1964a). Cognitive controls and exceptional states in children. *Journal of Clinical Psychology* 20:213–218.

———— (1964b). Development of cognitive controls in children. *Child Development* 35:939–949.

———— (1965a). Construct validity of the Miniature Situations Test: I. the performance of public school, orphaned, and brain-damaged children. *Journal of Clinical Psychology* 21:418–421.

———— (1965b). Relating self-report and overt behavior: the concepts of levels of modes for expressing motives. *Perceptual Motor Skills* 21:940.

———— (1968a). Miniature situations and methodological problems in parent–child interaction research. *Merrill-Palmer Quarterly of Behavior and Development* 14:285–312.

———— (1968b). Situational testing in personality assessment. In *International Encyclopedia of the Social Sciences*, ed. D. L. Sills, pp. 48–55. New York: Macmillan/Free Press.

———— (1971). Beyond nosology: diagnosis from the view-point of development. In *Perspectives in Child Psychopathology*, ed. H. E. Rie, pp. 130–177. New York: Aldine-Atherton.

———— (1976). Shepherd Ivory Franz: the father of research for clinical practice. *McLean Hospital Journal* 1:49–55.

———— (1977). Action, fantasy and language: developmental levels of ego organization in communicating drives and affects. In *Communicative Structures and Psychic Structures*, ed. N. Freeman and S. Grand, pp. 331–354. New York: Plenum.

———— (1978). *A Biodevelopmental Approach to Clinical Child Psychology: Cognitive Controls and Cognitive Control Therapy*. New York: Wiley.

———— (1980). Cognition in personality and the treatment process: a psychoanalytic view. *Psychoanalytic Study of the Child* 35:41–66. New Haven, CT: Yale University Press.

———— (1985a). *Cognitive Control Therapy with Children and Adolescents*. New York: Pergamon. Reprinted in 1995 under the title *Integrative Psychotherapy for Children and Adolescents with ADHD*. Northvale, NJ: Jason Aronson.

———— (1985b). Metaphor: an integration of action, fantasy, and language in development. *Imagination, Cognition, and Personality* 4:127–146.

——— (1986). Cognitive controls, metaphors and contexts: an approach to cognition and emotion. In *Thought and Emotion*, ed. D. Bearison and H. Zimiles, pp. 175–210. Hillsdale, NJ: Erlbaum.

——— (1988). *Cognitive Control Battery for Children and Adolescents.* Los Angeles, CA: Western Psychological Services.

——— (1995). Embodied meanings, cognition and emotion: probing how three are one. In *Rochester Symposium on Developmental Psychopathology. Vol. 6: Emotion, Cognition and Representation*, ed. D. Cicchetti and S. L. Toth, pp. 59–132. Rochester, NY: University of Rochester Press.

——— (1998). *A Handbook of Integrative Psychotherapies for Children and Adolescents.* Northvale, NJ: Jason Aronson.

Santostefano, S., and Berkowitz, S. (1976). Principles of infant development as a guide in the psychotherapeutic treatment of borderline and psychotic children. *McLean Hospital Journal* 1:236–261.

Santostefano, S., and Calicchia, J. (1992). Body image, relational psychoanalysis, and the construction of meaning: implications for treating aggressive children. *Development and Psychopathology* 4:655–678.

Santostefano, S., and Moncata, S. (1989). A psychoanalytic view of cognition within personality: cognitive dysfunctions and educating troubled youth. *Journal of Residential Treatment for Children and Youth* 6:41–62.

Santostefano, S., and Rieder, C. (1984). Cognitive controls and aggression in children: the concept of cognitive-affective balance. *Journal of Consulting and Clinical Psychology* 1:46–56.

Santostefano, S., and Stayton, S. (1967). Training the pre-school retarded child in focal attention: a program for parents. *American Journal of Orthopsychiatry* 37:732–742.

Stern, D. N. (1985). *The Interpersonal World of the Infant: A View from Psychoanalysis and Developmental Psychology.* New York: Basic Books.

25

On the Road: Vienna—Da Bronx—Vienna

MARTIN A. SCHULMAN

When Dr. Reppen invited me to contribute to *Why I Became a Psychotherapist,* it naturally led to a journey back to childhood, or, as Quentin Crisp calls it, "the deformative years." Interestingly enough, two analyses (with varying degrees of success, depending on whom you ask), years of self-analysis, and the obligations of relationships, parenting, and establishing a professional identity never really broached this seemingly obvious question: What was it that led me to become a therapist, an analyst, and a contemporary Freudian? I am grateful to Dr. Reppen for posing the question and helping on my journey of further self-exploration.

When I reconnoiter the terrain of growing up in the 1950s in the Bronx, little would indicate my future profession or identify. Psychoanalysis was unknown in my household and therefore unthinkable as a career. Coming from a progressive (the euphemisms of the McCarthy period still resonate in my writings and thoughts) Jewish background, I thought that the possibility of spending one's life listening to the "material from the couch," that socially isolating, individualistic profession, was as alien and unfathomable as becoming a Republican (God forbid). Even though my parents were from Vienna, and Viennese culture was integral to the ambiance of the family, Freud and psycho-analysis were, to the best of my recollection, mentioned only once. I remember as an adolescent reading the *Three Essays* (no, I wasn't an incipient Freudian, it simply was read along with the *Kama Sutra, Playboy,* and anything else having a sexual content). My father, in his usual genteel, nondogmatic way, looked at it and said something to the effect of, "What crap! While we were fighting the Fascists at the Karl Marx Houses [a story I had heard innumerable times], he was listening to the frustrated bourgeoisie talk about their sexual *mishegas.*" So much for Freud!

Introspection and self-discovery as ways to understand the "human condition" (forgive the cliché, but it actually was used in the household) were anathema to my parents. The solution to problems was quite simple. Change the social and economic conditions and people will change. Obviously, Marx's *Third Thesis on Feuerbach* was either unknown, or disregarded, otherwise my father would have realized that crude reductionism was antithetical to both a Marxist and, as I later came to realize, a Freudian analysis of society. But that is only part of the picture, a skewed representation at best. There was also an emphasis on music, art (realism, of course), and sports. I vividly recollect the radio being flung out the window when Bobby Thomson (that antichrist) homered off Ralph Branca in 1951. I remember with unambivalent pleasure the Friday nights spent with my father watching "The Gillette Cavalcade of Sports" (boxing, for those readers who are either too young or too politically correct to have been exposed to this), and most of all I remember going to the old Madison Square Garden to watch basketball, from the City College championship team to the fledgling NBA and my beloved Knicks. I still believe that except for two relatively minor factors, my lack of height and the total absence of ability, I could have played backcourt. (I still wait for the call, "Schulman, suit up, we need you.")

In essence, it was not, except for the political slant on life—the Yankees were the bad guys, only Westchester Republicans rooted for them; the Dodgers were the "people's team," having integrated base-ball; Paul Robeson and the Weavers were the height of the musical Renaissance; and it wasn't until late adolescence that I realized that

Sen. McCarthy's first name wasn't "that bastard"—an atypical child-hood. In fact the values were humanistic, caring, appreciative of cultural diversity, enlightened, and relatively nonnarcissistic. Simultaneously, they were tinged with a Central European elitism. Excellence and standards were required. There was contempt for superficiality and American mass culture. "Anyone can put on a suit in this country and think he's a somebody." Perhaps that explains my lack of sartorial concern. While my contemporaries were immersed in Elvis and the birth of rock, Mahler and Shostakovich were seen as modern. Oh, how I rebelled in this regard! And while Milton Berle and Sid Caesar were cultural icons, I was one of what must be a relatively select group that was exposed to the wit of Karl Kraus ("psychoanalysis is the disease it aims to cure") and *Die Fackel.* These are values that have become internalized, with some modification (perhaps Stalin wasn't the second coming, after all) and are integral to who I am and indeed my view of psychoanalysis and the analytic encounter. But we leap ahead too many years. Psychoanalysis is still in the future and arrived at only via detours of behaviorism and cognitive psychology.

Having not so long ago gone through the process of college applications for my daughter, I remember the contrast with my own decision. There was no choice! It was C.C.N.Y. Period. That certainly eliminated the conflict that options present. College, after spending much of my high school years in the pool hall, became a synthesis of two of my passions: intellectual immersion and political activity (ah the Name of the Father, to borrow from Lacan). Sprinkle that with a fair dose of sex, drugs, and rock and roll, and this encapsulates my undergraduate education. I started out as a biology major, with hopes of attending medical school. That choice was as appropriate and realistic as playing backcourt for the Knicks. I soon discovered that the best-looking women were in English and psychology. Since my style was never one of a Swinburnesque aesthete, and for the life of me I had no desire to teach literature, I simply loved reading, I opted for psychology. Even at City, where analytic oriented psychologists taught, and the department was an amalgam of orientations, the behaviorist "revolution" was still in vogue. Skinnerism appealed to me for the obvious reasons: it was environmentally oriented, inherently democratic, at least at first reading, and within the zeitgeist of scientific respectability. There also seemed a mission to the followers of B. F. Skinner; they were going to change the world. Little wonder that I gravitated toward this orientation. And yet, the pull was highly ambivalent. It didn't seem to explain my experience. There may be no legitimate inner world, from a "scientific" perspective, but I sure as hell had a world of desire, fantasy, and urges. To reduce it to reinforcement contingencies seemed rather simplistic (I still tend to euphemize). I "ran my rats" (actually Wister mice), as was required of all acolytes, while at the same time I searched for something deeper, more meaningful, and, lest I sound as elitist as my father, more intellectually rigorous.

In my junior year I signed up for a course in cognitive development. I can't remember who taught it or why I took it. The odds are that it was at a convenient time, or more likely that I was interested in some woman who was taking the course. In any event it exposed me to those theorists that I still consider the great thinkers of academic psychology: Werner, Piaget, Rapaport, and the Vygotsky-Luria perspective on development. While there are obvious differences, they all were, however, dialectic, totalistic, philosophical, and intellectually stimulating. Skinner and behaviorism quickly was deposited into that ubiquitous "dustbin of history" (a quote from Trotsky, just to show how emancipated from my father's influence I have become). This orientation was to become the entrée into psychoanalysis, but we are getting ahead of the unfolding tale.

The political identifications with my roots were also rather salient. I am eternally grateful to the wisdom of U.S. foreign policy and its decision makers for giving me the opportunity to carry on the family legacy. Involvement in groups such as the Congress of Racial Equality (CORE), the Student Peace Union (SPU), the Committee to Abolish the House Un-American Activities Committee (HUAC), and the antiwar movement became a second home and a second family. It was a rare gift presented to my generation to be able to act out one's oedipal in an arena where I felt then, and still do, that the power of duplicitous authority had to be confronted and overcome. During the mid-'60s, before disenchantment with the war in Vietnam led to a mass movement, there was a Congressional inquiry into "subversive" elements in the antiwar movement. I still take pride that when asked that infamous question, "Are you now or . . .." I responded by taking the 69th. When some Congressman replied by stating that he didn't know what that was (no Fifth Amendment Commie, me), I responded by telling him that that was exactly the problem. Some might feel that this was simply adolescent acting out; however, I may be the only person to get away with this, sans a contempt citation. One other political anecdote, before we return to my journey to Freud and psychoanalysis. During the early 1980s I was involved in the formation of an antinuclear group that centered on children's interests and anxieties. During a press conference, I spoke as a representative of this group. The *New York Times,* somehow confused me and a subsequent speaker representing Athletes For Peace. They reported, "Dr. Martin Schulman, two-time U.S. Olympic medalist, . . . " While perhaps not the Knicks, I still have, for posterity's sake, a framed copy of the article.

While the above may seem an unnecessary digression from the path of becoming an analyst, actually the two are intimately related. Political "burnout," the failure of the "revolution," and more important, the inability to sustain a relationship beyond a single-digit life span led me to enter my first analysis. Since the tendency to intellectualize has always been one of my characterological defenses, it also led me to read Freud and the early analytic literature. Perhaps on another level, I was going to know more than my analyst (the naïveté and arrogance of this youth was limitless) and undo the process. Oedipal victory lay ahead. I was fortunate; he called me on my resistances and I had to confront who I was. Can we conclude therefore that my encounter with Freud the theorist and with my analyst, the flesh-and-blood Freudian, determined my decision to become an analyst? One can, but it would be a premature transference interpretation. The beat will still have to go on for a few more years.

Graduate school in psychology continued to emphasize and center around my interest in cognition and the philosophical underpinnings of the psyche. Here luck, that unanalyzable factor, played a major role. I began graduate school and was soon "sent down," as the British say, due to my political involvements. No one informed me that my department chairperson was on a lifetime Air Force grant and politically a tad to the right of Attila the Hun. Being thrown out, and facing the possibility of a prolonged trip, via taxpayers' money, to Southeast Asia, led to a desperate move to reenroll somewhere. The New School had a relatively "open admissions" policy and they were willing to provide me with a graduate assistantship. There couldn't have been a better choice. While it was academically, in those days, antianalytical, it provided me with a continuation of the European tradition that I had been exposed to during my years at home. My interests in Freud, and my continuing analysis, were packaged to the side, and in a schizoid resolution unintegrated into my research and studies.

After completing my doctorate, and concurrently my first analysis, I was left with the necessity of determining what to do with the rest of my professional life. I was fortunate to have already had a full-time teaching position at a local college, and yet the thought of simply being an academic wasn't enough. Analytic training seemed the most viable option, and the National Psychological Association for Psychoanalysis (NPAP) the most viable choice. It had a history, was seen as the rebel child of the psychoanalytic movement, and was known for its openness to innovation and creative thinking. Add to this olio the infighting and schisms that personifies psychoanalysis and were played out within NPAP, and one can see from the manifest material I have already presented why the attraction was magnetic for me. Along with my studies there, I also entered a second analysis, more *glatt kosher* than the first. I still have the fantasy that my training analyst spent much of my sessions rolling his eyes and resisting the temptation to smack me on the head. But so be it.

My training coincided with the presentation of new models and paradigms within the psychoanalytic movement (allow me the luxury of calling it a movement, since this creates a continuity with my past). The object relations theorists, British and American, the self psychology of Kohut, and the challenge to ego psychology were all vying for adherents and legitimacy within the community. Lacan was still an unknown, Klein not included in the curriculum, and the relational model still housed in the Sullivanian tent. For reasons not entirely clear (time for a third analysis?) none of these tendencies particularly appealed to me. I saw them as too unidimensional, too focused on only one aspect of functioning or too exclusive to the clinical context. Freud and ego psychology (political correctness has obviously never been my forte, or perhaps I simply love lost causes) seemed to encompass the totality of human experience, the affective, the cognitive, and the connative (the voice of Rapaport still lives). At the same time I was uncomfortable with the reification and mechanization of the analytic process as I interpreted the writings of the ego psychologists. The "fetish of technique" seemed to leave little room for individuality and uniqueness, the sine qua non of what I envision as a successful analysis. Perhaps in response to the formulaic aspects of the way the world was viewed in the parental domain, I have always been reluctant to accept any system that is too neat, too predictable, too uniform in its presentation of case material. I recoil when patients seem interchangeable, when they all fit the model to a tee, and when the technique supersedes the psychic reality of the patient. While many colleagues whom I respect have become enamored of neo-Kleinian or Kernbergian views of treatment, these perspectives simply do not speak to me. I see people struggling with conflictual aspects of themselves, working out compromise formations and adaptations as best they can, and striving for an enhancement of their lives. I simply don't view people as Swiss cheese with missing pieces, or as arrested at early developmental levels. The recent emphasis on projective identification makes me want to grab a catcher's mitt, and the concept "borderline" seems to me a pejorative, scientific way of saying, "This patient is a pain in the ass." Have I become a conservative in my aging years? I think not. I still find Fenichel's *Problems of Psychoanalytic Technique* (1941), that oft-overlooked masterpiece, a predating of my voice. I am still fascinated by the brilliance and fervor of the classics in the field, and bemoan their relative neglect in our training programs.

Perhaps it is time for me to descend from my soapbox and return to the question posed at the beginning: Why did I become a therapist, an analyst, and a Freudian? Fascination with the mystery of who we are (my mother, lest she be ignored, devoured mysteries as if they were Bon Bons), the intellectual rigor of the field (identification with the aggressor), the need to relate to people in a nonexploitative way, and being part of a movement for improving life conditions are all obviously contributing factors. Whatever other reasons exist, either unknown or undiscloseable, the choice is one for which I have no regrets. The journey began for me intellectually and culturally, if not physically, in Vienna and with several detours ended up there again. Not a bad way to exist in this less than ideal world.

———— —— ————

Martin A. Schulman, Ph.D., is a Training and Supervising Analyst at the National Psychological Association for Psychoanalysis (NPAP) and the editor of *The Psychoanalytic Review.*

REFERENCE

Fenichel, O. (1941). *Problems of Psychoanalytic Technique,* trans. D. Brunswick. New York: Psychoanalytic Quarterly.

26

A Calling

JEFFREY SEINFELD

I was adopted at birth and grew up in financially difficult circumstances in Newark and later Irvington, New Jersey. My mother stayed home and cared for me during my first three years of life, while my father went to school to be an accountant and worked in a food market. My father died suddenly of an illness when I was 3½ years of age and my mother was forced to work long hours in a factory in Newark to support us. I was left alone for prolonged periods and drew on my imagination and play to entertain myself. I created a number of imaginary playmates for company and enactment of fantasy. I must have been frightened and angry because much of my play was around protecting myself against persecutors and enemies. My interest in object relations stems from this early childhood experience. The theory states that the person suffering separation anxiety or object loss attempts to fill the psychic void by internalizing objects and substituting fantasy for painful reality.

Throughout my childhood, my energy was concentrated in fantasy and in acting out. Since my mother worked long hours, I often went unsupervised. I joined with other youngsters who were prematurely independent and we often got into trouble for truancy, fighting, and petty thievery. I lived in a community where academic achievement was not valued. The children who did well in school were bullied and rejected. Therefore, intellectual achievement seemed frightening. I quit high school at 16 and passed my time with a local street gang. My adolescence occurred throughout the early and mid-1960s. At this time, street kids usually settled disputes by fistfighting. In ten years street fighting would escalate to the use of knives and then to the frightening proliferation of guns. Fortunately, when I was growing up, weapons were the exception and not the rule. As a teenager, I learned how to box and greatly valued this skill.

During my adolescence I was repeatedly sent to special rehabilitation facilities for acting-out youth. This was not an unusual occurrence in the neighborhoods I grew up in. I recollect my first time away feeling frightened in the yard and then being relieved at seeing the names of my local friends scrawled on the walls. They had told me where to look in the event I was sent away. In some ways I benefited from the reform schools in that they provided discipline and structure. My mother also tried to help by sending me to a Newark social service agency. I saw clinical social workers for once-weekly therapy for ten years. The treatment was very low cost—a one-dollar fee per session. It is fortunate that the focus of that period was not on short-term goals. If such low-cost, high-quality, long-term treatment was not available, my mother could have never afforded private therapy. This therapeutic experience with clinical social workers in a social service agency was by far the most important source of help that I received. These experiences of my youth influenced my theoretical outlook.

In growing up, I saw that the strong were often predators, preying on the weak. The latter typically found others who were weaker to prey on. My subsequent life experience has not changed this outlook. As I later encountered an educated and upwardly mobile social class, I have found these principles continue to hold true, except that the predator–prey struggle is manifested in the more civilized mode of envy, competition for success, wealth, and so forth.

John Bowlby (1969) states that humans are social animals who become preprogrammed regarding predators, based on their long evolutionary experience as prey. Bowlby considers the attachment instinct as an innate mechanism keeping humans together, thereby providing protection against predators. The tendency toward attachment and the formation of human groups is based on an innate, genetically preprogrammed apprehension of predators. The young among social animals have a much better chance of survival by remaining close to others. In modern times predators may be defined as all of the dangers a child may be exposed to when outside of the protection of responsible adults.

As an adopted child who suddenly lost a father and whose mother had to work long hours, I certainly felt abandoned to the danger of predators. The neighborhood I grew up in was constituted by individuals preying on one another. Joining a gang seemed the safest protection from predators. Unfortunately, such gangs are predators themselves.

Jean-Paul Sartre (1960) described how groups are formed when individuals experience alienation, isolation, and vulnerability to violence. The individuals come together for protection. There is the threat that if the group disbands, the individuals become isolated and alone. The group attempts to keep the threat of the danger of the external world alive to prevent its members from separating. My experience in youth groups fits the descriptions of Bowlby and Sartre.

While in special schools, I received a high school equivalency diploma and developed beginning good work habits. After returning home, I went to work for a blueprint factory and later for a construction company. I found my own apartment and eventually saved enough money to move to New York. As I felt better about my accomplishments, I became less frightened of my intellectual abilities. I read literature and was especially drawn to nineteenth-century Russian literature, especially the themes of spirituality versus materialism, original innocence versus original sin, and crime and punishment. I also discovered Freud and psychoanalytic theory. My therapists had never discussed their theoretical outlook but I quickly recognized their way of understanding in Freud's writings. I also discovered existential philosophy and its Eastern counterpart, Zen Buddhism. I have continued to study all of these areas and they have strongly influenced my own psychoanalytic writings.

When I first moved to New York, I barely had enough money to live and stayed at the old Greenwich Hotel on Bleecker Street, walking to work each day in midtown. I was eventually able to move to better accommodations in the 92nd Street YM-YWHA. I attended college at night. I realized that the only way a person in my financial situation would get anywhere was to work very hard and therefore I applied myself with much discipline to my studies and paid employment. I was now not so afraid of intellectual achievement and did well enough to matriculate after one year into the Borough of Manhattan Community College. I later transferred to City College where I received my B.A. I met my wife, who was also a student, while in college. We lived in a small apartment in the Bronx, both attending school and working.

While in City College, I was a literature and creative writing major. At this time I had not yet decided what I would do upon completing school. As I continued to study literature, I saw that my interests were not only in literary themes, but also centered on those authors who described psychological stages of characters in great depth. I especially appreciated the novelists Dostoyevsky and Kafka, and learned much about the dynamics of the unconscious from their work. For a time I was conflicted about whether to become a psychotherapist or a fiction writer and I eventually resolved this issue by becoming a therapist who writes a great deal. It is likely that I sublimated my wish to write fiction into writing clinical vignettes.

My own life experience motivated me to become a psychotherapist. In some way, I viewed my own psychotherapy as a form of salvation and I perceived this profession as a calling. I chose to be a clinical social worker because I wished to work with environmentally and emotionally disadvantaged individuals. I strongly identify myself as a clinical social worker who does psychotherapy based on psychoanalytic and existential principles. It is my belief that we, as human beings, are conditioned by our biology, our environment, our family relations, and the unconscious. We are strongly influenced by our social class, race, gender, age, and sexual orientation. However, we are not purely conditioned. We are shaped by these forces, but there is an existential factor that always tends to actively make something out of what we have been made into. This dialectic between conditioning and existential freedom has informed all of my professional beliefs and writings.

I received my clinical training at Hunter College School of Social Work and New York University School of Social Work. After completing my M.S.W., I went to work for a clinic in the Bronx of the Jewish Board of Family and Children's Services serving inner-city children, adolescents, and adults. I worked in the Bronx for over ten years as a line clinician and supervisor, and continue in the capacity of private consultant. One of my major clinical interests has been to help clients sort out and distinguish the difficult external and internal factors affecting their lives. My aim has been to enable clients to develop their inner resources to deal with their difficult life circumstances. It is also essential to help them make better use of the environmental resources that are available. Many clients become hopeless and discouraged and turn their aggression against themselves. To change their difficult circumstances, clients will need to have all of their aggression and energy available to fight the circumstances that impede them.

Upon completion of my Ph.D., I joined the full-time faculty of the Shirley M. Ehrenkranz School of Social Work. I identify with the school's mission of training students in clinical practice with the most vulnerable, at-risk populations living in the New York area. I therefore devote much time to teaching students assessment and treatment skills. I have a private practice in Manhattan and have treated a considerable number of schizoid and narcissistic patients, which has been a recent area of interest in my writing. I also continue to treat some of my original environmentally disadvantaged clients from the Bronx.

During my youth, I had some minimal involvement in the Chinese martial arts and always wished to pursue this activity. I had a long-standing interest in Zen Buddhism, the philosophy associated with the martial arts, and had read much in this subject. I have always been interested in philosophy, especially Hegel and the existentialists. I have been attracted to the psychoanalysts most influenced by philosophy: Fairbairn, Bion, Winnicott, and Lacan.

Nearly ten years ago, I started to study the Cheng Man-Ching style of Tai Chi Chuan. I also began to train in Shaolin Kung Fu, Chi Kung, and Zen Buddhism with a Shaolin monk in Chinatown. I have found that the martial arts of Tai Chi Chuan and Shaolin Kung Fu provide a fine balance of yin and yang. Whereas Tai Chi Chuan is slow, soft, and gentle, Shaolin Kung Fu is fast, vigorous, and dynamic. Chi Kung is a meditative health exercise focused on moving Chi throughout the body. In traditional Chinese medicine, Chi is the vital life force comparable to the life instinct in psychoanalysis. In addition to learning the physical aspects, I have also been studying Chinese history, philosophy, and culture.

I have found similarities between Chinese martial arts, Zen Buddhism, and psychotherapy. The soft, deflective methods of Tai Chi Chuan resemble the therapeutic strategy of not confronting defenses but gently deflecting the client's unconscious attempts to provoke the therapist into a repetition of early destructive patterns of relating. In psychotherapy there is the temporary letting go of oneself to accept the patient's projective identifications to experience and understand the patient's transference. In Shaolin meditation and Kung Fu, there is a letting go of self to experience and enact various forces and aspects of nature such as animal movements, stillness of mountains, flow of rivers, and so forth. In psychotherapy, the clinician often has to let go of narcissism and allow the patient to project various transference imagoes that sometimes are counter to the clinician's professional identity. In Tai Chi Chuan push-hands, the practitioner is taught to let go of self, invest in loss, and become one with the other player to develop sensitivity and to become skillful in anticipating the other's intended movement.

In Chinese philosophy, it is believed that tranquility leads to dynamic activity. This principle is manifested in the idea that the calm spirit of Zen leads to the dynamic activity of Kung Fu. In psychotherapy, the patient's restful therapeutic regression can often lead to dynamic change.

Jeffrey Seinfeld, C.S.W., Ph.D., is Associate Professor, New York University School of Social Work.

REFERENCES

Bowlby, J. (1969). *Attachment and Loss*, vol. 1. London: Hogarth.
Sartre, J.-P. (1960). *Critique of Dialectic Reason*. New York: Verso.

27

If You Love Your Job, You'll Never Work Another Day in Your Life

MARTHA STARK

When I was a little girl, I had a dream: when I grew up I was going to be an analyst, just like my dad. By day Dad worked at the National Bureau of Standards as a systems analyst, working with computers and numbers. He spent years on a project that involved taking aerial photographs of the traffic patterns along the major arteries in Washington, D.C.; then he did all sorts of fancy calculations to figure out how best to synchronize traffic lights so that drivers proceeding at "normal" speeds along straightaways would encounter one green light after the next. I always wanted Dad to show me what he was doing with the project; he would, but there came a time when I began to sense that although he was considered to be one of the best, for him his work as a systems analyst was still just a job—it neither fully engaged him nor fully satisfied him.

Where his passion lay was in his "contests," word and number games that he would work on for hours and hours every evening. His favorites were those sponsored by *The Prizewinner*, a national publication that came out monthly: you would pay, say, five or ten dollars to enter the contest; you would have six to eight weeks to work on getting the highest score possible; and then the winners would be notified. With respect to most of the contests Dad chose to enter, he would place in the top five: he often placed first (and would then receive something like one hundred dollars); sometimes he would be one of several tied for first place—and then the one hundred dollars would be split.

Dad's workstation was a rickety old card table that he had placed in the living room next to the fireplace; on top of the table were his yellow pads of paper, his "automatic" pencils (with #2 lead), several big erasers, his calculator, a ruler, boxes of index cards, and special dictionaries with all sorts of words in them. When Dad was busy at work on his contests, he was so happy.

Usually I did my homework upstairs in my own room, but some-times I would take my work downstairs so that I could join Dad in the living room. Those times, when I was working side by side with Dad, were some of the most peaceful times of my childhood. Dad would be busy with his contests, absorbed, happy; I would be busy with my homework, absorbed, happy. If I were working on a math problem set and got stuck, Dad would help me figure it out. I felt comforted by his presence. For the most part we were silent together, but every now and then one or the other of us would look up in order to smile at the other.

To this day, it makes me happy to see Dad (now 85) at work on his contests. He's not quite as quick as he used to be, but he continues to derive tremendous pleasure from working on his contests. He says he still has all his marbles—although they are rolling around inside a little more than they used to!

My family (which consisted of Mom, Dad, Susan, who was 2 years older, me, and Doug, who was 2 years younger) loved to play all manner of games. We had dozens of jigsaw puzzles (there was usu-ally a jigsaw puzzle "in process" and we would always do a big one on New Year's Eve), books of crossword puzzles and double crostics (Susan was so good she could do them in ink), board games (like the Chinese game of Go, Scrabble, chess, checkers, Parcheesi), and card games (like canasta, spit, pounce, spider, Russian bank, and double solitaire). We were all taught bridge from an early age. In fact, Mom and Dad told us that one of the reasons they had decided to have three children was so there would always be four people available to play bridge and one person who could be in the kitchen preparing popcorn for the others.

Whereas Susan loved to read and Doug spent most of his time playing outdoors, I loved mathematical games and puzzles. I learned how to multiply, in my head, without paper, two-digit numbers by two-digit numbers. Every Christmas, I would be given little puzzles to add to my collection of mind-benders. Dad and I had a number of games we would play together—including a Chinese ring puzzle that required a series of 128 steps to detach the rings from the rod and, in reverse order, 128 steps to reattach them. I would take it apart, Dad would put it back together; neither of us would ever do the other's job. (To this day, these forty or more years later, we still do that Chinese ring puzzle. Whenever I visit, the ring puzzle is waiting for me, assembled, waiting to be taken apart; by the time I leave, I will have taken it apart many, many times over. It never ceases to delight me.) In college I remember that Dad and I worked very hard to unlock the secret of Rubik's cube; after tens and tens of hours of work on it, we ended up stumbling on the solution but were never able to replicate the result— so we knew it didn't really count! Dad and I still enjoy games of Boggle; instead of competing with each other for the top score, we often work collaboratively to see how many words we can create between us—sometimes even cheating by changing some of the letters so that we can make longer words!

I remember with much pleasure a particular puzzle that Dad shared with me one summer. It involved twelve balls (eleven of which were equal in weight, the twelfth weighing either more or less than the other eleven). You have a simple Mettler balance and three chances to weigh any number of the twelve balls. After three weighings, you need to be able to ascertain which of the twelve balls is the "odd ball" and if it weighs more or less than the other eleven. I will never forget the sense of elation I experienced when I finally solved the riddle to the problem.

Whereas Dad loved to use his mind, Mom used her heart. She always delighted in talking to people, and they loved talking to her. Mom enjoyed people and hearing about their lives. People would confide in her and would end up telling her their life stories. Wherever we went, Mom would talk to people. She would ask people about their lives, about what mattered to them; then she would tell them her own stories, all kinds of wonderful stories about her life and (sometimes to my embarrassment) about all of us.

Mom has always had worlds of friends, many of whom have stayed in touch with her over the years. People who came over to our house to talk to her would often end up sitting with her on our back porch. Mom liked it when I would come downstairs to join them there, where I would settle into a little wooden rocking chair that was my favorite place to sit. It was situated unobtrusively in the corner, so that I could be a part of it all but still apart from it—both participant and observer. I spent many a wonderful summer afternoon on that back porch, listening to Mom and her friends talking. As the amazing stories of their lives unfolded, I would listen intently—in awe of the fact that there could be so many different people in the world with so many different stories to tell. Sometimes their stories made me laugh, sometimes they made me very sad. Every now and then I really wanted to say something, but usually I just sat very still, listening. I was really glad that Mom did not make me talk, because I didn't want to have to talk if I didn't want to.

Mom and her friends talked about everything: recipes, the meaning of life, their children, their husbands, the books they were reading, their jobs. Mom had, and has, a kind of wisdom about people and relationships that never ceases to amaze me. I would wonder, How did she come to know so much? It comforted me to listen to Mom and her friends talking.

Mom was as good a listener as she was a talker. She would remember all sorts of details about people's lives. I remember wondering if she wrote things down or if she was just able, somehow, to remember it all because she was truly interested in knowing. I think it was the latter. To this day, there are people I know whom Mom met only once, years ago, who still ask after her. I think people knew that she really did care and really wanted to hear about whatever was on their minds. She was able somehow to put them at ease; they would end up sharing with her all kinds of intimate details about their lives.

Later that day, around the dinner table, Mom would tell us about all that she had learned from talking with her friends during the day. Even though I would already have heard many of the stories, I still loved to hear her recount them again.

Every Sunday after church there would be a coffee hour. Dad, Susan, and Doug would long since have tired of the socializing and be lined up with coats and hats in hand, ready to depart, but Mom would still be talking away with her many, many friends and wide circle of acquaintances. I usually tagged alongside her, because I didn't want to miss out on any of the stories I knew would be forthcoming.

So I grew up with these two parts of me—a part of me very analytical, logical, interested in numbers and games (like my dad); another part of me more intuitive, more attuned to, and interested in, people (like my mom).

I entered Harvard College with plans to go on to graduate school in mathematics. I took all kinds of ever more advanced classes in pure math. Although I would eventually be able to master the material, I knew that doing so was a strain, that the kind of math we were being taught was not coming naturally or easily for me. I began to lose my passion for math.

The mathematics to which I was being exposed also seemed to be so much at a remove from the life I was living at school. I was in college during the late '60s, when hip-huggers, bell-bottoms, and tie-dye were in. I was very deeply into the music scene, organizing dances ("mixers") and concerts featuring local and sometimes nationally known rock groups. It was an exciting but anguished time for me, those years, as my friends and I struggled to make meaning of our lives. We would talk into the wee hours of the morning about our hopes, our dreams, what we thought we wanted to do with our lives, what contribution we thought we could make. I worked very hard in school and certainly developed my mind, but it was the connection I made with my friends that mattered the most to me.

As I look back now, I remember those years with a bittersweet nostalgia, and whenever I have occasion to walk through Harvard Yard, my heart quickens with the memory of those years when we were all so vital and alive and hopeful and young and so innocent.

It seemed to me that what I wanted to be able to do with my life was to pursue a career in which I could invest my passion. I knew that I would not be happy unless I chose a profession that was both intellectually challenging and emotionally rewarding. I also wanted to be able to feel that I was doing something with my life, that I was making some kind of contribution, that I was able to make a difference in people's lives.

It was only after much painful deliberation that I realized mathematics was probably not going to be fulfilling enough. Not only was math giving me less and less pleasure, but also it seemed to me to be so much at a remove from where my passion now lay. On the one hand was the abstract world of analytic thinking, mathematical conundrums; on the other hand was the world of people, emotion, engagement, relationship. The world of math seemed more and more sterile, more and more remote; the world of people was so much more immediate and where, I now realized, my heart really lay.

It was very difficult to think in terms of giving up my dream of being a mathematician like Dad. It's not that he ever put pressure on me to follow in his steps; rather, it was I who wanted to be like him. It took me some time to realize that maybe I should go more with the part of me that loved to feel connected to people—the part of me that was my heritage from Mom. I had had my heart set on doing mathematics, so it required some work on my part to relinquish that dream.

But when I finally let myself recognize the direction in which I was heading, I realized that I wanted to be able to do work that would involve talking to people, perhaps having an impact on them, perhaps actually making a difference in their lives. I didn't really know all that much about psychoanalysis, but what I did know about Freud and his ideas fascinated me. Perhaps, were I to become a psychoanalyst (not that at that point I had any idea as to what such training would entail), I would be able to combine my interest in analytic thinking with my interest in people. By becoming an analyst, I would be able to reconcile these two facets of my personality—the more rigorously analytic and disciplined with the more spontaneously intuitive and playful.

I remember well the moment, during my junior year in college, when I decided to shift from mathematics to premedical studies. I went off to Harvard Medical School, knowing that I wanted to be a psychiatrist upon graduation but wanting to learn as much as I possibly could about the body and the mind/body interface. I didn't like medical school much, but I certainly learned a great deal and came out of the experience a lot wiser and a lot more savvy than when I had started. But I feel that it was during my residency in adult psychiatry (and, later, my child fellowship) that I really came into my own.

I was now ready to pursue a career in psychoanalysis. I chose the more conservative of the two psychoanalytic training institutes in town, because I wanted to have a solid background in classical psychoanalytic theory and technique. Over the years, however, I developed an interest, initially, in self psychology and other deficiency-compensation models that speak to the importance of offering the patient some form of corrective provision and, more recently, in the relational perspective, which conceives of the therapeutic relationship as involving not just subject (the patient) and object (the analyst) but two subjects, both of whom bring their authentic selves to the interaction. No longer is the locus of the therapeutic action thought to be just "give" but "give and take," no longer simply corrective provision but negotiation of the here-and-now engagement between patient and analyst.

As I look back over my years as a psychotherapist, I recognize that part of what appeals to me about doing this kind of work is that it is so deeply engaging. In fact, it engages all of me—my mind and my heart. As I acquire more and more experience in my life, it enhances my skill as a psychotherapist. By the same token, as I acquire more and more experience as a psychotherapist, it deeply enriches the quality of my life. It feels deeply right to me to be spending many hours of every day sitting with people and being there for them. In terms of the parts of me that are engaged by such work, there is little disjunction between my professional life and my personal life. I feel that my work as an analyst enables me to live life deeply and richly; I pursue my work as an analyst with the same passion with which I live the rest of my life.

As I think about it, I realize that my two greatest skills as a therapist are probably my ability to listen (to which I owe thanks to my mom) and my ability to use my mind analytically (to which I owe thanks to my dad). Both are skills that I have been honing for many years now.

In more recent years, I have also been doing a lot of writing and teaching, my particular interest being the translation of theoretical constructs into the clinical situation. I spend several hours every morning at my computer, before my day officially begins, working on (and playing with) ideas about the interface between psychodynamic theory and clinical practice. I have had a long-standing interest in understanding how it is that the therapeutic process facilitates change; in other words, what is it that really heals the patient? I am also interested in the therapist's use of self (use of the countertransference) to find, and to be found by, the patient.

Parallel to my interest in doing psychotherapy has been my interest in dance; in fact, I have been dancing for as long as I have been doing psychotherapy—particularly disco dancing (which was very "in" during the '70s and early '80s). In more recent years, Gunnar (my dance partner as well as my life partner) and I have been taking swing and ballroom dance classes from an extraordinarily gifted teacher named Julius Kaiser. It was actually he who helped me to recognize that even as a student (a dance student) there are these two sides of me: part of me approaches new steps in a logical, analytical, disciplined manner, while another part of me is intuitive, goes with the flow, does not think much about it, just lets it happen. Until I develop a certain comfort level with a particular dance sequence, I will alternate back and forth between an analytic approach and a more intuitive one. It is only when I achieve a certain level of competence and confidence that I am able to integrate the two approaches—the net result being something better than either would have been alone.

I know that as I have matured as a psychoanalyst, I have been able to reconcile (in my work as well) these two aspects of myself: the more thoughtful, reflective, and analytical side of me with the more intuitive and empathically attuned side. I think I am at my best when I am able to be both observer and participant—when I am able to be present with both my head and my heart. I think that one of the reasons I am particularly drawn to contemporary relational theory is because it encourages the analyst to bring both her objectivity and her subjectivity to the analytic encounter.

At this point, I have been a psychotherapist for almost twenty-five years. It feels to me as if I am doing exactly what I was meant to be doing. The work is deeply, deeply challenging and rewarding, even as it is sometimes incredibly demanding and emotionally draining. But I feel that it draws out the best of me—the most of me. There is something so compelling about doing this kind of work. I feel that in this profession I am able to engage my head and my heart at the same time that I am able to do something worthwhile.

It is such a privilege to be doing this work. I never cease to be amazed that our patients will allow us to enter the innermost recesses of their hearts and souls. We are entrusted with what is most private, most personal, and most intimate—entrusted with what may never before have been exposed to the light of day.

These past years have been sometimes difficult, sometimes exhausting, often exhilarating, usually inspiring, never boring. When I sit with my patients, I feel deeply engaged, not alone, comforted somehow, at peace, at home. I love to hear people talk about what most matters to them; I love to hear about the details of their lives—the little things, the big things, whatever they might want to talk about. I have found that I remember well what they share with me. I also enjoy the process of reflecting upon the therapeutic process itself and upon what is involved, from a theoretical standpoint, in helping people to engage themselves more deeply and more authentically in both their own lives and the lives of others. It is then in the context of their engagement in the therapeutic relationship that they begin to dare to enter more deeply into the world.

A very wise teacher of mine named Leston Havens taught me the importance of not needing anything from the patient, including not needing the patient to change—not even needing the patient to want to live. Once I was able to master this profoundly important concept, the work became so much more pleasurable. The patient either will or won't get better; the choice is the patient's. It is not for the therapist to be invested one way or the other. The therapist is simply committed to helping the patient understand the internal workings of her mind; it is then for the patient to decide as she will about what she wants to do with her life. How many analysts does it take to change a patient? It doesn't matter; the patient won't change until the patient is ready to change. The two books I wrote on resistance speak directly to this issue.

As I look back over the past twenty-five years and the incredible joy that I have found in my work, it seems to me that I was pretty lucky. There are so many career paths I could have pursued that would have been so wrong for me. I think I am particularly well suited for the work of being an analyst because I so enjoy being with people and helping them to make meaning of things. I continue to find comfort from my work; I love the connection with people that doing the work affords. My experience has been that the deeper the work goes, the less afraid the patient becomes to be more fully present in the moment, the more able the patient becomes to put herself out there in her pursuit of fulfillment and meaning—no longer as fearful or held back.

The analytic part of me still loves to play with theoretical constructs but the people part enjoys the process of working collaboratively with patients to help them discover their truths. It is such a privilege to be able to accompany people on their journey.

I think that when I do my work as an analyst, I symbolically return to the comfort and the pleasure I got from being close to Dad (and his contests) and to Mom (and her interest in people). Doing my work as an analyst enables me to feel at peace and deeply engaged.

My work as a psychoanalyst, a teacher, and a writer have therefore enabled me to realize a personal dream that I had from way back— to use both my head and my heart to make a difference somehow. In the career I have chosen, I am doing exactly what I want to be doing; my dream has come true. Part of the pleasure I experience in doing the work derives from the fact that as a psychotherapist, I feel I am in a position to help my patients get a little closer themselves to realizing their own dreams.

Whenever I return home for a visit, there are my parents, now in their eighties, enjoying their twilight years together—they still play their games and they still enjoy talking to each other, even after all these years. In fact, with time, Mom has come to enjoy games more and more and Dad has become quite a conversationalist! I am deeply grateful to my parents for developing in me the capacity to pursue life with passion and for giving me implicit permission to do what would be most right, most meaningful for me. To Dad I owe the love of using my mind; to Mom I owe the love of using my heart. As a psychotherapist I have been able to do both—and I consider myself blessed.

Martha Stark, M.D., is a Training and Supervising Analyst at the Boston Psychoanalytic Institute.

28

The Endless Road

JAIME P. STUBRIN

In the late 1950s and early 1960s, the medical students' organization of the state university where I studied, Universidad de Buenos Aires (UBA), organized psychoanalysis courses, which I attended. They were held in the Aula Magna de Anatomía (large anatomy auditorium), which is an important amphitheater inside the college building. It is interesting that psychoanalysis should be introduced into the school of medicine in this huge auditorium, which represented the most authentic traditions of academic medical knowledge. These classes were taught by pioneers and founders of the Argentine Psychoanalytic Association (APA) such as Arnaldo Rascovsky, Angel Garma, and Arminda Aberastury, among others. In the mid-1950s the School of Psychology of the UBA was created, where these distinguished psychoanalysts from the APA used to teach.

By that time, I was an adolescent who had not yet finished high school.

The phenomenon generated was surprising. The auditorium became crowded with students, so much so that many had to sit on the stairs. Perhaps this explains, to some extent, the famous boom of psychoanalysis in Argentina, which arouses curiosity in so many people.

These public classes coincided with the important cultural renovation movement that took place in the country at the time. Psychoanalysis, which played a prominent role in that movement, reached, through its increasing expansion and reputation, not only the "learned" classes, but even people of the lowest socioeconomic conditions. This was the result of, on the one hand, the creation of psychopathology services in hospitals and mental health centers, and on the other, the fact that charismatic pioneers with good communication skills began to participate in radio and television programs speaking about psychoanalysis. Among them, I wish to mention particularly Dr. Arnaldo Rascovsky, who was one of the founders of the APA, and Professor Florencio Escardó, the eminent pediatrician, who was a real teacher, the only one I had throughout my entire career as a medical doctor. Dr. Escardó was the first to hospitalize children together with their mothers. He put an easy chair next to every bed. He used to say that no nurse was better than their own mothers. There had been no prior instance of this in the world, and it was recorded in many countries. He also prescribed psychoanalytic treatment to many people. I am proud to say that I also enjoyed the friendship of this model teacher, and that I have fond memories of Dr. Rascovsky too. He was one of the presenters of my book *Sexualities and Homosexualities*, one of his last scientific activities at the APA before his death.

To speak about oneself always implies the risk of falling into the narcissistic trap or at least into the exaltation of self-esteem.

Going back to the time I am describing, I was then an adolescent who was influenced by that movement. I was a keen reader, I still am, although I devote so many hours to psychoanalytic literature it hardly leaves any time for poetry and novels. When I was 16 or 17 years old, I began to read Freud, which was unusual in a youth of that age. I saw this in my own subsequent analyses without reaching a very clear conclusion. Why Freud? Because Freud was part of our everyday culture, as well as Nietzsche, Sartre, Dostoyevsky, Borges, Proudhom, Genet, Hesse, Gide, Faulkner, Poe, Tennessee Williams, Shakespeare, and Cervantes, among others. My friendship with Ernesto Sábato, the well-known Argentine writer and human rights advocate, made a deep impact on me.

Freud used to say that to know the human soul, it was necessary to approach the poets. I did so, both through their literature and in person. García Lorca, Rafael Alberti, Miguel Angel Asturias, Borges, Whitman, and Córdova Iturburu were important referents for me. Meeting Marcos Ana, a Spanish poet who was imprisoned for over thirty years during Franco's regime, was an unforgettable experience.

Undoubtedly, I was a distressed boy immersed in an intellectual and pseudointellectual universe, a young Jewish boy who had to become better than his elders because that was precisely what they expected him to do.

Drama has always had a crucial significance in my life, both as a spectator and as an actor. It somehow helped me improve my expressive skills and my capacity to understand, from a psychological perspective, different human characters.

Movies were very important as well. In the city of Buenos Aires, Ingmar Bergman and Federico Fellini nearly achieved cult status.

However, Sartre made the strongest impression on me. Existential anxiety was a permanent companion. We used to devour his books and discuss his ideas. Maybe that anxiety has never abandoned me. I think that an analyst who has never suffered from anxiety cannot be an analyst.

I started my first psychoanalysis (or my first approach to psychoanalysis) in a vocational guidance group, which was a service offered at the university. My clinical case was described in a book written by Irene Orlando (missing during the military government), who was my guide and friend, and there seemed to be no alternative for me other than taking up medicine. Perhaps this was obvious, perhaps it was a mistake. Later, I was a patient in a therapy group at Lanús Hospital, where Dr. Mauricio Goldemberg had created a psychopathology center. Psychoanalysis appeared in hospitals and started to displace traditional psychiatry. I had admission interviews in a car, as the facilities were inadequate for the large number of people who consulted. At that time I could not afford private treatment.

It was a time of great enthusiasm. We were encouraged by optimistic expectations about the results of psychoanalysis, which had chief importance in our lives. We shared a common interest, exchanged books, and got together to read and to discuss the interpretations of our analysts. We believed in the future of mental health. The prospect of happiness, of a Shangri-La, was at the end of the road, at the end of a therapy. Of course, we were very young.

For us, Buenos Aires was a psychoanalytic and Kleinian city. Melanie Klein and her followers were immensely powerful. The top ones traveled to London to supervise with her. Her portrait, not Freud's, hung on the front wall of the auditorium of the APA. Thus, in some of my successive analyses, the type that lasted many years, where the patient was presumed guilty of attacking the analyst until proven innocent, I saw flying penises and toothed vaginas. Some of them were not only Kleinian, but also pseudo-Kleinist.

When I graduated as a medical doctor, I felt an unexpected need to keep distance from psychoanalysis, so I began to attend services of different medical specialties for some time. I resumed psychoanalysis before long. I began to join private psychoanalytic study groups, which was then the way to develop a professional background. There were a lot of groups to choose from, most of which were taught by the analysts from the APA we idealized. A chronological study of Freud's work, which was a must, took many years. I used to go to a colleague's supervision session with one of the top ones only to listen (we shared the fee). By then, I did not yet dare to take patients under treatment.

Later, I attended courses at the Graduate School of Psychotherapy, founded by Rascovsky and others. I have a fond memory of Bernardo Arensburg, a great analyst and thinker, who lives in Spain now. This school was like the anteroom to the APA. Many colleagues of mine studied there, which seemed to be a condition to enter the APA. Besides, psychologists were admitted to this school, unlike the APA, since they were not allowed to practice psychoanalysis.

That was a very important experience. I studied, learned, and shared. However, the APA was highly idealized, and consequently inaccessible. I somehow felt like a child looking at the desired object exhibited in a shop window. The impression that developing a good professional background was too costly to afford was a myth. Up to a point, it was true because there were very few teachers; and besides, when we made an appointment for a training analysis we had to wait for ages. In 1974 a radical change in the association permitted all its full members to have access to the teaching profession, due to which costs were modified as a consequence of a pyramidal inversion.

I was then part of the staff of professionals who worked in mental health centers and assisted the community from the neighborhood where these centers were located (in general, very poor people).

Eventually, in 1976 I entered the APA and began my training analysis. Later, I attended seminars, supervisions, symposiums, and international congresses.

In my first interview with one of my formal supervisors, Mrs. Madelaine Baranger, after asking me about my background, she said; "But you are an analyst already." My experience as a candidate was excellent, and I had great enthusiasm.

I graduated and started teaching, with supervision from Dr. Luis Storni, a great man whose knowledge about the Freudian theory was extraordinary. I gradually made progress and became more and more Freudian. I was obviously acquainted with Klein, Fairbairn, Meltzer, Bion, Winnicott, and Lacan (another Argentine phenomenon), whom, however hard I studied, I never understood very well. Willy Baranger, a very distinguished analyst from my institution, was one of my Lacan teachers. I did not become a Lacanian. I got closer and closer to Freud and to skepticism.

I became more flexible about the setting and my expectations for therapy. I chose my last and present analyst on the ground that I agreed with him in part on his ideas about the prospects of psychoanalysis.

Classical psychoanalysis may only be suitable for future analysts who have been in therapy for years. Nowadays there are time limitations, and those who need assistance to improve their quality of life cannot wait so long.

Winnicott used to say that a good psychoanalyst had to be a lead violin in psychoanalysis.

I approached the topic of sexual perversions after years of working with drug addicts, as I realized their common features. Additionally, I discovered Joyce McDougall, who became not only an important theoretical referent but also a good friend. Although I had been working by myself on a similar line before becoming acquainted with her, her ideas transformed completely the way I thought about many aspects of human life.

It was hard for a Latin American analyst to gain a reputation in the Northern Hemisphere. We remain unknown because the language barrier is almost unbreakable. In addition to my great effort to spread my ideas, I was lucky. In spite of our theoretical differences, I am indebted to Dr. Charles Socarides for having invited me to write a chapter in one of his books.

That was my first approach to the American psychoanalytic movement, which I respect particularly for the importance it attaches to daily therapy.

I was invited to the University of Virginia by Dr. Vamık Volkan. Later, I had a professional relationship and a fond friendship with Joseph Reppen, who was responsible for many of my visits to New York City, which allowed me to communicate my ideas and interact with my peers. I certainly made very good friends in the United States, who became my referents as well, such as Dr. Owen Renik of San Francisco. And my book, translated into English, was a bigger success in the English-speaking world than in my world.

I have worked as a professor at the School of Psychoanalysis (Instituto de Psicoanálisis) where I lectured on the psychoanalytic technique in addition to the topic I have been concerned with for the last twenty years: perversions and homosexuality (which are not the same thing).

Time, experience, large amounts of literature, and perhaps my intellectual evolution have tempered my juvenile enthusiasm. Fortunately, today I am aware that psychoanalysis does not provide an answer to everything. Once, psychoanalysts were convinced it did.

In spite of the worldwide declining demand for psychoanalysis, I still consider it to be a very powerful tool to help people improve their quality of life, which, despite my theoretic gaps, is my one and only objective as an analyst. In writing, speaking, or teaching, I focus all my thoughts on the patient, who is always someone in distress—otherwise he would not consult. I know it is not an easy job to improve people's quality of life, but it is worth the effort. Paraphrasing Winnicott, I would say that I am not interested in analysis for its own sake; I am interested in people. I am interested in myself as a person. Patients also help the analyst improve, and I am constantly trying to improve the quality of my own life. Were I not interested in myself, I would not be able to be interested in other people. Words or theories do not interest me unless they are at the service of a particular patient. I never attempt to apply a particular theory to my work, as that would mean forcing the person under treatment to enter into the frame of some theory. Although I may be wrong sometimes, my basic interest is clinical. The setting, the couch, the fifty minutes, the transference are mere tools that ought to be used properly and wisely.

The time of great expectations and euphoria is over. Now that I am older and more down-to-earth, I live this life because there is no other life to live. I think there is still a lot to do in the field of psychoanalysis, but I don't want to give up reading poetry and things related to art. I work as an analyst, but analysis is not my whole existence.

Why did I become a psychotherapist? I do not know. Perhaps it is like neurosis choice. There is no answer. Who chooses anything? I am doubtful about the existence of strong vocations. A person who is reasonably intelligent can do many things reasonably well. The choice of this profession is undoubtedly related to a remedial need, probably with the need to remedy oneself.

Florencio Escardó used to say: "First a good person, then a good doctor. If you are not a good person, you will never be a good doctor."

Falling as I am into the narcissistic trap, I dare say that I am a good person.

Jaime P. Stubrin, M.D., is a Training and Supervising Analyst at the Argentine Psychoanalytic Association.

REFERENCE

Stubrin, J. P. (1994). *Sexualities and Homosexualities.* London: Karnac.

29

Family Influences

SAUL TUTTMAN

As a young child I found myself faced with a situation of sharply conflicting styles and values between my mother's and father's families. Curiously the two families had one feature in common—both had intense family loyalty and viewed members of the other family as outsiders. Any show of loyalty to one family was viewed as disloyalty to and rejection of the other family. For me, as a child, to feel secure in this situation, I had to develop a subtle awareness of what was wanted by the people upon whom I was dependent. In this way I was probably sensitized to the needs and feelings of others. Such pressures were undoubtedly instrumental in my learning to examine and try to understand human behavior around me from early life on. Eventually, and under the important influences of particular teachers, supported by particular books and films, I began to study mental processes and work toward a career as a psychotherapist.

In many ways, my parents were very caring and dedicated people, but I believe members of both parents' families somehow failed to develop a sense of autonomy and did not work through the problems that can bind youngsters in a state of emotional fusion and insufficient separation. This can interfere with achieving more mature stages of emo-

tional development. I believe that neither my mother nor my father nor
our close relatives were successful in reaching a more self-sufficient
way of living. As a result, conflict and underlying strife between members of both Mother's and Father's families ensued and created problems for both the older and the younger generations. In my case, as a
young dependent child, there was always a psychological dilemma (not
consciously understood until many years later, after maturing and having treatment). Within such a family structure, it was very difficult for
a youngster to learn how to maintain loyalty and to feel a secure bond
with both parents and with aunts and uncles on both sides. There was
guilt and discomfort when, as it inevitably happened, my feelings and
behavior would be construed as disloyalty to one faction or the other.
One example of this type of struggle ensued between my mother and
me involving her brother, Uncle Henry. When Mother and I were discussing who would be invited to my bar mitzvah, I entrusted Mother
with my feeling that Henry joked around in such a boisterous way that
I found it uncomfortable. When Mother heard me verbalize this feeling, she was very injured and informed me how hurt and upset she was
with my view of her brother! In retrospect, I believe this example reflects my experimenting with directly expressing loyalty to one of the
families. In this way I had sent a distressing message to Mother: I gave
her notice that, at least in part, I identified with Father's family values.

My parents were both born in New York and lived their lives
there, first in the Bronx and later in Brooklyn. Each time a move was
necessary, they always managed to relocate to an apartment almost
equidistant (and never further than walking distance) between Father's
parents (Bubbe and Zayde Tuttman) and Mother's widowed mother
(Grandma Stern, who lived with two unmarried daughters: Jennie and
Irma). Every Saturday, while Father worked at the store until late at
night, we were with Mother's family. Grandma cooked, Uncle Louis
played the piano, and we sang and danced and ate as well as gossiped
about relatives and neighbors. Mother's sisters especially criticized
Father's family. They believed that Grandfather Tuttman (Zayde) was
rich and withholding. They were angry that as a successful businessman, who gradually acquired two buildings with many tenants, Zayde
pressured his sons (my father and his younger brother) to work long

hours, six days a week, at low salaries. We had to live in a third floor walk-up apartment and Mother had to "shlep" shopping bags and baby carriages up many stairs. As I grew older, Mother's sisters, Irma and Jennie, appeared distressed that I was asked by my father to spend Saturday, from early morning until ten or later at night, helping out in Grandfather's store. They were enraged that I was paid one dollar for the entire day. My brother and cousin refused to do this, but in my need for approval, I willingly worked in the shop, where I learned all about antiques and fireplace equipment, sold to customers as well as polished metal, delivered things, and ran errands.

This might have been a good opportunity to share experiences with my father. In part it was, except that his rage (which I later came to believe had to do with his frustration) and his unpredictable temper were threatening and distressing. I dealt with it by avoiding contact with him. My cousins and others saw him as a gentle, caring person but I was upset by his anger as well as by his inclination to deny his anxieties and apprehensions. His denial of being unhappy or upset about anything seemed to me to contradict the way I sensed he often felt. Perhaps I needed him to be more secure and aware than he was able to be. It became clear in time that Father needed approval from relatives and contemporaries and that he carefully controlled himself in the presence of others. It was only with his wife and children that he expressed his strong negative feelings.

In contrast to her husband, Mother frequently complained and ventilated, quite hysterically, about what displeased her. As I grew older it gradually became clear to me that Father employed denial and repression to dispense with any potential conflict regarding authority figures.

When my father was quite young, his father, Zayde, pressed him to help polish metal and make deliveries. He often ran away and hid. He enjoyed telling the story of hiding in a flour barrel when trying to escape his father's call to work in the store. When found, he emerged covered in flour! Finally, in the 1940s, when my parents purchased their first television, I was impressed to note the intensity of sparring movements of Dad's body when he was watching boxing or wrestling matches, reflecting perhaps a deep identification with the combatants.

Grandma Stern, despite her swollen legs, did much shopping, meal preparation, and child care to help mother, who was experienced by her family as an attractive though nervous and somewhat deprived young woman. Throughout my childhood, I saw Mother taking that ever-present red, thick medicine elixir phenobarbital to try to calm her nerves. Mother's sisters had strong opinions about Mother's difficult plight and constantly tried to win my loyalty. Father's sisters (Eva and Elsie) were eager to share their values with me, especially as they became aware of my interest in music and theater. In Father's sisters' view, the Sterns were not sufficiently genteel and were too noisy and uncultured. The Sterns, for their part, regarded the Tuttmans as stingy, dreary, and righteous. I could see the points on each side but personally I enjoyed the food and music and card games at Grandma's, and took pleasure in the excursions to the theater and concerts that Eva and Elsie arranged. Due to their efforts I was encouraged to take piano lessons at an excellent music school, and was soon playing Bach on the piano. I valued the fine antiques the elder Tuttmans had and the pristine cleanliness of their home. My older cousin, Eva's daughter Rosalind, was studying opera and the beautiful arias she sang were enjoyed by all the Tuttmans. Zayde Tuttman was particularly appreciative, although his hearing loss eventually required him to use hearing aids. I was told that working for years as a coppersmith at the forge hammering metal had made him quite deaf.

Rosalind's father was an optometrist who only worked part-time and thus barely earned a living, probably because he was too busy teaching for left-wing organizations to dedicate himself to his practice. If he was not dealing with political issues or lecturing, he was reading constantly. His name was Israel, which was too difficult for young children like myself to pronounce, and so he became known to the family as "Sruel." It was one of my greatest pleasures to talk about ideas and politics with him. My mother and father and his brother disapproved of Sruel. They worked very hard for relatively low salaries while Eva, Sruel, and Rosalind had a rent-free apartment in a building Zayde owned. Father and his brother and their wives believed that much money went to subsidize Eva and Rosalind while the brothers and their families struggled. Some years later, when Sruel learned I was studying psychoanalysis, he expressed some enthusiasm but warned of the danger of coming to conclusions about human nature from observations of our society. He offered an image of psychologists sitting in a bathtub studying the dirty water and considering these samples to reflect the true state of the water supply without realizing how the contaminated social, cultural, and political predicaments of the world in which we live contribute to our misunderstandings and difficulties. He wondered how we can ignore the impact of economic and political issues if we really want to understand emotional health and pathology.

My Grandmother Stern and her daughters Jennie and Irma as well as Uncle Louis continually supplied me and my brother with food, clothing, money, and toys. Louis asked me to work with him one summer. It was a very different experience than working at Zayde's store. For one thing, he paid me generously and took me out for wonderful meals. After sound came to the movies, Louis lost his job as pianist at the silent movie theaters. He then applied his gifted ear to study piano tuning and we went together all over Long Island canvassing prospective customers for work. Soon Louis was repairing and tuning pianos. The customers enjoyed him and he was very successful, even during the Depression.

Despite many differences between the two families, in one way they were quite alike: the Sterns and the Tuttmans each had an intense commitment to their respective family rituals and values. Often I could feel myself to be a real Tuttman, in the eyes of the Tuttman family, provided I shared the common perceptions and loyalties of the other Tuttmans. A parallel problem existed in the Stern family. All the Sterns secretly demonstrated more loyalty to their own family than toward their mate's other relations. Aunt Jennie kept some of Uncle Abe's money hidden in case Grandma Stern needed it. This fact was kept secret from Abe's wife! The blood connection was stronger than any other bond. My mother could never be a Tuttman; my father could never be a Stern. If I behaved in a way not harmonious with one family's style and values, I might endanger my security with that clan. To survive in such an atmosphere, it was necessary to develop observational skills and to monitor functioning in a way that encouraged inauthentic and somewhat calculating responses in order to adapt and struggle to achieve a secure place in the family.

I remember one period, before my thirteenth birthday, when I repeatedly heard my mother crying and complaining to my father about his family rejecting her. It seemed that Father's family was somehow angry with mother, and did not want to communicate with her or Father about their feelings. Mother was distressed and upset to be so rejected and found guilty without explanation. It gradually came out that one of Eva's close friends, a very gossipy person, had told Bubbe and Zayde that Mother had complained that the elder Tuttmans were not providing adequate funding or help for my bar mitzvah celebration soon to take place, and that the Tuttmans encouraged a less costly option: Mother and helpers from both families would make an informal party at home. Mother insisted she had not pressed anyone to provide anything they did not want to provide. Father joined Mother, on this occasion, in anger toward the Tuttmans for upsetting Mother, on the basis of an outsider's comments. My parents did schedule a home celebration, and eventually the tensions subsided. This entire episode I monitored late at night from bed, overhearing them speak after Father came home from the store and he and Mother explored important issues.

My earliest formal interest in the field of mental health started at around the age of 12 when my parents joined one of the early book clubs, which sent announcements of selections each month. Although they were not particularly interested in the subject, it was my good fortune that my parents accepted the volume *The Human Mind* by Karl Menninger (1930). I found it fascinating to discover the varied patterns of behavior described by mental health experts, about which I had no knowledge. I found it stimulating to read about behavior patterns I had sensed existed in those around me and in myself as well!

At around this time, I engaged in some relatively innocent experimenting with a neighbor's daughter. The girl's mother complained to my mother that I had initiated some "sex play." Mother was very upset and took me aside and asked me, "What do you want to know? Come and ask me and *I will show you!*" She seemed terrified that I would somehow get into trouble because of my sexual curiosity. Certainly the prospect of her showing me her body, in some way related to my growing sexual interests, was very distressing to me. The following Sunday, Father, who rarely spoke with me about anything of substance, called me aside and said, "You had better not play around with yourself or anyone else down there" (pointing toward my penis). Mother, respecting Eva's and Elsie's greater knowledge about such things, told them about my behavior. They conferred briefly with a social worker who had been a customer at the family antique shop. She agreed to see me for a consultation and then reassured them not to worry. She encouraged me to meet with her and to try to arrange more private time with Father. Although I do not believe that her fee was unreasonable, the family decided it was too much money and unnecessary, and so therapy had to wait until I was old enough to arrange it for myself.

There was another incident during my childhood that reflected my parents' anxieties regarding the potential danger of either libidinal or aggressive behavior. After a winter storm, as the snow began to melt, I built a dam near the street curb, which was "engineered" to block the free flow of the melting ice. I was enjoying myself until a group of older boys approached me and threatened to destroy my creation. I armed myself with my shovel, warning the others to stay away. From three flights up, my mother, who had been watching from the window, became hysterical and shouted, warning me of the danger to myself if I hit the intruders, pleading with me that avoiding a confrontation was the only safe path. Again this reflected the view that it was dangerous to assert oneself even in self-defense. There were so many dangers and Mother was worried, once again, that I would suffer.

A number of films that I saw at that time also served to focus my interest in the field of psychotherapy. For example, the film *M*, in which Peter Lorre played the role of a psychopathic murderer and molester of young children, stirred my interest. Not exactly bedtime reading for youngsters, but interesting indeed for more than one reason. While the conventional reaction to such behavior would probably be to dismiss the crime with disgust and anger, the gifted director communicated the anguish and suffering of the disturbed character under study in the film. Also stimulating in terms of my growing interests were films such as *Now Voyager* with Bette Davis, which explored the behavior of a neurotic patient, abused by a controlling mother, and treated by Claude

Rains, the ideal understanding and reliable psychiatrist. This was followed by *Spellbound*, in which Ingrid Bergman, a hospital psychiatrist, deciphers the symbols creating great disturbance for Gregory Peck, her patient. These films as well as many books had a powerful influence on my developing a stronger interest in dynamic psychotherapy. The practitioner was in a sense the protective hero or heroine reassuring the rejected or injured patient by providing encouragement, sometimes technically valuable liberating help, and emotional support. I very much enjoyed the notion of receiving and offering help through understanding and concern. Another exciting possibility I learned is that if therapists can respond with sensitivity and skill, it is possible for them to liberate their patient from the bonds of mental illness. I could see myself as Claude Rains or the other liberators!

In graduate school I took courses with Abraham Maslow, Leopold Bellak, Saul and Karen Machover, David Wechsler, and Florence Halpern. I attended demonstrations of psychodrama conducted by Jacob Moreno and lectures by Abraham Brill. Of course, I obtained and read *The Collected Writings of Sigmund Freud* as well as other books and papers. In the context of this background, I decided to undergo analytic training. I applied to medical schools, but had difficulty gaining acceptance since the returning veterans filled the classes. I completed my doctorate in clinical psychology and eventually gained admission to medical school.

After graduating from medical school and attaining a Ph.D. in clinical psychology, I took residency training in psychiatry at New York University School of Medicine, and completed psychoanalytic training. I became an attending psychiatrist and faculty member at Downstate Medical School, returned to New York University School of Medicine as a faculty member, and finally joined the faculties of Albert Einstein College of Medicine and the New York Medical College (Psychoanalytic Division).

I believe that my sense of emotional isolation and hunger for empathy, understanding, and affection as a child has somehow contributed to my valuing a therapeutic stance and interaction that provided that sort of treatment atmosphere. My first psychoanalyst, Susan K. Deri (1988) of Budapest and New York, was one of the few therapists

I met who, at that time, understood Margaret Mahler's rather recent work regarding the symbiosis–separation-individuation developmental sequence. Deri provided a rich experience, which permitted me to work on the crucial task of defining boundaries and borders, a vital step in maturing that was so absent in my early home life. I learned from direct experiences with her the profound value of empathy and autonomy as well as the importance of nonverbal communication. When I began therapy, I did not know much about the field. To my surprise, I cried frequently during the first months of sessions with Susan Deri. It was a reflection of her skill that she patiently listened and did not offer any interpretations, allowing me to experience and sense my sadness and isolation. For me this was a unique opportunity. Having been "caught" between my mother's panicky overprotection and my father's anger, I found this new opportunity to experience an accepting and attentive listener especially relieving. Later, my second analyst, Andrew Peto, helped me appreciate my potential assertiveness and ambition in facilitating emotional growth and thereby furthering my effectiveness in life and work.

It is not surprising that nothing fundamentally new to me comes out of this review of the factors in my life and development that have influenced my choice of work. At the same time, I feel something profound emerges when I more clearly and fully recognize how important, how significant for my growth and work, were the precious connections and perspectives that I became aware of, especially those carrying emotional meaning and involving empathic attunement with analysts, supervisors, friends, lovers, and patients. Mirroring processes and sharing feelings and perceptions play a crucial role in facilitating growing up and understanding ourselves and others. The bonds of caring and communicating with others, certainly in my case, were central to learning about effective psychotherapy and developing more intimate relationships in life. I imagine that many others, like myself, pursued the field of dynamic psychotherapy in an effort to make up for crucial experiences that had been absent in our own early life development. It is invaluable when sincere and insightful treatment is made available by a caring and understanding therapist. At the same time it is important, if the therapy is to be realistic and productive, that the therapist understands what he/she needs from the treatment so as to ensure that the patient is not manipulated by the needs of the therapist. It is especially important that therapists understand themselves and their patients such that the dyad that develops between them does not involve an endless repetition and acting out of frustrations and longings from the past but provides a needed opportunity for therapist and patient to work through the unsettled issues and identify the inevitable repetition compulsions that result when unresolved feelings and needs come up again and again without meaningful resolution.

Over the years of my psychiatric-psychological-psychoanalytic practice, a considerable number of colleagues, former instructors, and friends, under varying circumstances, came to me for consultations and sometimes treatment. I tried to be helpful and naturally felt gratified that they found value in my understanding and availability. I believe that many in our field have had serious mental problems. I do not believe that having psychopathology is the prime credential for being an effective psychotherapist, but in many cases personal suffering and experience with pathology is useful and can contribute to constructive treatment of the suffering patient, provided that insight and perspective develop and permit the working through of serious pathology. However, it is essential that anyone with a predilection to "ego-lesions," as Federn (1952) called them, has worked through his/her own pathological tendencies if he/she is to function therapeutically in a consistently helpful manner. I worry about therapists who take pride in the extreme position of an alleged state of great rationality and mental health for the therapist and attribute serious psychopathology to the patient.

When I was a young therapist, I found treating seriously psychotic patients psychologically a very challenging and often satisfying activity. It states on the tombstone of Paul Federn, "He snatched many a mind from madness." I was also very impressed with the compassion and sensitivity of Edith Jacobson, Herbert Rosenfeld, Harold Searles, and others in their remarkable capacities to work effectively with the seriously disturbed.

My interest in group therapy was stimulated in part by meeting and interacting with Saul Scheidlinger, Len Horowitz, Asya Kadis, and

Wilfred Bion. I came to know Bion (1959) and his wife quite well when I invited them to New York for the first time to deliver lectures and conduct seminars, although I found Bion quite extreme in his reaction to the neediness of group members who, in the study group I had organized for the occasion, were relatively mature professionals in our field. The participants became frustrated and in fact enraged at his unwillingness to "feed" them. Personally I found his approach very interesting, but the extreme position of group leader and group members impressed me as unnecessarily frustrating to all, although he certainly made his point in that way as to how needy and angry those who feel like neglected children can be.

These days, I find the frustration of attempting to treat the more disturbed patients great, given the impediments devised by insurance companies who have seized upon managed care as a solution to their economic problems. In my presidential address (Tuttman 1997) to the American Group Psychotherapy Association in February 1996, I discussed the vital role of the therapeutic alliance in psychotherapy. Despite the present difficulties, what a privilege to have had the opportunity to work in a field I enjoy and value so much. I find it difficult to realize that I am approaching 71 years of age, and have been practicing for over forty years. These days I primarily do individual and group psychotherapy. I also continue to see some psychoanalytic patients, but there are fewer referrals nowadays for this approach. The newer psychotropic medications are often of help in treatment, but I remain convinced that the therapeutic relationship still is the critical element in successful therapy. I believe that a sensitive therapist can contribute significantly to a patient's welfare, but probably only when there is an empathic bond, a therapeutic alliance, as well as an understanding of the pain and anxiety people experience, and under the condition that the particular patient feels a need for that empathic connection. I know of many highly intelligent therapists who have an impressive grasp of the literature concerning dynamic psychotherapy as well as a keen appreciation of the key contributors to theory and technique, but who somehow lack the empathic accessibility to reach the patient. I recognize that the loneliness and suffering of many of us, both patients and therapists, may have added to our sensitization and understanding;

nonetheless, we need to recognize our personal motivation and work through our personal unconscious problems if we are not to become trapped in acting out our needs and treating ourselves through our patients, or obtaining pleasure and reassurance by offering understanding to others. The problem of becoming the "good object" we needed but could not find in reality, the problem of providing for others what we really want for ourselves, can interfere with our capacity to understand and help our patients.

So often there is an intimate connection between our personal suffering, the deficiencies in our histories, and our style of work, the theories and treatment techniques to which we subscribe. I have felt the enormous benefits that personal treatment brought to me in permitting a deeper understanding of myself, my motivations, and my problems, and the degree of freedom I could have in functioning helpfully to my patients. It is sad when we encounter therapists who need their patients to become self-objects or when the opposite to that happens, namely when we need to feel ourselves to be the saviors or self-objects of our patients. It is important that we learn to appreciate realistically how to help others and how to help ourselves! There is an incredible opportunity and temptation to use patients for our own needs or to be used by our patients. I do believe that empathic attunement is often a crucial factor in psychotherapy. Understanding the anxiety and isolation people experience can be a vital therapeutic factor, but it is only helpful when the patient can tolerate it and welcomes it. The therapist's sensitivity can be a vital determinant in facilitating successful treatment. Ferenczi was probably the first to appreciate these factors (Dupont 1988).

I concluded that the most valuable exploration of my decision to become a psychoanalyst would be to focus upon my personal psychological struggle with my own problems and difficulties. These are undoubtedly intimately related to my relationships with those who have had major influences upon my development. I could offer an impressive list of teachers and supervisors, but, despite the fact that those professionals with whom we identify or whom we emulate play a vital role in our development, I also consider the personal story of crucial importance, even though this requires the disclosure of personal details. In several other papers I have traced the history of psychoanalytic theory and treatment and the developments of the personalities of our theorists and clinicians. In this chapter I have endeavored to highlight the role of the personal struggle, which often motivates therapists to become sensitive and caring clinicians.

Recently there was a dedication in Washington commemorating the presidency of Franklin D. Roosevelt. One speaker described Roosevelt's background as having been very privileged and aristocratic, having helpful family connections and educational opportunities. The panel agreed that his greatness as a dedicated, caring public figure was strongly related to his sensitivity, which developed in the course of the tragedy and suffering he experienced after contracting polio. Although I have noticed similar reactions in many people, I do not want to imply that one only grows to become a sensitive therapist or an empathic person through great suffering. But I do believe that coping with adversity can have a sensitizing and beneficial effect on a person. In the spirit of the invitation to write about *why I became a psychotherapist*, I offer my story as I have come to understand it after long and sometimes painful effort.

Saul Tuttman, M.D., Ph.D., is Clinical Professor of Psychiatry at Albert Einstein College of Medicine, a Training and Supervising Analyst at the New York Freudian Society, and a Fellow of the Institute for Psychoanalytic Training and Research (IPTAR).

REFERENCES

Bion, W. (1959). *Experiences in Groups*. London: Tavistock.
Deri, S. K. (1988). *Symbolization and Creativity*. Madison, CT: International Universities Press.
Dupont, J., ed. (1988). *The Clinical Diary of Sandor Ferenczi*. Cambridge, MA: Harvard University Press.
Federn, P. (1952). *Ego Psychology and the Psychoses*. New York: Basic Books.
Menninger, K. A. (1930). *The Human Mind*. New York: Knopf.
Tuttman, S. (1997). Protecting the therapeutic alliance in this time of changing health-care delivery systems. *International Journal of Group Psychotherapy* 47:1–16.

30

Toward A State of Selflessness

STUART W. TWEMLOW

I am always "becoming a psychotherapist," and have realized that I will never finish that task. In fact, I hope that I never do. It has been said that when one thinks of oneself as a graduate in the school of experience, one becomes a public menace. I think, more importantly than that, one can cease to live one's life with a full sense of immediacy, commitment, and openness if fully fledged professional "expertise" encroaches!

George Bernard Shaw (1962) once said:

> This is the true joy in life, the being used for a purpose recognized by yourself as a mighty one; the being thoroughly worn out before you are thrown on the scrap heap; the being a force of Nature instead of a feverish selfish little clod of ailments and grievances complaining that the world will not devote itself to making you happy. [pp. 510–511]

The energy, commitment, and openness of the fully lived life, described by George Bernard Shaw, captures many of the features of a mentally healthy therapist and patient; moving from narcissistic self-absorption into being a piece of the puzzle, a member of a community, and expecting to and wanting to make a contribution to future generations, living, as one ancient Samurai described "as if a fire is raging in your hair!" Helping somebody become able to live life in this way implies a particular set of basic philosophical presuppositions and values. These values are the basis both of my evolution as a therapist and of what I am as a person.

I have realized that analytic work is at heart an embodiment of the person performing it. What I am is what I do. In a similar vein, Sati, an early disciple of Buddha, was once asked by him what he meant by consciousness. Sati's reply was, "It is that which expresses, which feels, which experiences the results of good and bad deeds here and there." Buddha agreed, saying that there is no arising of consciousness without conditions. He said that consciousness is named according to the condition through which it arises. For example, through the eye it arises as a visible form, through the ear as a sound, and so on. The implied aspect of this philosophy is that when the eye ceases to see or the ear ceases to hear, consciousness ceases also. Consciousness depends on sensations, perceptions, and thoughts, and does not exist independent of them. I take this principle to mean that the sorts of analytic attitudes that make my analytic work therapeutic are derived not so much from a particular theoretical position explaining an independent existing external reality, as from a particular way of perceiving reality and conveying that perception in many varied ways during the course of analysis. These basic philosophical presuppositions are both ways of perceiving reality and values, in the sense that they influence the choice of theory guiding the analysis, and the way in which the analyst manifests the theory in himself and in his practice.

Childhood experiences clearly mold and sculpt the ultimate form of the psychic reality of the person, and are thus pivotal in the gradual emergence of these ways of perceiving reality. In the course of my early life, I was often left to my own devices due to illness in my caregivers. I was left to help myself because those who wanted to help me could not. I was often to care for sick relatives even when quite young, and I was frequently exposed to death and to the process of mourning the death of those significant to me. I came to an early understanding that it was up to me to take hold of and direct the life that I was to lead if it was to come to anything. Being left to my own devices helped from the curiosity and energy that motivated my subsequent investigations of the "psychological cure," and also highlighted a later awareness that patients being left to their own devices (in the freedom to associate in the analytic hour) was also a very important part of analytic work.

I have always had a capacity to profit from experience and an urge to help others, beginning with a nursery for sick animals when I was a young child. I was frequently the child at school to whom my peers would come to discuss their personal problems. I do not remember ever feeling hopeless. I do remember feeling sad and feeling lost and alone but never without options, I may have been one of the children for whom the current parlance would be "resilient." Once, while in my latency years, I experienced coming very close to death by near drowning. Although a single incident, it was to shape a number of my attitudes and the way in which I pursued learning throughout my life. I remember the feeling of choking and sinking and the horror of a heaviness, making it impossible for me to move as I experienced my exhausted muscles giving up. The feeling of sinking was quickly replaced by an extraordinary feeling of lightness. In the days long before Cinerama, I experienced the wide-screen (a later déjà vu for me) replaying of all the sins of my short childhood, followed by a feeling of being drawn to a greater numinous light experience. I would have been happy to have remained in that remarkable nurturing and expanding universe, but was instead rescued. I remember feeling angry at that person for having interrupted what I felt was the greatest experience of all for me.

After this near-death experience, I remember feeling immediately that my life would never be the same again. I realized that I had come very close to death and later I also felt gratitude for having had a taste of the catastrophic terror of near annihilation. I remember both the submissiveness in the initial phase of drowning and a later expansion into what seemed to be a very different reality. From that moment on I became aware of an enhanced capacity to sense or empathize with others' experiences. Much of my reading and interest in Buddhist thinking and exploration of the martial and meditative arts began with that experience. To this day I remember the initial overwhelming wish to give up and the feeling of hopelessness and helplessness as I began to drown, and also the subsequent mastery of that fearfulness and desire to give up in the expansion into the numinous light. I believe this near-death experience has assisted me to help seriously ill patients and to not be overwhelmed by the seriousness of their illnesses. Instead I believe it has helped me become a better container for projections and less afraid of being damaged by them.

A later experience of the analysis of a psychotic woman over a twelve-year period extended and tested these containing skills. On more than one occasion she relived perverse sexual and physical abuse as a small child by a sadistic and psychotic stepfather. I would silently contain the projections of the bad parts of herself with the familiar experience of sinking and drowning. The metaphoric expansion into the numinous was a signal for me of the beginning of emerging understanding and transformation of these bad object and self representations, so that they could be reintrojected by her in a more helpful, less threatening form. On one occasion as I was speaking to her, she began to visibly recoil and sank down to her knees on the floor. I realized that it was my words that she was recoiling from as if they were missiles. When she became more and more fearful, I was eventually able to interpret to her this feeling of sinking as a response to the physical impact of sound, not its meaning. This seemed to help her own unconscious responses became more understandable to her with a subsequent reduction in psychotic anxiety. Experiences like this, where attending to the most immediate here-and-now enactments in the transference/countertransference dialectic, including nonverbal aspects, added an important quality in my psychoanalytic practice. A capacity to "regress in the service of the ego" became an important part of my practice, which I believe has enabled me to undertake the treatment of many seriously disturbed people and to help them.

It is such experiences in the immediate relationship with the analyst that I consider to be more therapeutic than connections with past experiences although work with past experiences has an anchoring and consolidating function for the therapeutic central relationship replayed in the analytic relationship in the here and now.

What led me into psychology had nothing much to do with any academic exposure. Indeed, I grew up in an atmosphere that discouraged thinking psychologically about patients. My medical school did not have a full chair of psychiatry, although several psychiatrists were helpful mentors, often fighting a losing battle with their more powerful medical and surgical colleagues. My interest in the field was initially stimulated through experiences as a part-time nursing assistant while a medical student. The very first psychiatric patient I "treated" was a psychotic physical education student who was admitted to the ward I worked on in the days before Thorazine had found its way to my country, New Zealand. I sat with this patient on a number of occasions and I vividly remember once when he emerged from a catatonic stupor, he said to me, "When are you going to come down in here with me? What are you afraid of?" I had no idea what he was talking about. His tight grip of my wrist, I remember, was like a dead weight pulling me down. He subsequently improved, completed his schooling, and kept in touch with me, thanking me for helping him preserve his sanity. My most vivid memory of the experience was knowing that I needed to remain calm and caring to prevent him from "drowning," with few words ever being exchanged. This was perhaps my initiation into an object-relational model. How I conducted myself in the relationship on a day-by-day basis, and how the transference was lived through and unconsciously enacted, partially fueled by unconscious remnants of the near-death experience, I now see was central to that "cure."

In my early experiences of medical practice as a general practitioner surgeon, I was thrust suddenly into performing major medical and surgical procedures under much less than ideal conditions. The lack of available anesthesiology in the area where I worked made early awareness of the importance of the patient's state of mind a central aspect of surgical recovery. I noticed that depressed patients had all sorts of problems with postoperative morbidity and mortality. It was this very pragmatic observation, together with reading Karl Menninger's *Vital Balance* (1963), that eventually led me to the United States and into psychiatry. While working as a GP surgeon, I had a striking additional experience of informal "psychotherapy." A friend and colleague who was the principal of a local high school was terrified by the compulsive urge to spit, which every morning he would do on the way to his school. It worried him that some of his students would see him spitting. I chatted with him on a regular basis each week, not yet aware that I was performing "therapy." I found that he had a quite rigidly organized view of life, which served him well as long as nobody, including his wife, asked for a close relationship with him. In the process of talking to me, he uncovered an early traumatic memory of a circumcision at age 6 and he became quite emotional and enraged, much to my chagrin. I found that by letting him "emote," he was helped. The urge to spit disappeared. He later thanked me for something that I was not sure that I had actually done. That particular experience remained intriguing to me, and eventually I called a local psychiatrist in what were then called "lunatic asylums." It was this man who introduced me to Freud and to my first reading of "The Psychopathology of Everyday Life" (Freud 1901). I remember to this day the experience of reading that essay. It was not only Freud's intriguing explanations of the unconscious origin of symptoms, but his obvious energy, excitement, and curiosity about the human condition that so enthralled me.

I came to the United States at a time when people were beginning to be disillusioned with psychoanalysis because it did not deliver what many of its pundits had promised, that is, relief from all the terrors and suffering of mental illness. By the time *DSM-III* was published in 1980, analytic thinkers were being exposed to extreme criticism about the validity of their work and the grandiosity of their claims to have all the answers to mental health problems. I remember vividly when the first patient in a psychoanalytically oriented hospital was denied continuing care after several years of inpatient treatment, and how outraged the psychoanalytic community was that its opinions were being questioned. In spite of arriving here at the beginning of the gradual decline of medically dominated psychoanalysis, watching that process made me aware early on that one needed to be limited in one's goals and satisfied with partial successes, certainly not the surgical cure I had been used to. One patient who shaped my awareness of this insight was a narcissistic man who had worked very hard in analysis to deal with his incapacity to have satisfying heterosexual relationships. It was not until a reenactment in the transference of an earlier experience of an incestuous relationship with his mother that he began to improve. The severe trauma of the betrayal by the mother and the "dead father," who remained a angry bystander but never really protected him, left permanent deficiencies in his capacity to trust. The treatment of this man enabled me to see that one is not always able to heal certain deficiencies that occur at critical times in the patient's early development. I probably prolonged that analysis longer than needed until I realized that my goals and the patient's capacities were somewhat different. I came across this patient many years later after he had married fairly successfully, become a father, and had entered a profession. In a brief interchange he mentioned, among other things, that the more uncomfortable parts of the process with me had been when he felt that he was not as healthy as I wanted him to be. I believe that having had to struggle as a child made me too active in the earlier stages of my analytic work, and although I consider that some of the more traumatic experiences in my life have been valuable in my development as an analyst, they have also at times been an obstacle, as indicated by this case study. I sometimes get impatient and have to remind myself that the pace should always be set by the patient.

The importance of having enough time to do the work without being hurried and the critical role of identification with the analysts' methods were also axioms that were brought home most clearly to me in one protracted ten-year analysis, with an initial three years of an almost exclusively negative transference. These three years represented attempts to drive me away with a constant barrage of criticism and contempt. My stoic survival of that barrage caused the patient to finally disclose hidden material after she realized that I wouldn't budge and that I would be with her as long as she needed. Her pathology contained primal perverse rage with many superego lacunae. She was eventually able to experience guilt, with emerging construction of a functioning supergo. I observed the gradual "plugging" of her "Swiss cheese" superego by the internalization of my persistent, even relentless, insistence on the self-analytic mode. When perverse or criminal acts were about to be indulged, my voice would intrude, like an intrusive thought: "Ms. ————, how do you understand what you are about to do?" When about to act out, she would usually think of my probable comments and cautionary reflecting on the self-destructiveness and risk taking. This experiencing of healthy identification with the "analyzing instrument" eventually enabled her to resolve much of the material, and she has become a happily married woman with a satisfying career.

If one considered the choice of career as a psychoanalyst as a symptom using Freud's principle of overdetermination, then my becoming a psychoanalyst was clearly overdetermined by many traumatic personal growing-up experiences and the influence of readings and teachers and other parental surrogates. In summary, the factors that influenced my development from early life included:

1. Early experiences of loss and the need to survive by my own wits, with these traumatic experiences occurring in an environment that was not inherently hostile and provided me with a basic means by which I could survive if I so desired. I believe that this basic environment of safety is what ameliorated the trauma sufficiently to give me the psychological space to profit from rather than to become impaired by it.

2. The pain of traumatic losses attuned me early to the value of close relationships with others to ameliorate such losses, and I became aware early of the importance of powerful, stable, parental surrogates in coping with the internal pain of such losses. Luckily these were available to me. I am grateful for such experiences and I believe part of my motivation as a helping person is the strong desire to repay some of the support that I was fortunate to have had as a child.

3. The unique near-death experience both heightened my capacity for empathy, and helped me deal with fear and victimization. It also stimulated my curiosity about human belief systems and the diverse ways in which people conceptualize the universe they live in.

Several basic values or ways of perceiving reality have emerged from these experiences, and have resulted in several foundational axioms of my practice. A definition of psychotherapy that I have developed is "the ethical use of the self in helping others." Two corollaries for that definition are that the therapist must be able to make whatever technique he or she chooses work, and that the techniques must be used ethically and in an informed way. The school of thought guiding my analytic practice is a broad philosophically based one that is not only focused on a specific way of thinking about thinking but instead closely examines how the mind itself works, particularly how basic presuppositions about the workings of the mind are used unconsciously in creating the world in which the individual lives. Thus psychoanalytic technique from my point of view consists not only of a body of basic techniques but also a body of assumptions about the nature and varieties of reality summarized in Twemlow (1994, 1996).

So far, this account highlights only a few of the incidents in a more complicated autobiographical process and leaves out references to major experiences like psychoanalytic treatment and training. There was, however, a very important parallel process that began early in my life but did not formally emerge as a direction in training until I came to the United States. I refer here to my interest and practice of the martial and meditative arts and the study of Zen. Although the near-death experience at a young age stimulated my readings in Buddhism and explorations of alternative realities, it was not until I came under the influence of certain teachers during my psychiatric residency and psychoanalytic training who gave me the opportunity to explore meditative and martial arts that this exploration began in earnest. In an early apprenticeship to a Tibetan meditation teacher and a parallel one with a psychologist who was an expert in body awareness, I began the long and continuing process of exploration of meditation and the martial arts. This process, which has been ongoing now for over twenty-five years, has had a major impact on the way I think about thinking. My conceptual framework now encompasses not only the content of the thoughts but also the process of thinking itself. This shift from content to process is the most recent phase in my becoming a psychotherapist. For about ten years of the initial practice of meditation I underwent a very important refining and deconstruction of my attentional and perceptual mechanisms, very difficult to translate into understandable psychological terms. As best I can tell, in sitting meditation and body work attention was focused on letting go of ideas, feelings, physiological reactions, bodily sensations, and external perceptions, leading eventually to a fundamental state of bare awareness. The mind settled down more and more with eventual transcendence into a state of selflessness. I experienced such a transition with my meditation teacher while listening to a lecture he was giving on the myth of freedom, an exposition of the idea that one can never be free from some forms of constraint (attachment) until one is also freed from the constraint of searching for tne self. I had a vivid visual image of a delicate ephemeral spiderweb sprinkled with dew drops and stretched across a shrub on a spring morning. When I discussed this with my teacher, he opened a book he recently finished containing, to my amazement, a photograph of exactly such a scene accompanying his lecture on the myth of freedom. He said that my image indicated to him that the emptiness of the self had finally been understood and lived within my unconscious. This unusual experience and many subsequent others began to open me up to a series of ideas that have become central to my thinking and practice:

1. Searching for the self is pointless, since the self has no spatial location. I identified a number of patients who had come to therapy searching for themselves and their identities. I found out in fact that many of them had not thought about the question for years and had given up the search and simply went about leading their lives. Kirshner's (1991) definition of the self as an emotional and intellectual expression of an experience of otherness in the present is a compact dialectical definition of the self that suits both my experience and my work with the meditative and martial arts.

There were many times during the practice of meditative arts that I became anxious that all the normal struts that seem to be supporting my mind were falling away. This questioning of basic assumptions about the nature of reality and of the self was luckily for me experienced in the context of a very receptive and open-minded training analyst who, far from seeing these investigations only as resistances, saw them as important ways in which I was experiencing and expressing my own idea of who I was.

2. I had always sought security in relationships throughout my life. Analytic treatment and these more esoteric explorations led me

to realize what Helen Keller (1940) perhaps best described more succinctly:

Security is mostly in superstition.
It does not exist in nature,
nor do the children of men as a whole experience it.
Avoiding danger is no safer in the long run than outright exposure.
Life is either a daring adventure, or nothing.
To keep our faces toward change and
behave like free spirits in the presence of fate is strength unde-
    featable.

Buddha had first described it as the principle of impermanence, and Helen Keller later embodied it in her life. The key idea is that nothing is fully reliable and that only continuing change is constant.

3. Bion (1967) talked about the mind as an apparatus for thinking thoughts. This metaphoric conceptualization was rediscovered by me in the process of integrating martial and meditative arts, including black ink brush painting, with psychoanalytic train- ing and insights from my childhood experiences. I realized that it is the training of attention and other cognitive processes that is one of the aspects missing from the modern training of psy- chotherapists and psychoanalysts. Current psychoanalytic train- ing assumes that if the therapists are healthy and aware of their own unconscious mechanisms, and are also well trained in tech- nique, they will be effective. What I have concluded from my experiences is that that effectiveness cannot be thus assumed. What is missing from this equation is the training of the mind itself. Bion's feeling was that thoughts are what force the psyche to develop the apparatus for "thinking or dealing with thoughts, or both" (p. 111). Perhaps this is, in a way, not dis- similar to the secondary autonomy of certain behaviors as con- ceptualized by ego psychology. As the mind develops from the stimulus of the thought, it achieves a certain independence of functioning that can mold and effect the thoughts that it con- tains. In his classic paper Freud (1912) perhaps erroneously dis- misses the training of the thinking by the analyst as simple. He

says, "The technique (of thinking of the analyst) however is a very simple one" (p. 324). Evenly hovering attention can be usefully further refined into several different forms of attending, which can vastly affect how the analyst listens, attends to, and hears the patient. I have considered these in much more detail in two publications (Twemlow 1997a,b).

CONCLUSION

If one sees a good theory as like a compass giving you general direction, the object relational and intersubjective theories are most useful conceptualizations for the work that I do with patients. In the year I have spent reflecting on this chapter and dealing with various difficulties that I have had with self-disclosure, anonymity, and privacy, I produced a Zen painting (Figure 30–1) as visual commentary and synthesis of this account of my becoming a psychotherapist. I dedicate this painting to the analyst, therapist, reader, of this book.

The original condition is not special but simply obscured by experience. The analyst below can be weighed down by his own enlightenment/knowledge. Shumpo Soki, who died January 14, 1496 at age 88, said on the day of this death:

> My sword leans against the sky.
> With its polished blade I'll behead
> The Buddha and all of his saints.
> Let the lightning strike where it will. [Hoffmann 1986, p. 115]*

---

*Excerpted from *Japanese Death Poems*, copyright © 1986 by Yoel Hoffmann. Published by Charles E. Tuttle Co., Inc., Rutland, VT, and Tokyo, Japan, and reprinted by permission.

FIGURE 30–1. SHOGO—WAKE UP!

Stuart W. Twemlow, M.D., is Training and Supervising Analyst at the To-peka Psychoanalytic Society and editor of the *Journal of Applied Psycho-analytic Studies*.

REFERENCES

Bion, W. R. (1967). *Second Thoughts*. New York: Jason Aronson.
Freud, S. (1901). The psychopathology of everyday life. *Standard Edition* 6:ix–291.
——— (1912). Recommendations for physicians on the psycho-analytic method of treatment. In *Collected Papers of Sigmund Freud*, vol. 2, pp. 323–333. New York: Basic Books.
Hoffmann, Y. (1986). *Japanese Death Poems*. Vermont, Tokyo: Charles Tuttle.

Keller, H. (1940). *Let Us Have Faith*. New York: Doubleday & Doran.

Kirshner, L. A. (1991). The concept of the self in psychoanalytic theory and its philosophical foundations. *Journal of the American Psychoanalytic Association* 39(1):157–182.

Menninger, K., Mayman, M., and Pruyser, P. (1963). *The Vital Balance*. New York: Viking.

Shaw, G. B. (1962). Dedicatory letter to Arthur Bingham Walkley of *Man and Superman*. In *Bernard Shaw: Complete Plays with Prefaces*, vol. 3. New York: Dodd Mead.

Twemlow, S. W. (1994). Misidentified flying objects? An integrated psychodynamic perspective on near death experiences and UFO abductions. *Journal of Near Death Studies* 12 (4):203–284.

——— (1996). The basic assumptions of psychodynamic psychiatry. In *Curriculum Outline for Psychodynamic Psychiatry and Psychotherapy Training*. Wichita: University of Kansas School of Medicine Department of Psychiatry and Behavioral Sciences.

——— (1997a). *The Zen of the therapist: I. The conceptual foundations for a new integrated focus in the training of a psychotherapist*. Manuscript submitted for publication.*

——— (1997b). *The Zen of the therapist: II. Stages in the training of a Zen influenced psychotherapist*. Manuscript submitted for publication.*

---

*Available on request from the author.

31

The Search for Understanding Human Beings

MILTIADES L. ZAPHIROPOULOS

"Theory is autobiography," said Paul Valéry, perhaps anticipating this volume's quest. On the subject of theory and practice, I am fond of quoting Goethe's Mephistopheles: "My worthy friend, gray are all theories, And green alone life's golden tree," and "Science is not enough, nor art; In this work patience plays a part." In what follows, I may take the name of some not in vain, but in a vein that carries aspects of my personal experience, and their impact on my choices.

"I was born long ago and far away," I wrote once. The statement remains true, and increasingly so its first part. For many years, beginning when I neither know nor remember, I believed that on the occasion of that blessed event my sea captain father was away, perhaps because he did leave and travel soon after my birth, for a year or longer, a hazy preoedipal or oedipal proposition at best, or at worst. One early memory is of crawling on a marble floor, picking up a piece of cheese and lifting it to my mouth, much to my mother's dismay, whose ideas about germs were not altogether phobic. She was young and must have felt an inordinate degree of responsibility for her solitary care of me. At some point, I interpreted that to mean that she saw me as an offering to my father, solicitously to be cultivated. Another early memory, with my maternal grandfather, is of horses and soldiers exercising in the sun of a nippy day. Thanks to an auspicious and opportune transfer, my father barely missed the torpedoing of his ship and the loss of its crew, something that it took us some time to find out. Upon his return, we moved from Alexandria to Port Said, where members of an extended family lived with us for a while.

The next memories are of bedsheets covered up to my chest with splintered glass from broken window panes, due to shelling by two German battleships, the names of which I have not forgotten, one of them eventually escaping to the high seas, the other being sunk by British destroyers. Make what you will of real fears of castration or of narcissistic injury, and, possibly, some budding preferential concerns with nations and cultures. Then came the threat of the town being blown to pieces if tankers in the port were bombed. It was conveyed in a cryptic note from my father to my mother referring to previous instructions about where and how to seek shelter, as he was preparing to take one of those tankers south through the Suez Canal. The job was done in a timely and effective way and the catastrophe was averted. By then I had a two-and-a-half years younger sister who was soon to demonstrate to me that penis envy is not necessarily self-evident and observable, and that being the good boy is not always or exclusively rewarding. Through it all, I began to experience uncertainties and constraints, and contrasts and discrepancies between relatively privileged positions and unpredictable vulnerabilities.

The ability to observe what goes on around me was fostered from an early age. I received some recognition for it, mostly from adults and girls, and became the object of envy and resentment among some of my male peers. Such ability obligated one to be, become, and remain objective. As with temptation, subjectivity, the observer's part, was neither to be denied nor ignored, but should be a matter of vigilant awareness and constant mistrust, to be reckoned and dealt with. Those who claimed pure objectivity, with attendant hold on the truth, not as a search but as a purported achievement, were to be questioned, boldly and painstakingly, and would usually be found to be highly subjective. Perhaps there were some intimations of the meaning of participant observation in the process. There were also admonitions as to how observations should be used, with emphasis on duty and discretion, pertinence and timing, involvement and detachment. Discerning among those entailed experience and taste, adherence to social norms and cultural tenets, and assumption of personal responsibility in deviating from them. Interpretations were a delicate matter. To this day, the question of whether, at times, discretion is the better part of valor remains open for me. Later yet, I was edified by Edmund Burke's admonition as to what good men should do about evil. And I came to appreciate Harry Stack Sullivan's musing that "evil is the unwarranted interference with living."

Another emphasis was on discipline, both as obedience to authority or its precepts, and as a desirable acquisition or achievement of one's own. Contending with the former was not often ego-syntonic. External necessities exposed me to various proponents and brands of authority at different stages in my development, and I noticed their vying for agreement in lording it over me while, otherwise, differing among themselves. Those who were wise taught me the improbability of anyone's readily availing oneself of the experience of another, but also the loss and waste entailed in interactions that fail to facilitate the development of one's own experience in conjunctive ways.

Debate had its attraction in dealing with opining or theorizing, at times succeeding in achieving reasonable and reassuring or redeeming consensus. It also proved useless in the face of blind faith, whatever its provenance. Much later, I came across a letter of Thomas Jefferson to his nephew, exhorting him to question everything, even the existence of God for, if there were one, He would want him to be upright rather than self-righteous. The same man wrote to Benjamin Rush: "I have sworn upon the altar of God eternal hostility against every form of tyranny over the mind of man." Whatever consistencies or lack thereof may be found in these declarations, I hasten to say that my decision to use them is simply my own. Therein also lie some reasons for my not needing or wanting to have heroes to worship or oracles to heed faithfully.

At under 16, I found myself in exciting and naughty Paris, loaded with parental admonitions as to what to do or not do, and burdened in some ways with parental confidence and trust in me to properly manage the tempting and the unfamiliar. Neither to fail them nor to betray myself became a task that proved to be recurrent in many areas of my life, personal and professional. Some of it pointed to lapses or lags in the parataxic to the syntaxic sequence, as I eventually came to understand. Curiosity kills the cat. It is also "one of the most permanent and certain characteristics of a vigorous mind," according to Samuel Johnson. Questions abounded and did not always make me popular. Ruth Benedict's viewing "answers as the attitudes taken by different temperaments towards characteristic problems" had not yet reached me. French chauvinism and xenophobia had me for a while partly identifying with the aggressor while not quite blaming the victim. I came to understand better the discomfort I had experienced with the fact that native Egyptians had seemed second-class citizens, compared to us Europeans, in their own country.

I had read the Greek and Latin classics with much emphasis and interest in language and philology and less so in ideas and ideology. I was impressed by their historical context and their recourse to mythology. I did not comprehend until much later the apparent fact that history succeeds myth, let alone how history may give rise to new myths, and what happens to myths when they become psychologized and scientized. My earliest reading of Freud (in French) consisted of *Totem and Taboo* and *The Psychopathology of Everyday Life*. I had to suspend disbelief regarding the former while I delighted in the latter. Previously, I had read about the subconscious (without attribution to any particular author) and about various ways and means of achieving consciousness, with a measure of wonderment at what was not part of consciousness, and with a healthy (or not so healthy) dose of the necessity to uncover that part and to subjugate it to consciousness. The process paid homage to will and willpower, invoked elements of asceticism and aestheticism, variously contrasted and commingled, much to my confusion and with some appeal to my conquering fantasies. Exposure to philosophical positivism left its imprint, confining my curiosity to seeking to understand but not to assume successful speculation as to ultimate causes or origins. I came to discard Descartes, methodologically so sure though in the long run doubting. Parsimony regarding highly uncertain ways of interpreting experience is probably still and always desirable. But uncertainties cannot be eliminated, and postulating axioms based on such presumably possible elimination is likely to give rise to theories that entail more certainty than is ever likely to exist. I developed a good clinical sense in medicine, but a fleeting exposure to Wundtian experimental psychology left me cold.

My first work in psychiatry was with children in a residential setting, split between looking for stigmata of degeneracy or congenital syphilis, and listening to two women psychoanalysts who had different ideas. In my psychiatric internship I sat for hours at the bedside (or, to more accurately describe prevailing conditions then, cotside or matressside) of catatonic patients who eventually emerged from that state without the use of somatotherapies. No wonder that later I took to the likes of Sullivan, Frieda Fromm-Reichmann, and Paul Federn. My doctoral dissertation challenged Kraepelinian prognostic pessimism in "dementia praecox" but also led me to indiscriminate etiological connections between pathogenic agents and clinical manifestations. Old habits had to die. I returned to the Sorbonne and to my old love, literature and philology. My modern comparative literature examiner was only mildly surprised when I responded to his question of what a nice young doctor is doing here by saying that there was much to those literary works, their use of character, ideas, and language, that taught me a lot of what I needed to know in order to be a better psychiatrist.

I chose to come to the United States for many reasons, ranging from the exalted to the plausible, this most basic human characteristic according to Sullivan. I knew of some indolent but stifling advantages I might predictably have elsewhere. Where opportunism grated, real opportunity had always excited me and scared me, lest I miss it or muff it. Again I was to be exposed to both organically and analytically oriented teachers and colleagues. It was nice to be doing psychoanalytically oriented psychotherapy at the New York State Psychiatric Institute and Hospital when, suddenly, a couple of my other patients were selected to be among the first ones to receive electric shock therapy in the United States. Two years later, I almost got fired from my twenty-five-dollar-a-month position at Rockland State Hospital for doing psychotherapy with psychotics instead of diligently filling out forms for the Department of Mental Hygiene. I got more respect serving with the Army of the United States, stateside and overseas, pervasive regional differences and a brush with death from smallpox notwithstanding.

I began to read and reread Freud, this time in English and in Greek. Questions arose: How about getting psychoanalytic training? And where? Columbia's program at the time was too taxing for a married man with one child and another on the way. Like a number of my friends, I applied to the New York Psychoanalytic Institute, had three pretty good interviews, and was pleased to be accepted. One of the interviewers commented that I didn't sound like a fellow who takes his friends by the buttonhole and tells them all he thinks. You would not believe in her perceptiveness after reading what I am writing here, but in many ways she was right. I was about to start classes when I was told that I would have to wait until my analyst, whom they would select for me, permitted it. I waited, did some more thinking, wondered if I was pouting or rebelling against authority. Hardly, I thought. Rather, a number of doubts and concerns were revived. What happened to me in rereading Freud? What had my New York Psychoanalytic colleagues been iterating? What did some of the journals talk about? What were they all assuming I *should* find in my patients? I began to inquire further and, like some others of my friends, I turned instead to the William Alanson White Institute and have never regretted doing so.

I had been delighted to learn about manifestations of unconscious activities and edified by corroborating these in my own and others' experience. Shedding light on the mystery of discontinuities in the stream of consciousness, as Sullivan put it in paying tribute to Freud's extraordinary contribution, was worth acknowledging gratefully. Topographizing or structuralizing the unconscious, or reifying it, seemed a different matter. Removing the stigma of degeneracy from sexual vicissitudes was a welcome view and opened up new vistas. Postulating libido and variously conceived drives or agencies utilizing it was again a different proposition. Psychologically reducing human beings to a status of appendage to one organ, and a frail one at that, has always seemed to me unreal and unscientific. Confessing perplexity as to what women want hardly justifies the use of a psychology painstakingly, if not painfully, derived from men as applicable to women. Attempting to resolve the riddle of man, generically speaking, by resorting to farfetched though fetching biologizing of life and death instincts, and by psychologizing their measure on the mind, makes for an interesting tour de force. It hardly explains the discrepancy between the alleged universal tendency to repetition compulsion parallel to a universally observable flux and change. Hypothesizing the function of dreaming in mental life and pursuing the study of processes within it need not result in the postulate of universal symbols in dreams when as symbolic par excellence an instance as language shows pronounced cultural differences, if not mutual exclusivities.

Also questionable seemed to me any mandated distinction between a purportedly narcissistic libido and an object seeking one, with attendant permutations and vicissitudes. Some essentially deterministic propositions needed to be reassessed and some exclusively energic assertions had to be recast or rechanneled. As time went on, I marveled at the variety of views, appraisals or appreciations, and ensuing espousals regarding what was thought of as necessary and what was thought of as sufficient, in both original and subsequent conceptualizations. If Freud had thought that his concepts, abstract and generalized as they grew to be, were vindicated by clinical findings, provided one looked long and deep enough for them, how was one to understand that later clinicians and theoreticians felt that such concepts failed the test of clinical relevance and applicability, thus becoming obsolete and otiose, pretty much in the way of leaves falling off after they allowed the tree of science to breathe, in Ernst Mach's poetic vision of theories? In a verbal discussion I ventured to say:

> As a first basic consideration, I submit that the tendency to search for one general theory not only for its neatness and completeness but, also, for the sake of a reassuring definitiveness and finality is likely to encompass more risk than resolution. It is also likely to engender adherence, on the one hand, and the need for additions, in the way of barnacles, on the other. This has led many psychoanalytic theoreticians to couch their contributions more in the way of a Procrustean bed, or of an ever growing pyramid, than in a way that allows for expansion through modification and change.

It is now sixty years since I first began to use psychotherapy in a

WHY I BECAME A PSYCHOTHERAPIST

professional way. Given my history, I did not go to medical school with the intention of becoming a psychotherapist. Yet soon enough in my medical education, almost unwittingly, I veered toward psychiatry, and soon again toward its more psychological and less organic aspects. At that time the humanistic part of medicine was valued, and reflected in it were experiences of somewhat removed family members and friends whose emotional problems intrigued me, parallel to my liking them and probably empathizing with their predicament and the impasses to which it led them. I continue to have a primary concern for benefiting the patient, in spite of the recognition of the broader concerns of psychoanalysis with an ever-expanding understanding of oneself, paying passing homage to Socratic or oracular injunctions. My early approach was psychoanalytically inspired. After analytic training it became psychoanalytically informed. In the process, I think that I paid respect to some classical psychoanalytic concepts and ensuing applications to therapy, became alert to the shift from the analysis of the id to the analysis of the ego and its implications, and responded naturally, so to speak, to the interpersonal theory of psychiatry which, together with developments in object relations theory, heralded the move from one-person to two-person psychology.

In the sixties, I became intrigued by certain varieties of countertransference apparently prevailing around me, which I dubbed "tender hearts and martinets," referring to nurturing as differentiated from confrontational attitudes. Whether or not a matter of individual style was accounting for these, it seems to me that they reflected probably unavoidable reactions to specific transferential developments, not to be suppressed or ignored, but to be brought into awareness, and, perhaps, to be used judiciously in the transference–countertransference continuum.

I did not mind, nor should I hide, my experiencing some satisfaction and some pride in being a participant in what I see as the cutting edge of psychoanalytic thinking and psychotherapeutic practice, which were enhanced by the fact that some frustration preceded my acceptance by, or at least the infiltration of, the mainstream of psychoanalysis. I was not meant to be a follower, and I have not sought any following. My heretofore analysands, supervisees, and students have chosen their paths, ranging from interpersonal to relational to self psychological. By the same token, my patients, I hope and trust, are offered a new experience meant to free them of unwarranted interferences with choices that they make in how to use themselves responsibly. Thomas Szasz has pointed out, perhaps a bit tendentiously, that there is no entry for the word *responsibility* in the general index of subjects in Volume 24 of the *Standard Edition of the Complete Psychological Works of Sigmund Freud*. I remain critical of many a not quite responsible innovation, whatever its provenance.

Recently, I titled a presentation of mine, "The Self of Myth and the Myth of Self." Among other things, I wondered what might have happened if Freud had used Odysseus as prototype of human development (as Kohut did) instead of Oedipus. In the therapeutic process I considered "controlled regression" an unfelicitous wording for the description of phenomena that cannot be understood, as Edgar Levenson has pointed out, in terms of a linear concept of time with developmental stages grafted on it. Nor can they be understood as independent of the time and place in which they occur, including the actual participants, neither of whom controls their occurrence, in spite of respective contributions to them. The corresponding concept of transference neurosis, as an absolute sine qua non for any analysis worth its salt, has been considered "a concept ready for retirement" by Arnold M. Cooper, yet it is perpetuated in the view of many an analyst that there are correct and irrefutable (only resisted against) interpretations, essentially if not exclusively based on drive derivatives as determinants. I am reminded of one of my Parisian psychiatric teachers reminiscing about Babinski's injunctions to some reluctant hysteric: "Unfortunate one! You are countersuggestioning yourself!" It is not only the willful hysteric that Leslie Farber revealed so well in discussing Freud's postscript to the case of Dora, who puzzles us still and always. Many patients of latter-day vintage, those who are not the way we used to know them, continue to bedevil us as to their resistance to change, while themselves not understanding why this is the case. It is difficult to give up something that seems to have worked out well, even if it no longer does, lest an alternative expose one to more hurt, or make one feel something of a fool over such a long time. Needless to say, this should alert us to ways in which some of our theories have become cherished beliefs that we find difficult to relinquish, feeling rather deprived when it becomes necessary to do so.

It has been said that psychotherapy relies on common sense as well as on uncommon sense. To paraphrase Morris Raphael Cohen's caution about any philosophy, psychotherapy would be cruel if it did not include nonsense. It is a necessary ingredient, not to be exalted and made into a virtue, but to be acknowledged and as much as possible brought into awareness, our patients' or our own.

As a corollary to the above and as a matter of perplexity to me, I shall mention the phenomena of velleities and entelechies. Velleities are wishes with weak effort toward their fulfillment. Entelechies are wishes that become goals, assiduously and energetically pursued. Why is it that with different persons or within the same person apparently strong and realizable wishes fail to command sufficient energy or commitment, while relatively nonpressing wishes become invested with tremendous and persistent energy, even if proving unfulfillable? We do not always elicit instinctual conflicts in these processes, or demonstrable anxiety in the prevailing pursuit of security over that of satisfactions. How are such differences likely to fare in the transference–countertransference interaction? Perhaps they have something to do with the vagaries of cognition and affects in early experience, and with nonretrievable aspects of these, no matter how diligent our inquiry or the patient's good will. Perhaps, also, advances in neuroscience may give us clues as to structures, closing or opening, allowing modification through events in the environment and interaction with them, and, eventually, suggest limitations as well as expanding horizons in psychotherapy.

Freud feared that therapy might undo theory, while maintaining the latter derived from the former. New theories arose from frustration, either due to bad therapy or because insistence on proving a theory right interfered with therapy. Determinism as a theory of tyranny may result in a tyranny of theory. I prefer thinking and exploring testable hypotheses to vindicating assumptions that have become dogma. Seeking does not mandate what is to be found while eschewing anything else that may be there. Recurrently, we have knowledge, with a sense of circumscription and temporality, which should be differentiated from rampant and all-encompassing belief. We should be responsible for our choices of treatment and in treatment: Is our choice of treatment the treatment of choice? And we should be fully aware of exercising personal preferences, conceivably based on empathy, and, we hope, reflecting intent as part of our contract with the patient. Our science is short, notwithstanding willful, capricious, pretentious, and pathetic debates or rebuttals about it. Our art oscillates between the inspired and the empirical. And we do need patience, since these other two may be necessary but not sufficient. Herbert Feigl said that the ability to live with an unfinished view of the world may be a sign of maturity. In exercising our impossible profession, we might minimize the risks if we remain patient enough to pursue our search for understanding human beings, let alone helping them, while being capable of living with an unfinished view of man, generically speaking.

Miltiades L. Zaphiropoulos, M.D., is Training and Supervising Analyst at the William Alanson White Institute.

Name Index

Adams, Michael Vannoy, 1–14
Aeschylus, 118
Aichhorn, August, 176
Alcott, Louisa, 42
Alexander, Franz, 127
Allport, Gordon, 102
Alpert, Augusta, 205
Anisfeld, Leon S., 15–21
Arensburg, Bernardo, 278
Augustine, Saint, 85

Babinski, J.-F.-F., 319
Bachelard, Gaston, 3
Balint, Michael, 140
Bally, Gustav, 140
Barmack, Joseph, 72
Bateson, Gregory, 209
Beethoven, Ludwig van, 27, 46
Beitner, Marvin, 160
Bellak, Leopold, 109, 290
Benedict, Ruth, 314
Benjamin, John, 243
Bergmann, Hugo, 26
Bergmann, Maria V., 23–37
Bergmann, Martin, 33, 35, 203
Binswanger, Herbert, 62
Binswanger, Ludwig, 62
Bion, Wilfred, 83, 84, 118, 131, 261, 293
Blake, William, 1, 7–8, 9
Bleuler, Eugen, 61

Blom, Gaston, 243
Bloom, Lawrence, 19
Blos, Peter, 36
Bohm, David, 10
Bolgar, Hedda, 39–49
Bornstein, Berta, 204
Bowlby, John, 162, 258–259
Brill, Abraham, 290
Bro, Ruth, 159
Brooks, William, 159
Brown, Norman O., 4–5
Buddha, 298, 307
Burke, Edmund, 313
Busch, Fred, 51–58
Bychowski, Gustaf, 204

Camus, Albert, 83, 140
Caruso, Igo, 63
Cervantes, Miguel de, 234
Chrzanowski, Gerard, 59–66
Coen, Arrigo, 91
Cohen, Morris Raphael, 320
Colbert, Claudette, 48
Conger, John, 243
Cooper, Arnold M., 319
Crisp, Quentin, 249
cummings, e. e., 82

Deason, Archie, 150
de Havilland, Olivia, 63
Deri, Susan K., 290–291

Hoffman, Irwin, 69–70, 71
Hogenson, C., 181–182
Holt, Robert, 73
Homer, 95
Hook, Sidney, 202
Horner, Althea J., 145–147
Horowitz, Len, 293
Hunter, Virginia, 149–163

Jacobson, Edith, 204
Johnson, Samuel, 314
Jones, Ernest, 125
Joyce, James, 82
Jung, C. G., 2, 3, 6, 9, 10, 83,
    181–182, 186–187

Kadis, Asya, 293
Kafka, Franz, 260
Kalinkowitz, Bernard, 106
Kant, I., 228, 231
Kapit, Hanna E., 165–177
Kearney, Richard, 2
Keller, Helen, 307
Kernberg, Otto, 204, 231
Kerouac, Jack, 78
Klein, George, 73, 105, 106, 243
Klein, Melanie, 83, 111, 126, 130,
    131, 142, 278
Kluckhohn, C., 209
Kohut, Heinz, 75, 83, 231
Kris, E., 195
Kris, Ernst, 202
Krüll, M., 213

Lacan, Jacques, 83, 87, 228, 261
Langs, Robert, 179–194
Laplanche, Jean, 230, 232
Lawrence, D. H., 78
Lax, Ruth F., 195–208
Lebovici, Serge, 225, 226, 227, 229,
    230
Lehrman, Philip, 214
Levenson, Edgar A., 209–214
Leyda, Jay, 6–7

Lopez-Pedraza, Raphael, 12
Lovelace, Richard, 146
Lukacs, Georg, 137–138

Mach, Ernst, 317
Machover, Karen, 290
Machover, Saul, 290
Mahler, Gustav, 28
Mahler, Margaret, 205, 207, 291
Mann, Thomas, 140
Marcuse, Herbert, 4–5
Maroda, Karen J., 215–223
Martin, Jay, 162
Marx, Karl, 28, 250
Maslow, Abraham, 290
Mason, Albert, 131
McDougall, Joyce, 279
Mead, Margaret, 211
Melville, Herman, 5–6, 7
Menaker, Ester, 106
Menaker, Esther, 204
Menninger, Karl, 288, 301
Metcalf, David, 243
Milner, Marion, 83
Modell, Arnold H., 12
Moore, Burness, 36
Moore, Thomas, 8
Moreno, Jacob, 290
Morgenthaler, Fritz, 140
Mulliken, Richard, 80
Mulliken, Susan, 80
Murray, Henry A., 5, 102

Nacht, Sacha, 228
Neubauer, Peter, 205
Nickerson, Arthur, 160
Niederland, William, 204
Noxzlopi, Laszlo, 138

Oppenheimer, Agnès, 225–232
Orlando, Irene, 277

Parker, Wanda, 163
Perls, Fritz, 160